INTERIOR FURNISHINGS SOUTHWEST

Interior Furnishings Southwest

THE SOURCEBOOK OF THE BEST PRODUCTION CRAFTSPEOPLE

SUZANNE DEATS AND JOHN VILLANI

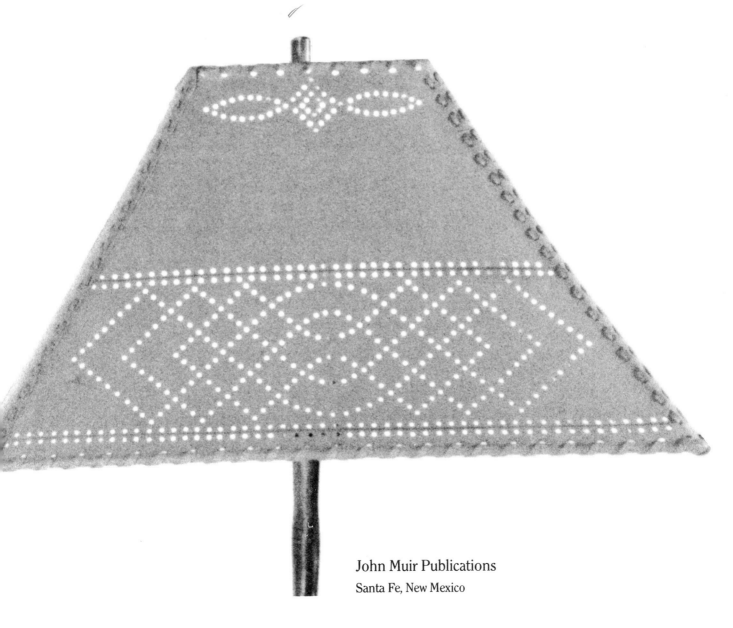

John Muir Publications

Santa Fe, New Mexico

ACKNOWLEDGMENTS

We would like to thank each craftsperson who responded to our questions and worked with us to make *Interior Furnishings Southwest* the finest sourcebook of its kind. We would also like to thank every designer and gallery owner who helped us find the best and most interesting people who create functional furnishings in the Southwest.

The information in this book has been provided by the craftspeople themselves and is subject to change. All craftspeople are included without charge to them. The craftspeople whose listings include photographs of their work have paid a fee to help defray the cost of publication.

John Muir Publications, P.O. Box 613, Santa Fe, NM 87504

First edition. First printing September 1992

Library of Congress Cataloging-in-Publication Data
Deats, Suzanne.
    Interior furnishings Southwest : the sourcebook of the best
production craftspeople / Suzanne Deats and John Villani.
        p. cm.
    "Sources": p.
    ISBN 1-56261-038-4
    1. Artisans—Southwest, New—Directories. 2. Decorative arts—
Southwest, New—Directories. I. Villani, John. II. Title.
NK824.6.D4 1992
745'.029'479—dc20   92-14413
                                                     CIP

Distributed to the book trade by
W.W. Norton & Co., Inc.
New York, New York

Cover photo by David Marlow. Cabinets by McMillan's Old Santa Fe
    Furniture Company; color finish and tin work by the Streck family.
Design: Susan Gutnik
Typography: Copygraphics, Inc., Santa Fe, New Mexico
Printer: Banta Company

Contents

Foreword

When I went to Santa Fe in 1980 to organize an exhibit of historic New Mexican furniture for the Museum of International Folk Art and to write a book on the history of furniture making in New Mexico, I was surprised and delighted to see that the tradition was still very much alive. My research brought me into contact with many people who were creating Southwestern home furnishings in traditional styles. Some had deep roots in New Mexico; others were new arrivals. All were attracted by the simple beauty of the Southwestern aesthetic. Today, I can say that that tradition is not only still alive but enjoying a renaissance.

The renaissance is due to the cultural syncretism that is a special characteristic of Southwestern life. This is where the nineteenth-century Anglo-American push to the west met the seventeenth-century Spanish push to the north, in the midst of Native American peoples who had been here for thousands of years when the Spanish arrived. Southwesterners are used to trading, absorbing, and reshaping ideas. They have had several centuries of practice in taking new materials, designs, and production techniques, putting a uniquely Southwestern stamp on them, and giving them back to the world in a new form. The Spanish brought wheat, pork, and chile to the Rio Grande Valley four centuries ago; Southwesterners transformed these ingredients into the fry bread, Navajo tacos, *posole*, and *carne adobado* that we enjoy today. In the early 1900s, traders on the Navajo reservation showed Navajo weavers how to incorporate designs from Turkish rugs into their traditional blankets, turning them into suitable floor coverings for Anglo-American homes. During the past ten years, contemporary Southwestern craftspeople have combined Hispanic and Native American forms and designs with elements derived from the ranch and the bunkhouse, the Rocky Mountains and the western logging camp, to create a dazzling variety of furniture, architectural details, lighting devices, floor and window coverings, and tableware with a distinctive "Southwestern Look."

This creative explosion is a response to a nationwide—indeed, worldwide—interest in the Southwest that seems to have its roots in both an age-old desire for a simpler, less complicated life and a new and genuine respect for the art and values of native peoples. The straightforward, just-do-it attitude of the cowboy has a strong appeal to a culture caught in the complexities of contemporary society. The reverence for nature and for the land that is shared by the Southwest's Hispanics and Native Americans seems to offer an alternative to industrial civilization's rapacious approach to its natural resources, and the continuity of those cultures in one place over time stands in stark contrast to the rootless mobility that has left most Americans without any ties to a specific piece of land. The land itself, with its rough textures and pastel colors and sometimes terrifyingly big skies (whoever wrote, "and the skies are not cloudy all day" had never seen a storm gathering over La Bajada), has an irresistible pull for people from greener, grayer places.

This attraction is not new, but it has increased dramatically in intensity over the past decade. In the 1920s, architects and craftsmen like Jesse Nusbaum, John Gaw Meem, and William Penhallow Henderson drew on New Mexico's Spanish and Pueblo heritage to produce buildings and furniture in the "Santa Fe style." Maria Martinez, the potter from San Ildefonso Pueblo, became world-famous in the 1930s through the new black-on-black glaze that she developed to accommodate a non-Pueblo aesthetic ("Black goes with anything," she is supposed to have remarked). At the same time, ornamental tinsmiths like Francisco Delgado, woodcarvers like Jose Dolores Lopez, and weavers like Nicacio Ortega popularized Hispanic crafts among a group of Anglo-American aficionados. But in the past ten years, Southwestern home furnishings have gained wider acceptance and are as sought-after in New York and Paris as they are in New Mexico.

The oldest blend of craft traditions in America has finally come into its own.

Interior Furnishings Southwest will play an important role in keeping those traditions alive by exposing Southwestern craftspeople to a larger audience and by serving as a sourcebook for people everywhere who feel the pull of the Southwest. It is especially exciting for me, as a historian of crafts, to watch the innovations that occur within the Southwestern tradition as newer and wider markets present new challenges and a regional craft tradition takes on national dimensions and becomes an American one. I hope that everyone who uses this book will feel the same excitement.

March 1992   Lonn Taylor
Washington, D.C.

Introduction

The American Southwest is a beacon that draws interest from designers, art collectors, and homeowners around the world. People are excited by the romance, glamour, and rambunctious humor of the West and by the mystique of the Native American and Hispanic influences that are reflected in the region's graphic design elements.

The look of the Southwest has never been more popular, particularly in the area of home furnishings. Until now, however, people have had to rely on catalogs and sporadic advertising for access to the furnishings through retail outlets. There has been no coherent way to locate the craftspeople who create these beautiful functional objects.

Similarly, these craftspeople have had no realistic way to reach the thousands of homeowners and residential and commercial designers who would appreciate having direct contact with them to acquire a deeper understanding of their work. For each artisan has a personal interpretation of the Southwest. And each enjoys the experience of direct contact with the people who will live with the lovely handcrafted objects produced in his or her studio.

Enter *Interior Furnishings Southwest* (*IFS*). It is for you. You may be a homeowner living in Atlanta, Portland, or Madison. You may be a designer living in New York, Tokyo, or Paris. You may be a furniture maker living in a remote village somewhere in the high desert of the American Southwest.

IFS is a real-world, supremely workable sourcebook. For the homeowner who wants to create a life-enhancing, very personal environment, this directory is a straight line to the craftspeople whose handmade objects are equally personal. *IFS* brings you behind the scenes and offers a rare look at the production studio. It supplies addresses and telephone numbers of these studios so that you may become directly involved in the process by which your furnishings are made.

For the interior designer seeking the finest Southwestern furnishings for businesses, hotels, restaurants, and high-end residences, *IFS* offers practical information and easy access, allowing intelligent choices with minimum research.

For the artist who creates functional furnishings, *IFS* is a connection with the right clients, the ones who understand and appreciate the intrinsic value of fine handcrafted pieces. *IFS* offers an in-depth look at two of these manufacturers. Collaboration is a joint venture of several brilliant designers, each of whom maintains a separate workshop and each of whom shares with the others in the design and production of special pieces. Collaboration represents the essence of *IFS*: the spirit of cooperation. McMillan's Old Santa Fe Furniture Company personifies an equally important facet of fine crafts production—the power of the individual. Dennis McMillan is a true pioneer, a maverick who has made his business work by relying on his own dynamic energy and a good measure of trial and error.

Interior Furnishings Southwest came about because of the extraordinary people you will find within these pages and because of our dedication to fine arts in the Southwest. We sought out the artist/craftspeople who are most interesting to you. We spoke with architects and designers who were enthusiastic about their own best sources. We spoke with the artisans themselves about their most respected peers. We traveled the back roads and visited the studios to find the unpublicized, the imaginative, the authentic. We found hidden treasures who create the furnishings that define the look of the Southwest today.

We have described these craftspeople and their work so that you may contact those who interest you. We have indicated the qualities that make each one different from all the rest. Whenever possible, we have allowed them to speak in their own voices about the nature of their designs and their businesses.

Creative people are by nature unconventional, so there are no two aesthetic frameworks and business formats exactly alike. One thing comes through unanimously, however. They all love the work they are creating and the area in which they are living.

It is these two elements that form the basis for Southwestern style. It is an exuberant, honest look made up of a wide variety of elements: the colors and natural materials of the high desert and the Rocky Mountains, the folk traditions of the early Spanish settlers, the bold designs of the Pueblo Indians, and the robust, humorous heritage of the American cowboy.

The Spanish influence survives in the strong furniture traditions and architectural accents that are alive today in the wood-carvers who are descendants of those settlers who arrived centuries ago. The Pueblo Indians were and are producers of fine hand-loomed textiles and world-famous pottery. The Anglo frontiersmen brought with them a strong practicality and a rustic elegance that survives in ranch furniture, ironwork, and rowdy accessories.

This rich amalgam has coalesced into a look that may be easily integrated into contemporary interiors worldwide. Its naturalism and human scale relate well to all ethnic strains; its vigorous charm is compatible with the most sophisticated decor. A great many of the craftspeople listed in *IFS* will customize their work to meet exacting requirements for interiors of all types, thereby providing just the right connection between the Southwest and the client's own environment.

This, then, is the true value of *Interior Furnishings Southwest*: it will work for you. If you are a designer of residential and commercial interiors, it will provide you with a gold mine of sources for your projects. If you are a homeowner, it will introduce you personally to some of the most interesting people you will ever meet, even if you only read about them here but especially if you visit their workrooms and acquire a functional work of art made for you alone.

Most of all, *IFS* will connect you to that gorgeous piece of geography, that enchanted landscape of the mind known as the American Southwest. It will furnish your life with the sunshine and blue skies, the romance and glamour, of this very special place.

THE BASICS
Furniture

outhwestern furniture falls into several categories that sometimes overlap and always look good together. These styles are influenced by the indigenous desert cultures, the early Spanish settlers, and the pioneer ranchers and loggers who homesteaded the plains and the Rocky Mountains.

Each of the five states covered in *Interior Furnishings Southwest* has its own traditions. Each state's craftspeople interpret those traditions in styles that adapt the classic motifs to contemporary usage or take them a step further into today's vanguard.

They are versatile artists, frequently using their ideas and their tools to create doors, fine cabinetry, and other items that are classified in the following sections of *IFS* according to production emphasis. Conversely, some of those craftspeople who are mainly known for structural components have developed a secondary line of furniture that is described in the listing of their primary medium in another section.

Arizona has developed a regional style that is gaining attention from designers and homeowners. Using woods and other materials such as cactus ribs that are native to the region, Arizona furniture makers have created a look that is sometimes called "Sonoran," after the name of the desert that covers this part of the country. Arizona's regional style incorporates elements such as hand-forged ironwork, punched tin, and leather that reflect earlier influences from pioneer ranch and Spanish colonial furniture.

The mountains of Colorado and Utah harbor the majority of Southwestern manufacturers of lodgepole and aspen furniture. Vacation home buyers at the local ski areas keep these craftspeople in business, because there is nothing more appropriate to a high country chalet than a lovely canopy bed made from hand-hewn lodgepole pine. Some of the region's more innovative furniture producers have started experimenting with surface treatments and random wood forms, adding an artistic element to the rustic charm of this casual furniture. Designers incorporate this romantic look into many different kinds of country and contemporary interiors, not just Southwestern ones.

New Mexico's Spanish wood-carvers have always found appreciative buyers for their carefully built furniture. They have the capacity to adjust their furniture's dimensions and aesthetic elements to changing popular tastes while retaining the handsome antique look. In recent years, the emergence of the New Mexico art scene has spawned a generation of artists who make strikingly original furniture, and their imagination has bonded with the solid Spanish colonial tradition to produce a vibrant, lively look that has become known as "Santa Fe style."

Wyoming's design roots are firmly set in the ranch furniture that most of us first saw in western movies. It is a simple, sensible design that occurs when craftspeople work with the elements at hand. The furniture from this part of the country is a distinctive blending of antlers, leathers, hand-forged iron, burled woods, and hand-planed softwoods. Wyoming craftspeople exhibit a contemporary attitude toward national design trends while bowing to nostalgic western traditions.

Southwestern furniture from all five states has in common a respect for regional customs, a robust humor, and an expansive creativity. It is solidly built and tends to look better and better as it is subjected to the wear and tear of the active western life-style. Southwestern furniture makers have given their homeowner customers carte blanche to prop their feet up on coffee tables, throw a dusty coat across the back of a chair, or even forgive a sleepy pet for finding a comfortable place to catch forty winks. And they have given interior designers witty, vigorous country elegance with which they can brighten even the most practical environment.

Acadia Woods

OWNER/DESIGNER: Edward Chipman

ADDRESS: P.O. Box 1256, Edwards, CO 81632

TELEPHONE: (303) 949-5124

FAX: (303) 949-5121

With a background in boat building, cabinet making, and timber framing, Ed Chipman brings tremendous woodworking knowledge to his Acadia Woods furniture line. His training in traditional furniture-making methods is a result of both self-taught knowledge and insights gleaned from the several furniture makers he has collaborated with in past ventures.

The Acadia Woods collection takes its design influences from several different sources, including American West, Southwestern, and Country French styles. Chipman is enamored of the challenge of bringing out the best individual characteristics in each piece of wood he chooses to work with, including "the different scales, shapes, textures, and colors one needs to deal with in the furniture-crafting process."

Acadia Woods uses both hardwood and softwood in its home furnishings designs. Because each piece is hand-tooled and hand-textured, there is a subtle degree of individuality that Chipman is able to impart to his products. He completes each piece with an assortment of clean, warm finishes he formulates himself.

PRIMARY PRODUCT: All types of interior and exterior home furnishings, including tables, chairs, sideboards, armoires, benches, chests, hutches, curio cabinets, shutters, bureaus, doors, windows, and wine cabinets.

PRICE RANGE: $150 to $1,500.

DIRECT SALES: Yes, through the production facility in Avon, Colorado.

CUSTOM ORDERS: Custom orders comprise the bulk of orders received at Acadia Woods. Chipman enjoys tailoring the furniture pieces in his line to the specific needs of clients.

ONE OF A KIND: Yes, will work on any special client projects.

CATALOG AVAILABILITY: No brochure, but a designer portfolio is available on request.

RETAIL DISTRIBUTION: No.

WHOLESALE SHOWROOMS AND REPRESENTATIVES: No.

HONORS AND SPECIAL COMMISSIONS: Acadia Woods has custom designed and installed one-of-a-kind pieces in large homes throughout Vail and Aspen, Colorado. First Place in the Vail Valley Woodworking Show, 1989, for his cherry pedestal table design.

Alpine Woodworks, Inc.

OWNER/DESIGNER: Steve and Kathe Porter

ADDRESS: P.O. Box 171053, Salt Lake City, UT 84117

TELEPHONE: (801) 278-3478

Alpine Woodworks builds a sophisticated line of lodgepole pine furniture, concentrating on developing a flawless, smooth finish on each piece. Their trademark style is lodgepole furniture that looks as refined and as visually perfect as possible. But Steve and Kathe Porter also create a more rustic line of furniture made from gambrel oak and willow. These pieces, which frequently incorporate rawhide strips and leather lacing into their seats and backs, have a true high country feeling. Alpine's fan back chair, which combines a willow frame with a black-on-white cowhide chair back, looks as if it would be right at home in a Gene Autry movie.

PRIMARY PRODUCT: Lodgepole pine bed sets in all sizes and several styles, bunk beds, sofas, easy chairs, armoires, coffee tables, nightstands, dining room tables and chairs, captain's chairs, bar stools, etagéres, and children's lodgepole pine furniture. Chairs and end tables made from gambrel oak and willow, featuring rawhide and leather webbings.

PRICE RANGE: $500 to $2,000.

DIRECT SALES: Telephone orders are accepted.

CUSTOM ORDERS: Yes. Installation services available at an additional charge.

CATALOG AVAILABILITY: Yes.

RETAIL DISTRIBUTION: Direct from the production facility.

WHOLESALE SHOWROOMS AND REPRESENTATIVES: Denver Design Works, Denver, Colorado.

Apodaca Designs

OWNER/DESIGNER: Steve Sovelove

ADDRESS: P.O. Box 265, Dixon, NM 87527

TELEPHONE: (505) 579-4392

Steve Sovelove is a talented young furniture designer who lives and works in rural northern New Mexico, in the Apodaca settlement near Dixon. His studio, Apodaca Designs, produces mostly one-of-a-kind furniture pieces of a lighthearted, essentially abstract nature. For example, his Aspen Grove table has a silver-finished wood top and a forest of peeled aspen poles for legs, giving it an almost anthropomorphic, centipede-like appearance.

Sovelove studied at Alfred University and the Wendel Castle School before establishing his design workshop in Apodaca. He produces contemporary sculpture in addition to his unique furniture.

PRIMARY PRODUCT: Custom furniture/sculpture in wood, metal, and glass. Chairs, tables, and architectural details. Contemporary design ranging from incidentally functional to practical but humorous.

PRICE RANGE: $300 to $6,000.

DIRECT SALES: One of the most charming workshops you will ever visit. Mail and telephone orders welcome.

CUSTOM ORDERS: Absolutely.

ONE OF A KIND: Most of the work is one of a kind. Sovelove deals directly with clients on a unique commission basis.

CATALOG AVAILABILITY: Photos, estimates, and other information on request.

RETAIL DISTRIBUTION: Call or write for current exhibition information.

WHOLESALE SHOWROOMS AND REPRESENTATIVES: Agnes Bourne Showroom, San Francisco, California.

HONORS AND SPECIAL COMMISSIONS: Publication: *Fine Woodworking*, Design Book 5. "Death and Taxes" invitational sculpture and painting exhibition, Shidoni Galleries, Santa Fe, New Mexico, 1992.

Arapahoe Flats Furniture Company

OWNER/DESIGNER: Steven Condie

ADDRESS: 427 East 3300 South, Salt Lake City, UT 84115

TELEPHONE: (801) 466-5933

Steve Condie, working with his furniture designer brother, A. Brian Condie, builds a line of furniture and accessories that combines both frontier and primitive influences. "Our furniture pays homage to mother earth, with enduring designs that echo the cultures that lived in Utah hundreds and thousands of years ago."

This stylized, limited edition line of furniture has a ranchlike solidity to its construction, yet incorporates artistic elements like mesa-cut wood, leather straps and handles, Indian blanket painted designs, carved cactus and horses, sandstone inlays with pictograph designs, and Mexican tapestries.

To build complete roomscapes, Arapahoe Flats also makes a line of accessories. Each piece is signed and dated by the craftsman.

PRIMARY PRODUCT: Beds, sofas, chairs, trasteros, dining room sets, armoires, dressers, tables, coffee tables, rocking chairs, hall trees, kiva ladders, wine racks, wall racks, hand-painted life-size wooden animals.

PRICE RANGE: $300 to $10,000.

DIRECT SALES: Retail clients are welcome through both mail and telephone orders direct from the production facility.

CUSTOM ORDERS: This is Arapahoe Flats' primary means of reaching clients. Each piece is individually crafted, and client participation in the design and decoration process of each piece is welcomed.

ONE OF A KIND: Yes.

CATALOG AVAILABILITY: Brochure and catalog are available at no cost. Finish samples are available for $10.

RETAIL DISTRIBUTION: The Eagle's Nest, 117 East South Temple, Salt Lake City, UT 84111.

WHOLESALE SHOWROOMS AND REPRESENTATIVES: Kathy Snow, "The Showroom," 1363 South Major Street, Salt Lake City, UT 84115.

HONORS AND SPECIAL COMMISSIONS: Utah Arts Festival, "Best of Show," 1989. Park City Arts Festival, Utah, 1989, 1990.

Arizona Ranch

OWNER/DESIGNER: Gerry Lemanski and Laura Urbanski

ADDRESS: 1300-A East 8th Street, Tempe, AZ 85281

TELEPHONE: (602) 921-4101

FAX: (602) 894-0204

The combined design and craftsman's experience of Gerry Lemanski and the financial and fashion acumen of Laura Urbanski have proven to be a successful mix for Arizona Ranch. Using Arizona pine, saguaro cactus ribs, woven manila rope, copper appliqués, and intricate carvings, Lemanski and Urbanski create furnishings that are, they say, ready for homes in the "New Southwest."

The Arizona Ranch collection uses lodgepole pine and ponderosa pine in building its furniture. Manila rope weavings are used as support elements for the seating components of the sofas and chairs. The design elements that are incorporated into these pieces range from a rustic, mountain country authenticity to a sophisticated, Southwestern contemporary motif. Arizona Ranch builds furniture that falls into either of these categories and also has a number of pieces that display elements of both design styles.

Lemanski designs and hammers out all the copper pieces used in Arizona Ranch furniture. From patinaed copper door pulls on entertainment centers to geometric design appliqués on cabinets and coffee tables to chair backs made from patinaed copper, Lemanski's metalsmithing work is one of the standout design elements in the Arizona Ranch collection.

PRIMARY PRODUCT: Ranch Western and "New Southwestern" furniture made from pine, incorporating copper patina design and functional elements, woven manila rope seat supports, and smooth, hand-buffed finishes. Complete furniture collections in lodgepole pine and ponderosa pine, using combined design elements that result in a contemporary Southwestern appearance.

PRICE RANGE: $495 to $8,000.

DIRECT SALES: Retail and wholesale clients may contact the production facility. Retail territories around the country are protected. Designers are welcome, by appointment.

CUSTOM ORDERS: Yes, with consultation charges added to the furniture cost. All pieces are designed and copyrighted by Gerry Lemanski Design.

ONE OF A KIND: Yes, often in conjunction with other artists. Art gallery and retail store installations are a specialty.

CATALOG AVAILABILITY: Catalog is available for $3. Color photograph requests are honored whenever possible.

RETAIL DISTRIBUTION: The Arrangement, Dallas, Texas, and Jacksonville, Florida. Su Casa, Phoenix; Que Pasa, Scottsdale, Arizona. Southwest Images, Sacramento, California. Time/Space Ltd., Milan, Italy. Kokopelli, Hamburg, Germany.

WHOLESALE SHOWROOMS AND REPRESENTATIVES: None, but work through dealers and special purchase programs.

HONORS AND SPECIAL COMMISSIONS: Phoenician Resort, Scottsdale. Chrysallis Women's Shelter, Phoenix. Numerous art galleries and retail store installations in Phoenix and Scottsdale, Arizona.

Arizona Traditions

OWNER/DESIGNER: Charles D. Rasmussen

ADDRESS: 555 West 2nd Avenue, #A-13, Mesa, AZ 85210

TELEPHONE: (602) 827-9742

Working from a full collection of furniture designs, Arizona Traditions puts together complete room sets and individual accent pieces and can also equip entire homes with its unique, Southwestern version of traditional lodgepole pine furniture. The emphasis in this line is on latilla pieces, the small-diameter sticks made from aspen and pine branches, which are used to accent the furniture's more substantial lodgepole components.

Charles Rasmussen says that by hand-pulling the bark off raw pine poles and by rough-sawing the ends of these poles, he is able to achieve a true mountain country appearance in the Arizona Traditions collection. All of the dowels that join the lodgepole frames of this furniture are hand-cut, using a draw knife to achieve the tightest fit and the most authentic appearance possible.

PRIMARY PRODUCT: Lodgepole pine furniture with a rugged, rustic appearance. Individual pieces include armoires, dressers, beds of all dimensions, nightstands, love seats, ottomans, entertainment units, easy chairs, and dining room sets.

PRICE RANGE: $100 to $2,200.

DIRECT SALES: While the primary business of Arizona Traditions is in the wholesale market, individuals may order direct via telephone or mail. Shop visits are welcome, by appointment.

CUSTOM ORDERS: Nearly half of the furniture business of Arizona Traditions is through custom orders from designers and individual clients.

ONE OF A KIND: On a limited basis.

CATALOG AVAILABILITY: Photographs are available.

RETAIL DISTRIBUTION: Only through production facility.

WHOLESALE SHOWROOMS AND REPRESENTATIVES: Call for information.

Art in the Dark/Wet Air Design

OWNER/DESIGNER: David R. Browne

ADDRESS: P.O. Box 8937, Santa Fe, NM 87504-8937

TELEPHONE: (505) 471-5182

David Browne has a distinguished reputation in Europe as a contemporary artist who creates functional furnishings. Since moving to the American Southwest, he has been influenced by the light and the hues of the high desert. His wife, a native New Mexican, and her family's history have also inspired a change in his designs. Currently, he is producing a new collection of tables and screens influenced by New Mexico.

PRIMARY PRODUCT: "Glow in the Dark" tables of all sizes and room screens of three to seven panels, completely illustrated and painted, then lacquered with an anti-graffiti clear protective coating. Southwestern, Native American, and Art Deco motifs.

OTHER LINES: Interior and exterior murals. Glow in the dark ceramics.

PRICE RANGE: Tables: $1,500 to $25,000. Room screens: $3,000 to $40,000. Murals: quoted on contract.

DIRECT SALES: Orders accepted by mail or telephone.

CUSTOM ORDERS: Custom product orders welcome. Many of the pieces can be customized to specific interior designs. Large quantity commissions for hotels or restaurants can be met if time is available.

ONE OF A KIND: Most pieces are one of a kind. Will travel to complete major projects and installations.

CATALOG AVAILABILITY: Inquire for photographs/slides.

RETAIL DISTRIBUTION: Brinkman Galleries, Frozen Fountain Gallery, Amsterdam. Dartmouth Street Gallery, Albuquerque. Others in United States: please inquire.

WHOLESALE SHOWROOMS AND REPRESENTATIVES: Ann Ward, (505) 471-5182, Santa Fe; John Cacciatore, (505) 266-7751, Albuquerque, New Mexico. Ricki Renna, (415) 776-3772, San Francisco; Frank Newell, (213) 466-2911, Los Angeles, California.

HONORS AND SPECIAL COMMISSIONS: Major murals in Holland and England. Other commissions: Cheech & Chong Foundation, private foundations and collector groups. Racing cars painted in "glow in the dark" in England and Puerto Rico. New York exhibit with Amsterdam Diamond Exchange.

Arroyo Design

OWNER/DESIGNER: Elaine Paul and Stephen Paul

ADDRESS: 224 N. 4th Avenue, Tucson, AZ 85705

TELEPHONE: (602) 884-1012

Arroyo Design is a custom furniture company specializing in classic designs incorporating woods native to the Sonoran desert. The furniture made by Stephen and Elaine Paul is designed and produced in a nine-employee shop in which individual creative concepts often find their way from a craftsperson's mind onto a showroom floor. The Arroyo Design collection has made inroads into several metropolitan markets around the country and has received national media attention. Law firms, architecture firms, Hollywood studios, and high-end hotels are but a few of the long list of clients owning Arroyo Design pieces.

"We build and market our furniture as an investment to be passed along to future generations," says Elaine. She and Stephen have renovated homes in Tucson's historic district and have studied architectural history and historic preservation. As a result, the Pauls have an appreciation for classic design elements and a designer's sensibility for contemporary evocations of their regional, Southwestern motifs. Each of their collections reflects distinct influences: Presidio draws from Victorian and American West sources, Mission reflects the American Arts and Crafts movement, and Neo-Classic echoes European Deco and contemporary forms.

Working in mesquite wood is a particular interest of Arroyo Designs. The wood is dried according to the Pauls' specifications, and sawed boards are kept together so that wood panels can be bookmatched in doubly patterned markings. Bookmatching, along with mortise and tenon joinery and a high degree of hand-worked craftsmanship set Arroyo Design furniture apart from the rest of the field. Where else could one hope to find a Victorian-inspired mesquite armoire decorated with intricate carvings of agave plants?

PRIMARY PRODUCT: Classic designs in mesquite wood that has been finished, oiled and stained to enhance its natural coloration or to resemble other woods, such as cherry, oak, and pecan. Three furniture collections: Presidio, Neo-Classic, and Mission. Each collection includes armoires, dressers, beds, desks, dining tables, sofas, arm chairs, bookcases, and coffee tables.

PRICE RANGE: $600 to $6,000.

DIRECT SALES: Arroyo Design furniture is sold through the company's Tucson showroom and through catalog orders from around the country. Visitors are welcome in the showroom, which displays 30 pieces from the company's three furniture collections.

CUSTOM ORDERS: Absolutely encouraged. Clients with specific needs are invited to join the design process and to stop in the Arroyo Design production facility to see their work-in-progress.

ONE OF A KIND: Corporate office and professional office installations are a specialty. The Pauls have designed and built one-of-a-kind home entertainment centers for some of the biggest names in Hollywood and the recording industry.

CATALOG AVAILABILITY: Standard lines are depicted in the Arroyo Design catalog. Specialized and custom pieces can be photographed, depending on client's needs.

RETAIL DISTRIBUTION: Through the production facility/showroom at 224 N. 4th Avenue, Tucson.

WHOLESALE SHOWROOMS AND REPRESENTATIVES: Through the production facility/showroom.

HONORS AND SPECIAL COMMISSIONS: Corporate headquarters, Professional offices, Hollywood studios, international custom installations. Numerous museum exhibitions and regional design industry awards.

Top: Lorraine chair, neoclassic armoire, Photo by Tim Fuller
Bottom: Seated writing desk, Pasadena chair, Mack table, Photo by Tim Fuller

Aspen Log Furniture Company

OWNER/DESIGNER: Gale Bryant

ADDRESS: P.O. Box 4084, Aspen, CO 81612

TELEPHONE: (303) 925-1821

FAX: (303) 963-0145

Starting with dead lodgepole pine stands around his Colorado home, furniture craftsman Gale Bryant set out five years ago to inexpensively furnish a few rooms of his own residence. What was at the time a sideline diversion for the contractor/builder has gradually become his professional passion. While he no longer has time to seek out and haul into town his own supply of hand-selected lodgepole pine, Bryant still works as a one-man, quality-conscious operation.

The pine that Bryant uses has been killed by beetle infestations and is filled with natural imperfections that he incorporates into distinct design elements. He starts by hand-peeling each log (a process that eliminates the beetles) and gradually moves through a series of steps that allows bumps, knots, and other cosmetic flaws to be retained for their "character appeal."

Each of the Aspen Log Furniture Company's pieces is designed to be a comfortable addition to the interior scheme of a customer's home. The large-scale dimensions, unique foundation and down feather cushioning systems, solid joinery, and hand-rubbed finishes all contribute to the ultimate test of one of his furniture pieces—whether its builder can easily take his afternoon nap on it.

PRIMARY PRODUCT: Lodgepole pine furniture characterized by a rustic, hand-carved appearance. Canopy beds, headboard beds, footboard beds, bunk beds, sofas, sectional sofas, love seats, easy chairs, otto-mans, benches, dining tables, banquet tables, desks, coffee tables, end tables, nightstands, bar stools, mirrors, and frames. Bryant also builds a line of hand-painted pine furniture that includes armoires, home entertainment cabinets, benches, folding room dividers, medicine cabinets, and mirrors. Architectural elements include fireplace mantels, structural columns, stair railings, and outdoor ramadas.

PRICE RANGE: $450 to $5,000.

DIRECT SALES: Direct sales are welcome through the Aspen Log Furniture Company showroom in Carbondale, Colorado. Telephone and mail orders are accepted.

CUSTOM ORDERS: Client participation in the design process is welcomed.

ONE OF A KIND: In most cases involving one-of-a-kind installations, Bryant travels to the site to determine the client's individual requirements.

CATALOG AVAILABILITY: Brochure is available free of charge.

RETAIL DISTRIBUTION: The only retail outlet is the company's showroom in Carbondale, Colorado.

HONORS AND SPECIAL COMMISSIONS: Bryant has completely outfitted residences across the United States, including Hawaii, with his distinctive lodgepole pine furniture.

Autumn Wood / Fox Manufacturing Co., Inc.

OWNER/DESIGNER: Dale Fox, Luana Fox, Mike Hendricks, Tim Fox

ADDRESS: 5105 Williams S.E., Albuquerque, NM 87105

TELEPHONE: (505) 873-1432

FAX: (505) 873-1873

Autumn Wood is a large custom furniture line with showrooms in three New Mexico cities. The many pieces and sets are produced to customer specifications at the factory in Albuquerque. Designer Dale Fox has created a vast array of elegant, practical furnishings for residential and commercial settings. They are tailored to the real world and styled to the warm, natural look of the Southwest.

Several years ago, the Fox family drew national notice and acclaim for their businesslike handling of a fire that destroyed their factory. Thanks to a well-backed-up computer system, they were able to advise every customer of the situation immediately and to be back in production in a record eight weeks. Clients were reassured by this speedy response to crisis, which translates to excellent business practices during normal times. After the fire, sales actually increased over the previous year, due in no small part to the beauty, practicality, and long-term economy of Autumn Wood's custom furniture.

PRIMARY PRODUCT: Contemporary and Southwest furniture for home or office, in oak or pine with selection of fabrics, dimensions, and stain or wash colors. All furniture is custom designed and built: living room, dining room, bedroom, den, wall units, desks, computer centers. The Southwest designs are not rustic but have finished detailing and full support seating.

PRICE RANGE: Moderate to moderately expensive.

DIRECT SALES: Visitors are welcome at the factory. Mail or telephone orders accepted. Examples of Autumn Wood's full line of custom furniture and the many available options may be seen at the company's three large showrooms (see below).

CUSTOM ORDERS: All orders are custom.

CATALOG AVAILABILITY: Call or write for free information brochure. Photos of specific items available. Ask about video.

RETAIL DISTRIBUTION: Autumn Wood's own showrooms: 3900 Menaul N.E., Albuquerque, NM 87110; 3501 Cerrillos, Santa Fe, NM 87501; 1340 South Solano, Las Cruces, NM 88001.

WHOLESALE SHOWROOMS AND REPRESENTATIVES: No wholesale sales.

HONORS AND SPECIAL COMMISSIONS: Member: Chambers of Commerce and Better Business Bureaus in Albuquerque, Santa Fe, and Las Cruces, New Mexico. U.S. Chamber of Commerce: Blue Chip Enterprise Award, 1991.

Beaver Works, Inc.

OWNER/DESIGNER: Jonathan Frykholm

ADDRESS: 5959 Omaha Boulevard, Colorado Springs, CO 80915

TELEPHONE: (719) 380-0921

FAX: (719) 380-1425

By adding its own design features to a complete line of lodgepole pine furniture, Beaver Works has developed a distinctive signature style for its high country Colorado home furnishings line. Each furniture piece uses mortise and tenon joinery and is offered in a full range of colors and finishes. Jonathan Frykholm, owner of Beaver Works, says that his furniture can be made to suit the needs of practically any customer who wants a Western, Southwestern, or Country design motif.

Beaver Works makes furniture out of all types of lodgepole pine log pieces but especially enjoys the challenge of creating unique furniture from naturally curved logs. According to Frykholm, these curved logs are ideally suited for headboards, benches, and chairs. Another design feature of the Beaver Works line is hand-peeled log surfaces that can only be achieved by the use of a draw knife instead of lathes and sanders.

There may not be another lodgepole pine furniture manufacturer in the country that incorporates colorful, Mexican-made tiles into the surfaces of its pieces the way Beaver Works does. Frykholm has made a national reputation by using these handmade tiles in completing the tops of his dressers, dining room tables, nightstands, and occasional tables.

PRIMARY PRODUCT: Lodgepole pine furniture, including complete room sets for the bedroom, dining room, and living room. Also entertainment centers, coat racks, captain's chairs, benches, coffee tables, barstools, mirrors, and kiva ladders.

PRICE RANGE: $200 to $2,000.

DIRECT SALES: Only wholesale accounts may purchase directly from the production facility.

CUSTOM ORDERS: Custom sizes and design requirements, such as color and shape, are welcome.

ONE OF A KIND: Since each log that Beaver Works furniture starts from is unique, each piece is unique. Commissioned, one-of-a-kind pieces are regularly built by the production facility.

CATALOG AVAILABILITY: Brochure is available at no charge; a designer portfolio is available for a refundable charge of $25.

RETAIL DISTRIBUTION: Country Classics Furniture, Colorado Springs; Kacey Fine Furniture, Denver, Colorado.

WHOLESALE SHOWROOMS AND REPRESENTATIVES: None.

Big Horn Antler Furniture and Design

OWNER/DESIGNER: Michael V. Wilson

ADDRESS: P.O. Box 306, Jackson, WY 83001

TELEPHONE: (307) 733-3491

During the long, cold winters of Mike Wilson's youth, he would observe the men in his family as they fashioned a traditional Wyoming craft, furniture made from antlers. Over the years, this unique style of making chairs, lighting fixtures, and sofas has become Wilson's profession. Today he is known as the region's premier craftsman working exclusively in antler products.

The deer, elk, and moose antlers that Wilson uses in his craft are naturally shed each spring. Wilson spends a good deal of time trying to determine where and when the best antler harvesting will take place. When that time arrives, he ventures into the Wyoming wilderness and literally picks the naturally shed antlers off the ground.

Wilson produces one piece of furniture at a time, making certain that the complex structure of an antler chair, for example, is solidly built, comfortable, and sits squarely on the floor. As each of his pieces uses at least several curved, hooked, forked, and pointed antlers in construction, the progress of each piece must be carefully followed.

PRIMARY PRODUCT: Since 1972, individually designed antler chandeliers, antler tables, antler chairs and love seats, antler sofas, and antler lighting fixtures such as floor lamps, table lamps, and wall sconces. To enhance the Western flavor of these pieces, Mike Wilson adds customized, hand-wrought ironwork, rawhide webbings, leather cushionings, and textile upholsterings, depending on customer's needs.

PRICE RANGE: $450 to $12,000.

DIRECT SALES: Call for an appointment.

CUSTOM ORDERS: While Wilson uses traditional Wyoming designs, he will work with clients to adapt his pieces to suit their needs.

ONE OF A KIND: Most of the pieces are one of a kind, due to the nature of the materials Wilson works with.

CATALOG AVAILABILITY: Yes, along with special project design information.

RETAIL DISTRIBUTION: Jack Dennis Outdoors, Contract Design, Fighting Bear Furniture; all in Jackson, Wyoming.

WHOLESALE SHOWROOMS AND REPRESENTATIVES: Index, Dallas, Texas. Elsie Farrie, San Francisco; Tobane, Los Angeles, California.

HONORS AND SPECIAL COMMISSIONS: Beretta Firearms Corporation, Anheuser Busch Corporation, Houston Livestock and Rodeo Association. Hunting lodges and retreat homes around the world. Trophy case design for big game hunters.

John Becking Designs

OWNER/DESIGNER: John Becking

ADDRESS: P.O. Box 521155, Salt Lake City, UT 84152

TELEPHONE: (801) 277-7957

A woodsman as much as he is a craftsman, John Becking says that he really should be putting in more time at his one-man shop. But that would take away from his true enjoyment, trekking through the forests of Utah, Wyoming, and Colorado in search of the most unlikely pieces of aspen, lodgepole pine, and fire-etched pine that he can turn into exquisite furniture.

Without using any lathing or doweling process, Becking has developed his own system of joinery. This allows him to take crooked, forked, and fire-damaged pieces of wood right from the forest and incorporate them "au naturel" into finished furniture pieces. The wood must be structurally sound yet unusual and artistically challenging to work with.

While Becking takes full advantage of the unique structure of this special wood, he is careful to find enough similarly shaped pieces to be able to complete closely matched sets for full room installations.

PRIMARY PRODUCT: Furniture made from aspen, chocolate aspen, lodgepole pine, and fire-etched pine, including beds of all dimensions, easy chairs, end tables, coffee tables, sofas, dining room tables, and living room chairs. Pedestal tables made from pale ivory-colored juniper, in coffee table, end table, dining table, and entryway console sizes. Pedestal tables made from sandstone-colored incense cedar. Pedestal tables made from weathered desert cedar with bark still on the wood. Table bases, consoles, and wall hangings made from incense cedar roots and red cedar roots, in colors ranging from light tans to rich browns and reds.

PRICE RANGE: $275 to $5,000.

DIRECT SALES: Yes.

CUSTOM ORDERS: Pedestal table heights are adjusted to the thickness of the material the customer selects to use on the table's top. Log furniture is frequently sized and finished to meet customer needs. Becking travels to complete custom installations.

ONE OF A KIND: See above.

CATALOG AVAILABILITY: Brochures are available for both the pedestal tables and log furniture. A charge may be applied for the designer's binder.

RETAIL DISTRIBUTION: Coast to Coast Designs, Park City, Utah.

WHOLESALE SHOWROOMS AND REPRESENTATIVES: Tasha Leonard, Fort Collins, Colorado, (303) 482-3364.

HONORS AND SPECIAL COMMISSIONS: Scottsdale Hilton, Scottsdale, Arizona; Paramount Studios, Hollywood, California.

Collaboration

Collaboration is a uniquely structured design group. It arose spontaneously when three creative people began working with each other on individual pieces of furniture. When Hillary Riggs and Peter Gould experimented with new ways of carving and coloring wood that resulted in lovely pieces like the Iris Bed, they were interested only in producing furniture that reflected their mutual vision. When Peter Gould and Ernest Thompson first began talking about a selected pooling of their production resources, they were seeking stronger design capability within existing work spaces and markets. There was no thought of joining forces on a commercial venture. In fact, there was no thought of any organized effort at all. At the beginning, there was only the sheer joy of combining ways and means, skills and talents to increase the beauty and quality of their work.

The joy still shows, but now it has been translated into a large, beautiful showroom and a flexible design and production system. The workshops are tucked away in various convenient locations, and design ideas as well as actual pieces of furniture flow freely between them. The showroom itself, which opened in 1991, is situated on the busy corner of Guadalupe and Paseo de Peralta in Santa Fe, where its eye-catching windows full of colorful, exuberant furniture draw people like magnets.

Inside is a high, bright space with a wraparound loft reminiscent of a palatial

The Sunflower Cabinet by Hillary Riggs and Peter Gould

contemporary residence. From the balconies and the windows below them one can see beautifully arranged furniture, accessories, and fine art. On the two-story back wall is a mural by Walter Green depicting that artist's special vision of the high desert landscape.

Tucked unobtrusively into this glorious environment is a highly efficient, full-service design system that is accessible to the private residential client, the industrial decorator, and everyone in between. In a matter of minutes, the showroom can connect with any or all of the individual collaborators' workrooms and can get exactly the right custom order tailored to the site specifications and the client's tastes.

The three principal furniture designers whose paths have converged at this unique juncture are each at the top of their respective disciplines. Hillary Riggs is the owner of The Sombraje Collection, home of the famous twig shutters and furnishings, and was the originator of that company's color system. She has since carried her color expertise further, developing new ways to impregnate wood surfaces with brilliant hues that allow the wood grain to remain visible as a design element. She designs a line of furniture that uses these translucent polychrome glazes as integral formal components. The subjects, which are mostly flowers in many hues, become the basic elements rather than decorations. She is also a talented painter whose radiant canvases are exhibited at Collaboration.

Peter Gould has been an

influential presence on the New Mexico furniture scene since the mid-1970s. He is widely recognized for the attractive, superbly finished furniture pieces he crafts in a contemporary vision derived from Spanish Colonial and Shaker design themes.

Gould designs and manufactures furniture with Chris Sparks, a native-born Texan who has been trained in the American Colonial and German Shaker schools of design. Their line is marketed under the Sparks Brothers name and is a contemporary embodiment of Southwestern and Texas Hill Country furniture motifs.

As a design-oriented workshop, Sparks Brothers is able to concentrate on the design details that enhance the beauty and functionality of their furniture. The finishes and hardware that complete a Sparks Brothers piece are custom-designed and carefully considered. Each finish, whether translucent or rich, is applied with attention given to bringing out the wood's best qualities. Hardware is hand-forged and built to enhance the furniture's design integrity.

While most of the beds, cabinets, credenzas, tables, chairs, and desks built by Sparks Brothers use ponderosa pine and sugar pine, their recently introduced Texas Hill Country collection relies on the rich hues of Texas pecan, a traditional hardwood furniture building material. The designs used in this collection are an incorporation of the best aspects of the features seen in furniture in the Southwest. Starting in mid-1992, this collection will be available at the Hamilton Sparks furniture store in Austin, Texas, as well as through Collaboration in Santa Fe.

The Ernest Thompson Furniture Company is the state's largest, most widely marketed home furnishings manufacturer. While Thompson himself has assumed an advisory role with the company, his successors, Mike and Doreen Godwin, have continued to produce the unique furniture designs that have made the name Ernest Thompson synonymous with Southwest furniture craftsmanship.

The signature style of Ernest Thompson Furniture is actually a combination of bold, complex hand carvings and solid, mortise-and-tenon joinery. The design motifs that characterize the company's several individual furniture collections range from the geometric and crazily colored Wild West Collection to the subdued, timeless lines of the Sandia Collection. The Ernest

Iris Bed #2 by Hillary Riggs and Peter Gould

Thompson Furniture designs are so broadly positioned in the national furniture market that when Mike Godwin tracks the line's sales patterns, he is able to predict when and where the popularity trends of one of the company's furniture collections will start rising or tapering off in a given area.

Understanding the national furniture market and being able to adjust its production accordingly is the reason Ernest Thompson Furniture has remained at the forefront of Southwestern home furnishings fashion trends. Mike and Doreen Godwin have used their industry savvy and marketing know-how to establish themselves in the European home furnishings market.

As both an individual corporation and as a part of Collaboration, Ernest Thompson Furniture has the ability to design and produce in quantity any specific

Trastero, shutters, table, and chairs by Peter Gould

or hybrid furniture piece an individual or corporate client may desire. If one member of Collaboration needs a chair to be made with features from the Ernest Thompson line, the Godwins are capable of producing such a piece to specific customer dimensions. Similarly, if a customer requires a substantial number of furniture pieces from any of the Collaboration designs, Ernest Thompson's production capacity can be tailored to fit that client's design or delivery requirements.

Thompson, Riggs, and Gould had known each other in business circles for some time, but the right elements did not fall into place until early 1991. At that time, Peter Gould had his woodworking operation in the magnificent space now occupied by the Collaboration showroom. Conversations between one and another of the designers and their partners led to a meeting from

Sombraje shutters, table, and chair; Peter Gould cabinet

which ideas flowed, built up, and finally took off. Changes started immediately, and by the end of the year, each of the manufacturing and retail situations had been altered to everyone's satisfaction and the showroom had become a reality.

The multifaceted group known as Collaboration is rapidly evolving into a formidably efficient and creative supplier of large design projects, whether those projects are built around an authentic Southwestern theme or are bright, innovative, and all-American in their total look. In addition to being available as a very flexible custom design venture, Collaboration has also created a regular collection of furniture lines.

The most interesting development is a new group of outdoor furnishings. The elegant design of this line, like the rest of Collaboration's furnishings, embodies the spirit and substance of the American Southwest. And the collaborative venture itself embodies the spirit of the American craftsman.

Ernest Thompson's carved and painted chest

Ernest Thompson's signature carving designs on a bench

The Tesuque trestle table and chairs by Ernest Thompson, with spiral, sunburst, keyhole, and chip carving

Dennis McMillan

*A*t the age of forty, Dennis McMillan has become known throughout the Southwest and the United States for his line of handcrafted furniture. From contemporary to Southwest designs, from the home to the office, his furniture has become synonymous with quality, prestige, and elegance.

Throughout his career, McMillan has been learning business the old-fashioned way, by doing it. That has meant setting goals, taking chances, failing, succeeding, but always keeping one thought in mind: "Do the best you can, be honest and fair, and don't demand absolute perfection all the time. Nature is not perfect, man is not perfect, and, it is true, I am not perfect either," he says.

McMillan's furniture career started in junior high school. He won the "Who's Who" for wood shop in the ninth grade because of his enthusiasm and skill, which pointed him toward his first professional goal of becoming an industrial arts teacher. He went to the University of Northern Colorado in Greeley and, on graduation, returned to his junior high and high school in Palo Alto, California. There, he taught beside those teachers he had admired and appreciated. This was a real achievement and honor for him, one he says that he appreciates as much today as he did then.

McMillan could not turn away, however, from the excitement of moving to a small mountain town and

Corner cabinets with some of the available finishes and details

starting his own business when the opportunity presented itself. In 1973, after spending a couple of weeks looking at the clear blue skies of New Mexico, enjoying the casual atmosphere, and appreciating the artistic energy of the area, he moved to Santa Fe. Hence, McMillan's Woodworks was born.

He found a 2,000-square-foot shop in what was then an undesirable part of town. But McMillan could see the possibilities the area had to offer and correctly assessed it as a high visibility location that would attract a lot of walk-in traffic.

He vividly remembers finding the old boarded up body shop, calling the telephone number on the For Lease sign, and making his first real business deal. He entered into a ten-year lease, one that left only him to answer for the successes or failures that were to come. The day he opened, a fellow woodworker dropped by to tell him he was crazy, that the shop was too big for one man, and that he would be out of business in six months. But the business grew despite this pessimistic prediction.

Exciting things began to happen. A famous photographer asked him to build "a coffee table that would sing." McMillan gave it a try. When the client returned, he was told, "Here's the table. I don't know if it sings yet." Evidently it did, because the client was delighted. It was a good omen.

McMillan continued to set goals for himself. One goal

was to remodel his woodshop into an extraordinary showroom and fabulous art gallery. His dream was to attract top artists to show with him. The way to do this, he knew, was to create an exciting environment for their work as well as his own.

The result was a gallery that people still talk about more than a decade later. It was the factory showroom by which others were measured. It was beautifully lit with Saltillo tile floors, a loft, and a quirky fireplace/fountain. Some of the most exciting art of the time hung on the walls: Charles Collins, Loren Willis, Kevin Red Star, and the late Helen Hardin, for whom McMillan hosted three lavish Indian market exhibits.

He added new lines, which today include a wide variety of furnishings crafted in ponderosa pine and Appalachian red oak. In association with the esteemed Streck family of Santa Fe, he also produces modified reproductions of very old Spanish Colonial pieces, crafting them to a scale and sturdiness suitable for modern interiors. The Strecks collaborate with him by providing special painted finishes as well as punched tin and copper panels.

Over the years McMillan's business continued to prosper. He worked toward other goals, such as buying a beautiful piece of land on the outskirts of Santa Fe with wonderful views and seclusion and building his home himself. Today, twelve years later, he still lives in that home. He appreciates the beauty, simplicity, and solitude that he, his wife, Nancy, and their two dogs and two cats experience each day.

McMillan describes it as an "in-town haven while I'm between visits to my mountain sanctuary." That small two-room retreat, high in the mountains of northern New Mexico, has "no phone, no running water, and no people. Just lots of deer, elk, turkey, and bear and lots of raw beauty with which to become one—to learn, to

The look and feel of the Southwest in a handsome conversational grouping

reflect, to enjoy, and to let the creative juices flow." He says the sanctuary provides him with relaxation that is otherwise impossible while running a small business. He and his wife and two dogs sometimes spend as much as two weeks at a time there.

McMillan talks a lot of his mother and father, whom he credits with helping him develop his creative ability and his appreciation for the outdoors. He wants to carry on the legacy of his loving father and to continue to be a source of pride to his mother, in his failures as well as in his successes.

Somehow, he finds time for a very special personal activity, teaching woodworking at a local retirement center one day a week. His enthusiasm is plainly evident as he talks about how he loves to teach his older students to build shelves, bird houses, and folk animals. "They tell me it's the one activity they look forward to all week," he says. "They just can't get enough. They work until they have to quit for dinner, and then they start planning for next time." Evidently, they have caught McMillan's dynamic spirit.

Echoes of old Santa Fe in an elegant dining ensemble

A luxury custom residence furnished entirely by Dennis McMillan

During the recession of the mid-1980s, McMillan had to give up the gallery/showroom concept that had been ahead of its time. To concentrate on furniture, which was what he knew best, he did not renew his lease on the magnificent space on old Guadalupe Street. He moved his furniture business to a more reasonably priced showroom. Soon after this move, McMillan reached an agreement with American Furniture Company, a family-owned company of large stores with whom he enjoys a friendly professional relationship, to be his exclusive New Mexico representative. He has also opened his own showrooms in Tucson, Arizona; Las Vegas, Nevada; and Dallas, Texas. He travels frequently to his various showrooms, continually adapting and refining his approach to an ever-changing market.

Obviously, Dennis McMillan is a man on the move.

Dennis McMillan teaches woodworking to an enthusiastic retiree

He knows that big rewards come from taking calculated risks, and he has the courage to do so. Sometimes an idea does not work out exactly as he had planned, so he moves on to a better one. More often, his daring efforts pay off.

McMillan says that his business was summed up in a poem written by a young friend. At the time, he was a "big brother" with the Big Brother/Big Sister organization. It was his little brother, John Howell, who wrote:

We are McMillan Woodworks from Santa Fe.
We build furniture the old-fashioned way.
Mortise and tenon construction and kiln dried wood
Means we can build your furniture better than
  anyone else could.
If it's quality you're looking for, come in and see
Our showroom full of Southwest furniture and
  wonderful accessories.

Comfortable Southwestern bedroom furnishings

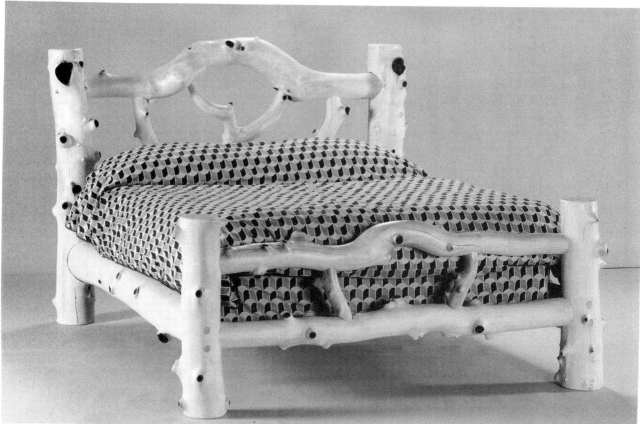

Top: Sand-blasted cedar root table
Bottom: Aspen wood king-size bed

Blue Canyon Woodworks

OWNER/DESIGNER: Larry Hulsey and Judy Hulsey

ADDRESS: 1310 Siler Road, #1, Santa Fe, NM 87501

TELEPHONE: (505) 471-0136

Larry Hulsey, owner/designer of Blue Canyon Woodworks, is a second generation woodworker. He assists clients by custom designing furniture to fit individual needs and tastes. His stately furnishings are solidly crafted, richly detailed, and brought to a high finish.

Blue Canyon's traditional New Mexican pieces feature hand-planed surfaces for a smooth texture that is distressed to give an original appearance. These antique reproductions are scaled for comfort and high standards of design for home or office. Hulsey also creates original variations such as carved Mimbres designs in door panels and deeply etched petroglyph figures in cast stone tabletops.

PRIMARY PRODUCT: Fine Southwestern furniture, custom designed per individual order. Traditional New Mexico antique reproductions scaled for modern comfort and practicality. Contemporary designs to clients' specifications. Mortise and tenon joinery. Ash, alder, cherry, oak, poplar, walnut, or pine.

OTHER LINES: Cabinets, doors, screen doors, gates, shutters, moldings.

PRICE RANGE: $400 to $6,000.

DIRECT SALES: Workshop has a separate showroom of representative pieces. Customers are welcome from 8:00 a.m. to 5:00 p.m. Monday through Saturday and by appointment to view designs, woods, colors, and workmanship. Mail and telephone orders per company specifications. Blue Canyon will ship, blanket wrapped, anywhere.

CUSTOM ORDERS: Client participation is encouraged. Working drawings with all elevations and dimensions, plus finish sample on the wood of choice, provided as part of Blue Canyon's custom design service.

ONE OF A KIND: See above.

CATALOG AVAILABILITY: Brochure $1.00.

RETAIL DISTRIBUTION: Through Blue Canyon's Santa Fe showroom.

HONORS AND SPECIAL COMMISSIONS: Renovation of the New Mexico State Capitol, commission work. Art furniture produced for the New Mexico State Capitol. Presidential home, West Texas State University. Furnishings, Saint Thomas the Apostle Catholic Church. Residences and offices throughout the United States.

Top: Galisteo bench, 33″ × 33″ × 20″, Honduras mahogany, custom upholstery
Bottom: Blue Canyon's Rio Grande desk, 33″ × 72″ × 29″, walnut

Blue Stone Woodworks

OWNER/DESIGNER: Bill Cheatwood

ADDRESS: 637B South Broadway, #205, Boulder, CO 80303

TELEPHONE: (303) 494-1785

Like many craftsmen who are creating furniture in the American West, Bill Cheatwood has made furniture for nearly his entire adult life. Having been raised in the Midwest, he was exposed to traditional Shaker furniture styles in the homes of his friends and relatives. After moving to Colorado, he became an admirer of the colonial furniture styles that were brought to the Southwest by Spanish settlers in the 1600s.

The Blue Stone Woodworks furniture line emphasizes these influences in its design motifs. Some of the pieces are exact reproductions of historic Spanish Colonial designs, while other pieces blend the updated versions of these designs with elements of Shaker furniture pieces found in the East and Midwest. While all of Cheatwood's creations use mortise and tenon joinery with square pegs for added support, he has also reconfigured the dimensions of his pieces and added a sophisticated upholstery system for modern comfort.

Blue Stone furniture is mostly pine in its construction, although other softwoods and hardwoods are often used for specifically commissioned pieces. The stains and paint finishes are lightly applied, resulting in a washed or slightly weathered appearance.

PRIMARY PRODUCT: Spanish Colonial and Shaker/Southwestern furniture. Pieces include chairs, benches, dining tables, shelves, kitchen tables, mirrors, and mantles.

PRICE RANGE: $350 to $2,000.

DIRECT SALES: Yes, through the Blue Stone production facility in Boulder, Colorado. Mail and telephone orders accepted.

CUSTOM ORDERS: Clients are invited to select among the several fabric and finish options offered by Blue Canyon, as well as among the company's design motifs.

ONE OF A KIND: Many pieces have been crafted to fit specific designer requests. On-site design and installation services are available.

CATALOG AVAILABILITY: Price list and brochure are available at no cost.

RETAIL DISTRIBUTION: Great Things West, Breckenridge; Soho West, Denver, Colorado. Red Rock Trading Company, Washington, D.C.

Brenden & Company

OWNER/DESIGNER: Robert Brenden

ADDRESS: Box 175, Dixon, NM 87527

TELEPHONE: (505) 579-4696

Robert Brenden is in a class by himself. His furnishings resemble no one else's, yet they are a genuine expression of the brightest and most fanciful Southwestern designs today. He studied art and ceramics at the Instituto Allende in San Miguel de Allende, Mexico, and received his degree in art and Spanish at the College of Santa Fe. He also attended the University of New Mexico, where he took courses in the Russian Studies department.

Out of this background came his joyous furniture designs. "My work reflects Latin American and Russian Baroque influences, with Territorial motifs including Second Empire stylistic variations," Brenden explains. "I call it 'Territorial Baroque,' as I fuse elements of these styles in unusual ways."

PRIMARY PRODUCT: Unique trasteros, tables, chairs, benches, and repisas (wall shelves) in sugar pine, basswood, and poplar. Tables frequently have turned legs. Mortise and tenon joinery. Architectural millwork. Vivid colors in bold contrast, stained rather than painted so that the wood grain shows through.

OTHER LINES: Constructions or shrines utilizing found objects and old architectural pieces. Extravagant bird cages.

PRICE RANGE: $150 to $3,000.

DIRECT SALES: Clients are always welcome at Brenden's brightly colored workshop on Highway 75 in beautiful downtown Dixon, New Mexico. Mail and telephone orders are graciously accepted.

CUSTOM ORDERS: "Custom orders are always welcome, as long as they are interesting to me."

ONE OF A KIND: Most pieces are one of a kind. Brenden will travel to meet with clients.

CATALOG AVAILABILITY: Color Xeroxes available on request.

RETAIL DISTRIBUTION: Brenden Workshop, Dixon; LoFino, Taos, New Mexico. Museum of American Folk Art, New York City.

WHOLESALE SHOWROOMS AND REPRESENTATIVES: Johanna Welty, Ltd., Walnut Creek, California.

HONORS AND SPECIAL COMMISSIONS: Absolut Vodka, Southwest Ad campaign, *Country Home Magazine*. Museum of International Folk Art, Santa Fe, display/lecture kiosk. Studio Tour Coordinator, Dixon Arts Association. Award of Merit, Taos Furniture Show, 1988. Examples of Territorial woodwork at Andrew Dasburg House and Hughston House, Taos, and Coburn House, Dixon, New Mexico.

L. D. Burke III Cowboy Furniture and Mirrors

OWNER/DESIGNER: L. D. Burke III

ADDRESS: 1516 Pacheco, Santa Fe, NM 87501

TELEPHONE: (505) 986-1866, (505) 983-8001

In a classic understatement, the *New York Times* reported several years ago, "L. D. Burke III, a cowboy furniture maker from Santa Fe, is doing some of the most adventurous work coming out of the Great Southwest today." Adventurous is not the half of it. Burke's imagination is boundless, and his sense of humor is the stuff of legend.

"As an artist, I'm working the fine line between cornpone and slick stuff," he admits cheerfully. His idiosyncratic furniture, ruggedly built to last for three generations, is frequently emblazoned with original cowboy sayings, sometimes picked out in brass nail heads: "Ya can tell a real winner by the way he plays a losin' hand," and "If you take life seriously, how do you explain yesterday?"

Burke's furniture is also embellished with a variety of artifacts including horseshoes, spurs, horns, silver dollars, and other Western paraphernalia. The overall look is unabashedly romantic, recalling the bygone glories of range life and the Code of the West. L. D. Burke's furniture brings it back alive.

PRIMARY PRODUCT: Original and one-of-a-kind furniture, hand adzed, painted, and waxed for "a finish that feels like a newborn calf." Beds, daybeds, headboards, chairs, dining room tables, trasteros, chests, sideboards, and wonderful children's furniture.

OTHER LINES: Mirrors, lamps, chandeliers, cabinet doors, horn racks. "In fact, anything to furnish the ranch or home."

PRICE RANGE: $175 to $20,000.

DIRECT SALES: Complete showroom open by appointment only, at 1516 Pacheco, one mile from the Plaza in Santa Fe. Call (505) 986-1866 for appointment.

CUSTOM ORDERS: "Custom orders are becoming the rule."

ONE OF A KIND: Many unique commissions and installations with the help of a small, highly trained staff. Work can be shipped anywhere.

CATALOG AVAILABILITY: Send $15 for a full-color catalog and price list.

RETAIL DISTRIBUTION: Jane Smith's, Santa Fe, New Mexico, and Aspen, Colorado. Yippee-Ei-O, Scottsdale and Phoenix, Arizona, and Santa Monica, California. For Heavens Sake, Dallas; Blue Coyote, Houston, Texas. Gene Autry Museum and Rituals, Los Angeles; Raffia, Van Nuys; Painted Desert, Salinas, California. Philbrook Museum of Art, Tulsa, Oklahoma. Santa Fe Connection, Kansas City, Kansas. Comina, Hartford, Connecticut, and Providence, Rhode Island. Spirit of the Earth, Fall River, Massachusetts.

HONORS AND SPECIAL COMMISSIONS: One hundred seventy-five national and international awards over a thirty-year period.

A corner of L.D. Burke's showroom in Santa Fe

Captured in Colorado

OWNER/DESIGNER: Tom G. Urlacher

ADDRESS: 1207 Highway 65, Eckert, CO 81418

TELEPHONE: (303) 835-8462

FAX: (303) 835-8514

From a tiny roadside workshop in the heart of Colorado's apple orchard country, Tom Urlacher designs and builds an extensive line of pine, willow, and lodgepole pine furniture. His Captured in Colorado line is a testament to his Old World standards of craftsmanship.

What is important to Urlacher is how a piece will look and function years from now, not how long it has taken to create it. While his most popular furniture collection is the one made from willow, Tom also specializes in handcrafting his own unique collection of lodgepole pine furniture for clients outfitting custom homes in the Colorado ski resort regions.

Each fan-back or heart-shaped willow furniture piece that leaves his showroom is branded with his back-to-back "CC" mark, which carries with it an indication of the pride and honest effort Urlacher builds into each of his creations.

PRIMARY PRODUCT: Adirondack-style willow furniture, designed with an updated, contemporary appeal. Heirloom designs such as fan-back chairs and love seats, heart-back chairs and love seats, wedding arches, sofas, tables, children's furniture, and lighting fixtures.

OTHER LINES: Lodgepole pine furniture, stone-top tables, burl wood tables, clocks, and glass-top root tables.

PRICE RANGE: $75 to $13,500.

DIRECT SALES: Visitors willing to make the trip to Urlacher's roadside workshop and showroom are welcome, but call ahead to let him know you are on your way.

CUSTOM ORDERS: Yes. Designers and clients are welcome to contact Urlacher.

ONE OF A KIND: Urlacher enjoys doing on-site commissions and specific installation projects. Much of his custom work is in the Phoenix and Denver areas, but he has undertaken projects from coast to coast.

CATALOG AVAILABILITY: Catalog is available at a moderate cost.

RETAIL DISTRIBUTION: Captured in Colorado, Scottsdale, Arizona. In Home, Santa Fe, New Mexico. Malo Interior Design, Cambridge, Massachusetts.

WHOLESALE SHOWROOMS AND REPRESENTATIVES: Through the Captured in Colorado production facility in Eckert, Colorado, and through the Captured in Colorado showroom in Scottsdale, Arizona.

HONORS AND SPECIAL COMMISSIONS: Several stores for Ralph Lauren Polo.

David E. C'de Baca

OWNER/DESIGNER: David E. C'de Baca

ADDRESS: Rt. 14, Box 234D, Santa Fe, NM 87505

TELEPHONE: (505) 438-3211

"After spending a lot of time watching my father make furniture," recalls David C'de Baca, "I knew deep down that of his five sons, I would be the one to continue the tradition established in my family. This tradition is important to me. I want to do what I can to see that those who come after me can learn from, use, and enjoy the Spanish furniture I make today. Spanish New Mexican furniture is my heritage."

C'de Baca stays as close to the authentic styles as possible while satisfying the needs of his customers for furniture that will work in a present-day setting. Like his Spanish wood-carver ancestors, he uses pine, the wood most commonly found in New Mexico. He uses the same carving designs and techniques they used. Many honors and commissions have come to him because of his fine craftsmanship and his devotion to tradition.

PRIMARY PRODUCT: Traditional Spanish New Mexican furniture in ponderosa and sugar pine: from night-stands to hand-carved office desks.

PRICE RANGE: $300 to $5,000.

DIRECT SALES: Yes, by appointment at the workshop.

CUSTOM ORDERS: Frequently.

ONE OF A KIND: Not very often.

CATALOG AVAILABILITY: Photos of specific items a client is interested in.

RETAIL DISTRIBUTION: Santa Fe, New Mexico, Spanish Market, summer and winter shows.

HONORS AND SPECIAL COMMISSIONS: Spanish Market, annual summer event recently expanded to include a winter show: 1st, 2nd, and 3rd places plus special awards since 1978. Collections: New Mexico State Capitol Renovation Project, Santa Fe Public Library, and International Folk Art Museum, Santa Fe; La Cienega Village Museum, La Cienega; Millicent Rogers Museum, Taos, all in New Mexico. Restaurants, luxury condo developments, churches, residences.

Chew Design

OWNER/DESIGNER: Keith Chew

ADDRESS: 1516 17th Street, Denver, CO 80202

TELEPHONE: (303) 534-0322

A graduate of London's Tailor & Cutter Academy, Keith Chew holds the title "Tailor of Bespoke Clothes for Men." He also spent a few years as a professional ski racer. Chew has turned his considerable talents to the design and manufacture of custom home furnishings, crafted for both adults' and children's living environments.

"I deal directly with clients, determining what their specific needs are, then using any materials available to me to meet their requirements for unique, one-of-a-kind furniture," Chew says. Ironwork becomes a gravity-defying mass of smooth metal forms under his experienced hands. Wood is bent and joined in a series of unexpected shapes, while filling its precise design needs and functional requirements.

The furniture pieces designed by Keith Chew are varied in terms of both materials and form. He has provided corporate suites, downtown condominiums, and palatial homes throughout the Denver area with furnishings of distinct design and flawless construction.

PRIMARY PRODUCT: Custom, one-of-a-kind adult and children's furniture.

PRICE RANGE: $300 and up, depending on client's needs.

DIRECT SALES: Keith Chew deals directly with each client.

CUSTOM ORDERS: Exclusively.

ONE OF A KIND: Exclusively.

CATALOG AVAILABILITY: No, but photographs of individual pieces are available.

RETAIL DISTRIBUTION: Chew Designs, Inc., 1516 17th Street, inside the historic Barth Hotel, Denver, Colorado.

Collaboration:
Ernest Thompson & Co., The Sombraje Collection, Sparks Bros./Peter Gould Design

OWNER/DESIGNER: Mike Godwin (Ernest Thompson); Hillary Riggs (Sombraje); Peter Gould and Chris Sparks (Sparks Bros./Peter Gould)

ADDRESS: 544 S. Guadalupe, Santa Fe, NM 87501

TELEPHONE: (505) 984-3045

FAX: (505) 982-5281

Several major furniture designers and manufacturers recently pooled their resources and markets to create a unique showroom and cooperative production enterprise called Collaboration. Ernest Thompson, a fifth-generation northern New Mexican, is influenced by the history and beauty of the region. He is known for his dedication to maintaining the traditional techniques of Old World master craftsmen. Hillary Riggs, owner/designer of Sombraje, has degrees in painting and art history from the Instituto Allende/University of Guanajuato, San Miguel de Allende, Mexico. She is influenced by the land and colors of the Southwest. Peter Gould studied architecture at Texas A&M and spent many years visiting the wood-carvers of Texas and getting a feel for the region. He recently became partners with Chris Sparks, a similarly trained designer. Together, these artists form the core of the multitalented, sophisticated design group that is Collaboration. (Also see special profile.)

PRIMARY PRODUCT: Handcrafted Southwestern regional furniture and twig shutters, primarily produced in pine, but other wood choices are available. Full range of residential, outdoor, office, and commercial furniture. Architectural elements such as doors and corbels. Functional art furniture: beautiful art pieces that have a practical use as well. Wide variety of finishes, including color washes, available.

OTHER LINES: Paintings, lighting, accessories.

PRICE RANGE: $225 (chairs) to $2,495 (buffets). Art furniture $4,000 to $15,000.

DIRECT SALES: Collaborations showroom is open six days a week. Clients and visitors welcome. Orders accepted by mail or phone.

CUSTOM ORDERS: Custom orders are welcomed at Collaboration. Custom finishes are available.

ONE OF A KIND: Unique commissions are accepted. Can provide on-site installations. One-of-a-kind pieces a specialty; an example is the well-known Iris Bed.

CATALOG AVAILABILITY: Ernest Thompson catalog $5, Sombraje brochure (shutters and furniture) and Sparks Bros./Peter Gould brochure.

RETAIL DISTRIBUTION: Collaboration showroom, Santa Fe, New Mexico.

HONORS AND SPECIAL COMMISSIONS: Member ASID, ISID. Most recent major commissions: Plaza Real Hotel; Eldorado Hotel; Bishops Lodge; Inn of the Anasazi; Vermejo Park, all in Santa Fe; University of New Mexico, Albuquerque, New Mexico. McCormick Ranch Inn, Scottsdale, Arizona. Disney Dolphin Hotel. Numerous large (and famous) residential projects.

Columbine Mountain Crafts

OWNER/DESIGNER: Richard Dunham

ADDRESS: P.O. Box 444, Lake City, CO 81235

TELEPHONE: (303) 944-2245

From his workshop at the 8,700-foot elevation of Lake City, Colorado, Richard Dunham produces furniture pieces that are built to withstand the temperature extremes common in this part of the country. He has almost twenty years of experience in the cabinetry and home-building fields. He even builds the foot-powered lathes on which his furniture pieces are crafted.

Columbine Mountain Crafts specializes in the manufacture of marquetry furniture pieces, particularly headboards for beds. Using locally grown aspen and pine as a starting point for his furniture, Dunham crafts marquetry inlay plaques that are set into the headboards. Several marquetry designs are available; the hummingbird design is the most popular.

The design style used in these furniture pieces is one Dunham has developed over the years. He calls it a "Colorado-Rocky Mountain Motif," a style that reflects both Victorian and Shaker influences.

PRIMARY PRODUCT: Furniture featuring marquetry plaque inlays, designed in a traditional Victorian/Shaker motif.

OTHER LINES: Handcrafted wood lathes made of aspen wood.

PRICE RANGE: $500 to $8,500.

DIRECT SALES: Yes, just call him at home.

CUSTOM ORDERS: Dunham welcomes the opportunity to design his marquetry plaque inlays to fit the stylistic requirements of his clients.

ONE OF A KIND: Special commissions are welcome, as is the opportunity to complete on-site installations of his work.

CATALOG AVAILABILITY: Photographs and prices are available on request.

RETAIL DISTRIBUTION: Main Street Gallery, Cedaredge; The Colorado Peddler, Writer Square, Denver, Colorado.

WHOLESALE SHOWROOMS AND REPRESENTATIVES: None.

HONORS AND SPECIAL COMMISSIONS: Member, Lake City Mountain Crafts Co-op; American Association of Woodturners. Dunham's work is installed in homes on the East and West coasts and across the Southwest.

Contents Contemporary & Southwestern Furniture

OWNER/DESIGNER: Ken Smalley and Linda Smalley

ADDRESS: 4380 East Grant Road, Tucson, AZ 85712

TELEPHONE: (602) 881-6900

FAX: (602) 322-6900

Working in the furniture styles that are specific to their Sonoran desert environs, Ken and Linda Smalley manufacture a full line of residential and commercial interior furnishings. They define their genre as "Arizona Style."

Contents offers handcrafted furniture made from mesquite wood, sugar pine, cottonwood, Arizona walnut, acacia, and palo verde wood. The company also uses saguaro cactus rib inserts in many of its furniture pieces.

PRIMARY PRODUCT: Handmade, custom furniture for residential and commercial use. Materials are primarily Arizona-grown hardwoods and softwoods and cactus ribs.

PRICE RANGE: Midrange prices. Call for details.

DIRECT SALES: Yes, retail clients are welcome.

CUSTOM ORDERS: Yes, unique commissions are accepted.

ONE OF A KIND: Yes, including fireplaces made from mesquite wood.

CATALOG AVAILABILITY: No.

RETAIL DISTRIBUTION: Through the company's production facility.

Corrales Furniture Company

OWNER/DESIGNER: Mike Gandy

ADDRESS: 4605-4607 Corrales Road, Corrales, NM 87048

TELEPHONE: (505) 897-0348

Mike Gandy refers to his furniture designs as "Hotel Lobby Style—massive old-timey stuff." Each piece has a special quality. It is the kind of thing you would find in an out-of-the-way place and then would refuse to tell your friends where it had been purchased.

Gandy presides genially over the woodshop where his designs are created and also operates a small retail shop on the premises. He is fond of putting a few pieces outside, perhaps a couple of chairs and a trastero. Passersby can seldom resist stopping in to see what else Corrales Furniture Company has to offer.

PRIMARY PRODUCT: Custom furniture: primitive, cowboy, country, Southwest. Mortise and tenon joinery. All pieces constructed of pine.

OTHER LINES: Decorative accessories.

PRICE RANGE: Stools and benches from $50. Furniture $300 and up.

DIRECT SALES: Visitors to the shop are always welcome. Open 8:00 a.m. to 7:00 p.m. Monday through Saturday, 11:00 a.m. to 5:00 p.m. Sunday. New Mexico artisans have consignment spaces in the shop. Mail and telephone orders accepted. MC/Visa (no AmEx). Shipping via UPS available. Gandy delivers locally and defines "local" as Arizona, New Mexico, Colorado, and Texas.

CUSTOM ORDERS: Custom orders are major part of the business.

ONE OF A KIND: Yes. Also install special pieces such as bookcases and cabinets.

CATALOG AVAILABILITY: No.

RETAIL DISTRIBUTION: Corrales Furniture Company, Corrales; Gift 'n' Gourmet, Santa Fe, New Mexico. Y Pico, Tucson, Arizona. Hoshoni, New York City; Kiva Trading Company, Cold Springs Harbor, New York.

WHOLESALE SHOWROOMS AND REPRESENTATIVES: Dallas Market, Phoenix Oasis Show.

Country Furnishings of Taos

OWNER/DESIGNER: Mary Shriver

ADDRESS: P.O. Box 2047, Taos, NM 87571

TELEPHONE: (505) 758-4633

"Taos Country Furnishings is a Southwest version of Williamsburg," said one of the clients of this thriving cottage industry. Certainly, there are similarities, notably, in the use of soft, friendly colors that create a pleasant mood. Taos Blue is one color that is almost a hallmark of the local style.

Mary Shriver coordinates marketing for a group of individual folk artists who do the building, carving, and painting in their homes and studios. "Painted furniture and custom painting has become a style all its own," she has found.

PRIMARY PRODUCT: New Mexican folk art painted furniture. High Mesa line of viga furniture, featuring aspen and spruce beds, chairs, end tables. Pine furniture by Harry Lundberg.

PRICE RANGE: Small retail items $10; furniture to $1,800.

DIRECT SALES: Country Furnishings of Taos is a showroom located in a small adobe house on the main road just north of the center of town. Unique retail items are available. The shop does a lot of business by mail or telephone, from taking orders to working with clients on specific requests.

CUSTOM ORDERS: Many custom orders, for example, building special VCR cabinets and custom painting them.

ONE OF A KIND: All pieces are one of a kind. The painting is always unique and can be done to the customers' specifications. One of the painters, Cassie Demmin, flew to California to paint friezes in a kitchen to match table and chairs purchased in Taos at Country Furnishings. Christine Waszak went to Vail to paint designs around door and window frames to match a bed frame sold to the customer.

CATALOG AVAILABILITY: Call for color Xerox catalog. Moderate charge. Free information package including price list with dimensions and brochure and postcards with photos.

RETAIL DISTRIBUTION: Taos Country Furnishings, 534 North Pueblo Road, Taos, New Mexico.

WHOLESALE SHOWROOMS AND REPRESENTATIVES: Taos Country Furnishings sells to forty galleries and shops around the United States and is transacting future business with shops in Amsterdam and Milano.

Covert Woodworking

OWNER/DESIGNER: Jimmy Covert and Lynda Covert

ADDRESS: 907 Canyon Avenue, Cody, WY 82414

TELEPHONE: (307) 527-6761

As the former owner of a sawmill, Jimmy Covert brings an expert knowledge of different woods and their unique properties into his furniture creations. For several years, he was Cody's acknowledged master repairman and reupholsterer of Thomas Molesworth furniture pieces. Now that Covert's original furniture designs are becoming popular, he has less and less time for restoring classic pieces. But on occasion, if he is attracted to a particular piece, he will agree to rebuild and refurbish it.

Working with woods ranging from juniper to maple to hand-peeled fir poles, Covert's creations can range from Molesworth reproductions to his own modern interpretations of traditional ranch furniture. Combining a range of materials like antlers, hand-woven blankets, driftwoods, and Chimayo blankets from New Mexico into his pieces, Covert has made his own place in Cody's bustling furniture scene.

PRIMARY PRODUCT: A full range of nearly fifty furniture pieces, including couches, easy chairs, end tables, coffee tables, and armoires. Bedroom pieces include frame beds in all sizes, chests, dressers, bureaus, and nightstands. Lighting creations by Covert include chandeliers in cast bronze with cowboy, Indian, and wildlife scenes and also Molesworth-type floor and table lamps.

PRICE RANGE: $150 to $15,000.

DIRECT SALES: By appointment, the public is invited to visit Covert Woodworking at 907 Canyon Avenue, Cody, Wyoming.

CUSTOM ORDERS: With the exception of certain pieces created for industry shows, all of Covert Woodworking's furniture is made for custom orders.

ONE OF A KIND: See above.

CATALOG AVAILABILITY: Photographs of specific pieces available on request. Portfolio available for $35 (refundable). Telephone before ordering.

RETAIL DISTRIBUTION: Big Horn Gallery in Cody and Jackson, Wyoming. Dampierre & Co., New York City.

HONORS AND SPECIAL COMMISSIONS: Member of Master Artisans Guild. Commissions include corporate offices in New York and Los Angeles, ranch residences in Wyoming, Montana, Colorado, and Germany, and room groupings installed in homes on the East and West coasts.

Elise Covlin Designs

OWNER/DESIGNER: Elise Covlin

ADDRESS: P.O. Box 2989, Taos, NM 87571

TELEPHONE: (505) 776-8862

Elise Covlin's furniture is instantly recognizable for its bold design sense and its trademark details such as variegated stripes and slash marks. Her long-legged animals and birds frisk across the surfaces of furniture that she constructs in her workshop in Ranchos de Taos, New Mexico. Covlin is a former petroleum engineer who feels that the discipline of precision drawing and balance has enhanced her artistic career. "I love what I am doing," she says. "If I were asked to conjure up an ideal life, this would be it."

PRIMARY PRODUCT: Contemporary pine furniture, hand painted, carved, or ornamented with pounded tin. Nightstands, coffee tables, trasteros, buffets, armoires, dining room tables, chairs.

OTHER LINES: Lamps, three-dimensional wooden wall constructions, contemporary paintings, and pen and ink drawings.

PRICE RANGE: $100 to $2,000.

DIRECT SALES: High-end store and/or gallery owners are welcome to schedule appointments for private viewing of collection. Orders accepted by telephone or mail or in person.

CUSTOM ORDERS: Frequently accepted, with stipulations regarding artistic freedom.

ONE OF A KIND: Commission pieces are an enjoyable aspect of Covlin's work.

CATALOG AVAILABILITY: Covlin deals mainly with galleries and stores. Their approved clients may request photographs of currently available work.

RETAIL DISTRIBUTION: Taos Connections, Denver, Colorado. Galisteo, San Francisco, California. Mesa Arts, Franklin, Michigan. Chevignon, Paris, France.

WHOLESALE SHOWROOMS AND REPRESENTATIVES: No.

HONORS AND SPECIAL COMMISSIONS: Several solo exhibits in Denver, Colorado, Santa Fe, New Mexico, Detroit, Michigan, and Frederick, Maryland. Featured in numerous articles in national periodicals.

Crazy Horse Enterprises

OWNER/DESIGNER: Dale Thomas and Claudia Thomas

ADDRESS: P.O. Box 421, Gunnison, CO 81230

TELEPHONE: (303) 641-1590

Dale Thomas produces a unique line of free-form furniture from his workshop deep in the mountains of central Colorado. While his designs are influenced by the lodgepole pine furniture so frequently found in this part of the country, the furniture produced by Crazy Horse Enterprises bears little resemblance to its stylistic forebears.

Using a variety of woods, including willow, pine, and juniper, Thomas seeks out raw materials that have bends, forks, bows, and twists. He takes these unsightly pieces of wood, strips them down to their smoothest form, and then sands, waxes, and polishes them into beautiful, sculptural wonders. He then fits these finished pieces together, using similarly sized tree limbs and trunks to achieve a furniture form that is original yet functions effectively as a usable, durable piece of furniture.

Thomas, a woodsman, outdoorsman, and craftsman, enjoys the constant challenge of solving the puzzles presented by the natural curves and variations of the wood pieces he uses in his furniture. During his search for wood in the Colorado forests, he gathers naturally shed deer, elk, and moose antlers he finds on the forest floor. Back in his workshop, he turns these materials into a line of home accessories, including lighting fixtures, mirrors, and picture frames.

PRIMARY PRODUCT: A line of free-form, handcrafted furniture, including tables, chairs, stools, benches, and sofas. In addition, Crazy Horse Enterprises also produces a line of antler products, including picture frames, mirrors, and lighting fixtures.

PRICE RANGE: $100 to $1,400.

DIRECT SALES: Orders are accepted through the Crazy Horse Enterprises showroom, located in Gunnison, Colorado. Telephone and mail orders are accepted, and visitors are welcome.

CUSTOM ORDERS: Custom orders are the mainstay of Crazy Horse's business, as certain materials, characteristics, and design dimensions can be incorporated into finished pieces to meet client's needs.

ONE OF A KIND: While similarities exist in the designs produced by Crazy Horse Enterprises, the nature of the furniture's material dictates that each piece is one of a kind. On-site installation and design work is available.

CATALOG AVAILABILITY: Brochure is available at no charge.

RETAIL DISTRIBUTION: Home Outfitters, Vail; Interiors, Gunnison, Colorado.

Creative Woods by Fred Romero

OWNER/DESIGNER: Fred Romero

ADDRESS: P.O. Box 155, Santa Cruz, NM 87567

TELEPHONE: (505) 753-6270

Fred Romero is a shining example of the native northern New Mexico woodworker who conveys the look of his region by means of traditional detailing. His furniture incorporates notches, bullets, sunburst carving, and other motifs. He cites his father and the culture of his Hispanic heritage as his major influences. He earned a degree in woodworking and carpentry from TVI in Albuquerque and has since established a strong reputation for authentic furniture design and production.

PRIMARY PRODUCT: Custom furniture for the home or office. Traditional New Mexican, Southwestern, and contemporary designs. Ponderosa pine, domestic sugar pine, Appalachian red oak, and sometimes exotic hardwoods. Specializing in gallery furnishings and showcases.

OTHER LINES: Kitchen cabinets.

PRICE RANGE: $50 to $6,000.

DIRECT SALES: Clients are welcome to visit the studio and showroom located in Santa Cruz, New Mexico, twenty miles north of Santa Fe. Call for appointment. Mail and telephone orders accepted.

CUSTOM ORDERS: Romero will work with clients to custom design individual pieces. He will visit your home or office or gallery to measure and consult on the design, size, and color.

ONE OF A KIND: Unique commissions are accepted; will travel to do specific consultations and installations.

CATALOG AVAILABILITY: Color brochure, $3. Call for photos of other available pieces.

RETAIL DISTRIBUTION: Creative Woods, Santa Cruz; Dear and Co., Espanola (Arroyo Seco), New Mexico.

WHOLESALE SHOWROOMS AND REPRESENTATIVES: Own showroom.

HONORS AND SPECIAL COMMISSIONS: New Mexico State Fair Hispanic Art Exhibit: 1st Place, Furniture. Publications: *Once a Tree* (3/90), *Southwest Sampler* (3/91), *Wood Products Magazine* (4/91). Custom commissions: Frank Howell Gallery and High Mesa Inn, Santa Fe; Los Alamos National Laboratory, Los Alamos, New Mexico. Contemporary Southwest Galleries, La Jolla, California. Breckenridge Hilton, Breckenridge, Colorado.

David Cunningham

OWNER/DESIGNER: David Cunningham

ADDRESS: P.O. Box 8307, Santa Fe, NM 87504

TELEPHONE: (505) 982-3941

David Cunningham creates fine art that has functional furniture as its base. He cuts, paints, and collages an uproarious assortment of subjects such as pueblos, mesas, television sets, and mushroom clouds. (One such piece is entitled "There Goes the Neighborhood.") The Pueblo Koshare, a ritual clown figure striped in black and white, appears in many of his pieces. "With his anything-goes personality, Koshare has both personal and historical associations for me," says the artist.

Cunningham is a native Southwesterner, basically self-taught, whose influences are "Robert Crumb, Dr. Seuss, Keith Haring, Lynda Barry, Picasso, Rick Griffin, George Herriman . . ." He creates one piece at a time, in the manner of an artist who works at an easel. Each piece is completely original. Cunningham refers to his art as "furniture-form cartoons."

PRIMARY PRODUCT: Painted trasteros, buffets, television and stereo cabinets. High-quality kiln-dried pine, screwed and doweled together. Linseed oil finish over a painted, sanded wash.

PRICE RANGE: $500 to $5,000.

DIRECT SALES: Clients are welcome to visit the studio. Orders by mail or telephone are gladly accepted.

CUSTOM ORDERS: Whenever possible.

ONE OF A KIND: All the work is one of a kind.

CATALOG AVAILABILITY: Photographs sent to interested parties on request.

RETAIL DISTRIBUTION: Charles and David Interiors, Santa Fe. Elaine Horwitch Galleries, Santa Fe, New Mexico, and Scottsdale, Arizona. Adobe East Gallery, Millburn, New Jersey. Southwest Expressions, Chicago, Illinois.

HONORS AND SPECIAL COMMISSIONS: Nationwide collections.

Dell Woodworks / Santa Fe Concepts

OWNER/DESIGNER: Jim Dell

ADDRESS: Dell Woodworks, 1326 Rufina Circle, Santa Fe, NM 87501

TELEPHONE: (505) 471-3005

ADDRESS: Santa Fe Concepts, 7001 N. Scottsdale Road, Suite 124, Scottsdale, AZ 85253

TELEPHONE: (602) 483-8433

Jim Dell has the right idea about Southwestern furnishings. "If designers stay on the move at all times with new ideas," he says, "the Southwest look will survive for a long time." He knows that any strong regional style must continue to respond to changing times. "The roots of American furniture are right here. It's up to the artist to fulfill the challenge of the new."

Dell himself is the best example of his philosophy in action. He designs furniture that reflects his own vision of a growing Southwest and makes that furniture with a measure of honesty that is rare in today's fast-paced market. He obtains ponderosa pine from northern New Mexico and southern Colorado that is milled with one of the few circular saws still in operation, producing a unique texture that cannot be duplicated. The wood is then air dried to maintain its integrity.

The manufacture and marketing of the furniture from this point is a family endeavor, with individual members overseeing every step from planning the cuts in the wood at the workshop in Santa Fe to managing the stunning new showroom in Scottsdale.

Dell holds a degree in music and teaches privately. From that grounding in rhythm, interval, and texture comes a design sense that is in perfect harmony with interiors throughout the American Southwest and beyond.

PRIMARY PRODUCT: Four main lines of handcrafted wood furniture: Pueblo, the most popular because it represents the Southwest so well; Santa Fe Colonial, a substantial, classic design; American Southwest, a composite of Southwestern themes; and the Desert Collection, incorporating saguaro cactus ribs. A full line of residential, commercial, and office furniture in each of these designs. Full selection of finishes, including soft colors as well as wood stains.

OTHER LINES: Doors.

PRICE RANGE: $350 to $3,500.

DIRECT SALES: Santa Fe Concepts, Scottsdale. A small selection of prototypes at the Santa Fe production facility.

CUSTOM ORDERS: About 50 percent of all orders are customized through Dell's "design brochure."

ONE OF A KIND: No, but prototypes are sometimes available.

CATALOG AVAILABILITY: Dell Woodworks has created a unique "design brochure." Clients can work with it and create their own custom designs through interchangeable parts such as spindles or panels.

RETAIL DISTRIBUTION: Santa Fe Concepts, Dell's big new showroom in Scottsdale.

WHOLESALE SHOWROOMS AND REPRESENTATIVES: Showrooms double as wholesale sources to designers. Trade show participation is planned.

HONORS AND SPECIAL COMMISSIONS: Office furnishings for the Museum of New Mexico.

Denver Design Works, Inc.

OWNER/DESIGNER: Pauline A. Clark

ADDRESS: 1780 Wazee Street, Denver, CO 80202

TELEPHONE: (303) 292-9475

FAX: (303) 295-3724

When Pauline Clark, the owner of Denver Design Works, moved to Colorado in the mid-1970s, she fell under the spell of the primitive, yet comfortable, home furnishings indigenous to the American Southwest. Working with a designer and an expert in the furniture manufacturing field, she developed the several home furnishings lines she is now marketing under the Denver Design Works name.

Denver Design Works' line of home furnishings includes the Kiva Steps Collection, a grouping of tables, lighting fixtures, and pedestals sheathed in copper and built with the geometric design features associated with Southwestern furniture motifs. Easy chairs, sofas, sectionals, and other chairs are contained in the Rio Grande Collection. One of the strongest features offered in the Rio Grande pieces is their comfortable, down-filled, upholstered cushioning systems.

For children's rooms, Denver Design Works offers the Enchanted West Collection, a group of hand-painted furnishings made from maple and pine. These pieces are colorful evocations of the dreams every young cowboy and cowgirl fall asleep to, complete with carved horse, buffalo, and coyote figures on top of each finished item. Finally, the Aspen Log Collection is Denver Design Works' grouping of wash-finished tables, chairs, side chairs, and bar stools. These pieces feature a unique seating system made from woven sisal.

PRIMARY PRODUCT: Furniture for adults and children in several distinct collections, including Kiva Step, Rio Grande, Enchanted West, and Aspen Log.

PRICE RANGE: $395 to $4,000.

DIRECT SALES: Denver Design Works maintains a showroom at the Soho West Gallery, 1780 Wazee Street, Denver, Colorado. Mail and telephone orders are accepted with a check or credit card.

CUSTOM ORDERS: All furniture pieces sold by Denver Design Works are custom made to order. The customer selects the finish, size, color, and upholstering for each piece.

ONE OF A KIND: One-of-a-kind pieces are welcome commissions at Denver Design Works. The company just completed restoration of a railroad car for the Denver & Rio Grande Railroad and has renovated numerous cabins at Woody Creek, Colorado.

CATALOG AVAILABILITY: Catalog sheets and price lists for individual collections are available at a small cost by mail or by telephone.

RETAIL DISTRIBUTION: Soho West Gallery, 1730 Wazee Street, Denver, Colorado.

WHOLESALE SHOWROOMS AND REPRESENTATIVES: Kailer-Grant Design, Santa Fe, New Mexico. Howard Mathew, Ltd., Design Center at the Ice House, Denver, Colorado.

Desert Song

OWNER/DESIGNER: J. Alan Wreyford and Mary M. Wreyford

ADDRESS: 6300 S. Highway 60, #102, Apache Junction, AZ 85219

TELEPHONE: (602) 844-3102

Alan and Mary Wreyford etch petroglyph designs onto flagstone tabletops. They do not work from textbook sources but from images they have found while sketching and photographing ancient Indian petroglyph sites. The effect is one of making each piece of furniture into a storytelling medium.

They build lodgepole pine and aspen wood bases for these tabletops and continue the theme into a full line of furniture designs. The cross-beams of their rustic pieces are secured with leather straps, creating a sophisticated yet rustic flavor.

PRIMARY PRODUCT: Complete collection of lodgepole pine and aspen wood furniture using mortise and tenon joinery, leather securing straps, and flagstone tabletops. Leather and glass tabletops are also available. Collection includes dining tables, chairs, beds of all dimensions, sofas, settees, benches, and coffee tables. Retail merchandise display units are also available.

OTHER LINES: Hohokam collection, influenced by Sonoran desert and saguaro cactus motifs, will be introduced in mid-1992.

PRICE RANGE: $250 to $2,500.

DIRECT SALES: Yes, through the production facility.

CUSTOM ORDERS: Yes. The Wreyfords are eager to work with customers who have a definite sense of what they want.

ONE OF A KIND: Yes, especially in the sense of reproducing new sets of Indian petroglyph designs on tabletops.

CATALOG AVAILABILITY: No catalog, but photograph portfolio is available to designers.

RETAIL DISTRIBUTION: Cogswell Gallery, Vail; Squash Blossom, Denver; Santa Fe Ambiance, Boulder, Colorado.

Designer Southwestern Furniture

OWNER/DESIGNER: David Slocum

ADDRESS: P.O. Box 767, Medanales, NM 87548

TELEPHONE: (505) 685-4688

David Slocum's furniture is noted for its Old World craftsmanship, which he learned while studying cabinetmaking during a twelve-year residency in Germany. He also traveled extensively in Spain. His education includes history and art history, which gives him a broad perspective on functional art.

Today, he lives and works in a rural area of northern New Mexico. His neighbors include respected crafts-people and artists, some of whom collaborate with him on producing fine Southwestern furnishings.

PRIMARY PRODUCT: Contemporary Southwestern furniture of ponderosa pine featuring mortise and tenon joinery. Very comfortable chairs with rounded backs and woven wool cushion covers by well-known Medanales weaver Cordelia Coronado. Armoires or roperos, buffets, dining sets, Parsons tables, end tables or coffee tables, benches, beds, couches or daybeds, dressers, mirrors, writing tables, desks.

OTHER LINES: Professional photography.

PRICE RANGE: Estimates per job.

DIRECT SALES: Slocum maintains a private client list. Inquiries are invited.

CUSTOM ORDERS: Custom orders only. "No assembly line or production-type pieces." Slocum always works with clients on measurements and drawings of new ideas.

ONE OF A KIND: "Each piece is unique. I don't have a line of furniture. Except for chairs, I seldom build the same piece twice." Slocum will, for instance, measure, design, produce, and install cabinetry for a complete kitchen.

CATALOG AVAILABILITY: Photographs and drawings on request.

RETAIL DISTRIBUTION: Direct sales only.

Doolings of Santa Fe

OWNER/DESIGNER: Rob Dooling

ADDRESS: 525 Airport Road, Santa Fe, NM 87501

TELEPHONE: (505) 471-5956, (800) 835-0107

FAX: (505) 471-1568

Rob Dooling already had seven years of cabinetmaking experience when he established his workshop in Santa Fe in 1976. In the interim, he has become known for his furniture, which takes its design influence from the authentic Spanish Colonial pieces found in very old adobe homes of the area. "It's the oldest American look, comparable to, say, an English period piece or Shaker classics," Dooling points out.

He has invested this ageless look with some contemporary technology. His cushions are stuffed futons, never foam rubber. They are hand wrapped and upholstered at the workshop. Base cushions are suspended on an upholstered webbed deck. This provides a degree of comfort unheard of in antique pieces.

Drawers are dovetailed and cedar bottomed. They run smoothly on a hidden system developed by Dooling specifically for his pine chests. A light touch opens or closes them. The joinery has been engineered to allow for the natural movement that occurs in wood due to the loss or gain of moisture content, allowing Dooling to ship his furniture with confidence to all parts of the country as well as overseas.

PRIMARY PRODUCT: Complete lines of Southwest and Country West furniture for home, office, or the finest hotel or resort suites.

PRICE RANGE: $250 to $10,000.

DIRECT SALES: Exclusively. "There's always a little sawdust on our showroom floor."

CUSTOM ORDERS: Custom products are developed only for projects or volume runs.

ONE OF A KIND: Whole projects only, such as restaurants or public areas.

CATALOG AVAILABILITY: Full color catalog, $5. For faster delivery, call the 800 number. MasterCard and Visa accepted.

RETAIL DISTRIBUTION: Dooling's lines are available exclusively through the Santa Fe showroom or the catalog. Other locations are planned.

WHOLESALE SHOWROOMS AND REPRESENTATIVES: Commercial and other large accounts are handled on an individual basis from the main office.

HONORS AND SPECIAL COMMISSIONS: Member, Board of Directors, Furniture Guild of New Mexico. Chair for Pope Paul's visit to Phoenix, 1987. Anthony's at the Delta, a luxury restaurant in northern New Mexico: design, furniture, and architecture throughout.

S. R. Drost Furniture Manufacturing Company

OWNER/DESIGNER: Susan Drost and Ronald Drost

ADDRESS: 7740 East Gelding Drive, #1, Scottsdale, AZ 85260

TELEPHONE: (602) 998-8977

FAX: (602) 998-8978

From casual and Southwestern to traditional American design, S. R. Drost has an enormous amount of flexibility in its offerings. More than simple furniture craftsmanship, the emphasis here is on creating a fully designed product, from upholstery to fabric to finish and functionality. Underneath the exterior of an S.R. Drost piece are canvas webbings, hardboard backings, spring cushionings, and feather fillings. The company specializes in adjusting the dimensions of its pieces to fit specific design requirements, like lengthening a seat's proportions or introducing a special finish that matches an existing furniture collection.

S. R. Drost produces private label furniture lines for designers and retailers across the Southwest. The commercial accounts served by S. R. Drost include hotels, country clubs, government offices, and professional offices. Susan Drost has an extensive background in the design field; Ronald Drost has a strong business background.

PRIMARY PRODUCT: Custom-designed furniture collections for retailers, architects, designers, commercial enterprises, and private residences. Most of the furniture pieces are fully upholstered, but several Southwestern designs are available.

PRICE RANGE: $300 to $15,000.

DIRECT SALES: To the trade, by telephone or fax.

CUSTOM ORDERS: Custom orders are the most frequent types of projects undertaken by the company.

ONE OF A KIND: Yes, for residential, commercial, and government clients.

CATALOG AVAILABILITY: Catalog is available for $10.

RETAIL DISTRIBUTION: Beyond Horizons, Scottsdale, Arizona. Crystal Farms, Aspen, Colorado. Tops, Malibu, California.

WHOLESALE SHOWROOMS AND REPRESENTATIVES: Westgate, Laguna Niguel, Los Angeles, San Francisco, California. Phoenix, Arizona. Dallas, Houston, Texas. Atlanta, Georgia. Washington, D.C., Dania, Florida.

The Paul Duke Conglomeration

OWNER/DESIGNER: Paul Duke

ADDRESS: 4040 Pacific Avenue, Riverdale, UT 84405

TELEPHONE: (801) 393-7865

FAX: (801) 393-9425

The Paul Duke Conglomeration specializes in a complete line of lodgepole pine home furnishings. Pieces can be finished in a number of methods, including a clear, hand-rubbed wax, antique crackle lacquers, white or colored washes. The tables offered by Paul Duke Conglomeration are available with a selection of tabletops, including wood, glass, or acid washed metal.

Paul Duke, the company's founder and president, said that his main consideration in the design of a furniture piece is the availability of natural materials found in and around Utah. His basic designs are influenced by nineteenth-century Utah, a land of wagon trains, pioneers, and missionaries. From these people, a style evolved which Paul Duke refers to as "Contemporary Mountain West Style."

PRIMARY PRODUCT: Complete room and home furnishings made from lodgepole pine. Bedroom sets include canopy beds, mirror frames, nightstands, dressers, armoires, tables, and lamps. Living room sets include entertainment centers, sofas, easy chairs, end tables, coffee tables, ottomans, gun cases, and storage trunks.

PRICE RANGE: $250 to $1,150.

DIRECT SALES: Yes, through the Paul Duke Conglomeration showroom in Riverdale, Utah. Catalog sales by telephone or mail are also welcomed.

CUSTOM ORDERS: Yes.

ONE OF A KIND: One-of-a-kind work in lodgepole pine, such as store fixtures and commercial office projects, are welcomed.

CATALOG AVAILABILITY: Catalog is available at no charge.

RETAIL DISTRIBUTION: Vignettes, Las Vegas, Nevada. The Plant Plant, Dallas, Texas. Scan Design, Longwood, Florida. Santa Fe Way, Elliot City, Maryland. Higgins Furniture Shops, Orange, California.

WHOLESALE SHOWROOMS AND REPRESENTATIVES: Paul Duke Conglomeration is a regular exhibitor at the annual National Furniture Market in High Point, North Carolina, and in Los Angeles at the Southern California Furniture Market.

Expressions in Wood

OWNER/DESIGNER: Scott Collin Rikers

ADDRESS: P.O. Box 682, Ophir, CO 81426

TELEPHONE: (303) 728-6274

Scott Rikers specializes in the design and construction of one-of-a-kind and limited production contemporary furniture. A recent graduate of Prescott College, Scott concentrated on woodworking and furniture design. The furniture he crafts is sold under the Expressions in Wood name and is a collection of clean-line pieces that use several types of wood and elements of Southwestern and Japanese design to achieve a unique artistic statement. "This is not a shop that turns out one piece after another but a small studio in which attention to detail and absolute customer satisfaction are our primary interests," Rikers says.

PRIMARY PRODUCT: Contemporary line of chairs, armoires, lighting fixtures, dining tables, and entertainment centers.

PRICE RANGE: $500 to $5,000.

DIRECT SALES: Yes. Visits to Rikers' studio may be arranged by appointment.

CUSTOM ORDERS: Custom orders represent the majority of work performed by Expressions in Wood. Rikers is anxious to work with designers and clients who have specific notions about their own design needs.

ONE OF A KIND: Yes. Travel to perform on-site design and installation is possible.

CATALOG AVAILABILITY: No, but photographs of individual pieces are available.

RETAIL DISTRIBUTION: Ellison Gallery, Colorado Avenue, Telluride, CO 81435. (303) 728-3980.

Fine Additions, Inc.

OWNER/DESIGNER: Kingsley Hammett

ADDRESS: 2405 Maclovia Lane, Santa Fe, NM 87501

TELEPHONE: (505) 471-4549

"We spend at least a third of our lives in bed," says Kingsley Hammett. "I believe that should be a comfortable, comforting place. The majority of our furniture line is beds, night stands, roperos, and other bedroom pieces.

Hammett's designs are simple, straightforward, and clearly influenced by the classical pieces of the Works Progress Administration-led revival of Spanish New Mexico Colonial furniture of the 1930s. The most unusual aspect of Fine Additions, Inc., is the availability of the furnishings in kit form as well as drawings for those who wish to build their own furniture from a Kingsley Hammett design.

PRIMARY PRODUCT: Custom-made beds, tables, roperos, and night stands in ponderosa and Idaho white pine. Mortise and tenon joinery. All finished in low-toxic and nontoxic materials.

OTHER LINES: Precut kits, shipped UPS for the customer to assemble and finish. Architect-developed, fully detailed drawings complete with construction suggestions for the more adventurous craftsperson.

PRICE RANGE: $350 to $1,850.

DIRECT SALES: Customers are welcome to visit the workshop at any time. Mail orders are welcome, as is close contact with the client concerning design, detail, or proportion changes.

CUSTOM ORDERS: "Send us a sketch, a photograph, an idea and we will make you a bed or table to complement your surroundings."

CATALOG AVAILABILITY: A free brochure is available on request.

RETAIL DISTRIBUTION: None.

Fine Pine Shop

OWNER/DESIGNER: Terry K. Thompson and Irene Sally Thompson

ADDRESS: 335 North Cascade Avenue, Montrose, CO 81401

TELEPHONE: (303) 249-8359

With a background of twenty-two years in various aspects of homebuilding, cabinetmaking, and furniture making, Terry Thompson has an expert's knowledge of how to solve the joinery and fabrication problems that arise in the furniture-building process. He has applied that knowledge to his line of Fine Pine home furnishings, a group of handcrafted lodgepole pine furniture pieces that he makes in his western Colorado workshop.

The Fine Pine line emphasizes a sophisticated, smooth exterior finish that is applied to updated, contemporary designs. Thompson takes many of his design cues from modern home furnishings, then interprets those designs in the form and rustic feeling of furniture made from lodgepole pine. Using pieces of wood that have grown into a variety of shapes and configurations, he adjusts the joinery and bulk of each piece to arrive at a free-form appearance that is completely functional and built to last.

PRIMARY PRODUCT: Contemporary lodgepole pine furniture interpreted with a sophisticated flair and an appreciation for free-form design. Furniture pieces include beds of all dimensions, canopy beds, nightstands, chests of drawers, dressers, armoires, dining tables and chairs, couches, lounge chairs, coffee tables, and end tables. Couches and lounge chairs made by Fine Pine come with padded spring seat decks that allow the customer to select the fabric to finish the piece.

PRICE RANGE: $340 to $4,000.

DIRECT SALES: Retail clients are welcome at the Fine Pine Shop, 335 North Cascade, Montrose, Colorado. Mail and telephone orders are accepted with a 50 percent deposit at time of ordering.

CUSTOM ORDERS: "I specialize in Dreams Made to Order."

ONE OF A KIND: Thompson frequently travels to design and install one-of-a-kind pieces in both residential and commercial interiors. His specialties are custom handrails for complex stairways and conference tables for professional offices and corporate boardrooms.

CATALOG AVAILABILITY: Photographs of specific pieces are available at no cost.

RETAIL DISTRIBUTION: Fine Pine Shop, Montrose, Colorado.

Fine Wood Furniture

OWNER/DESIGNER: Chris Manzanares-Sandoval

ADDRESS: 901 3rd Street N.W., Albuquerque, NM 87102

TELEPHONE: (505) 247-9725, (800) 827-9725

Chris Manzanares-Sandoval is one of the best-known younger furniture makers in New Mexico. His distinguished record of public commissions is supported by a long list of satisfied private collectors of his work. He grew up in his father's small furniture business, where he began carving and turning spindles at the age of nine. His mother, a graduate of the Chicago Art Institute, influenced his love of art and his furniture design. Manzanares-Sandoval studied classical guitar at the University of New Mexico, and the rhythms and flow and precision of fine music are reflected in his clean, solidly crafted, beautifully proportioned furniture.

Fine Wood Furniture has recently joined forces with Artisans of the Desert.

PRIMARY PRODUCT: Sofas, coffee tables, end tables, dining room tables and chairs, trasteros, buffets, benches, desks, headboards, dressers, blanket chests, nightstands. A new series of small wine cabinets, some of which are in Southwest Deco style with a stonelike finish. Their size (15″ deep × 18½″ wide × 33″ high) allows shipping by UPS, the cost of which is included in the cabinets.

OTHER LINES: Hand-carved doors, carved beams, posts, and corbels.

PRICE RANGE: From $325 to several thousand dollars, depending on design requirements.

DIRECT SALES: All retail clients are welcome at the workshop. A small adjacent showroom is open 8:00 a.m. to 5:00 p.m. Monday through Friday; Saturdays by appointment only. Mail and telephone orders accepted (see 800 number). MasterCard and Visa.

CUSTOM ORDERS: "We specialize in custom orders."

ONE OF A KIND: Chris Manzanares-Sandoval is noted for his commissions (see below).

CATALOG AVAILABILITY: Available on request for $3.

RETAIL DISTRIBUTION: Only outlet is Fine Wood Furniture workshop and showroom at 901 3rd Street N.W. in Albuquerque.

HONORS AND SPECIAL COMMISSIONS: Furnishings, Pecos National Monument; restoration carving, La Posada Hotel, Albuquerque; sofas, chairs, and tables for State Capitol renovation, Santa Fe, New Mexico.

Greg Flores of Taos

OWNER/DESIGNER: Greg Flores

ADDRESS: 120 Bent Street, P.O. Box 2801, Taos, NM 87571

TELEPHONE: (505) 758-8010, (505) 758-9516

Greg Flores designs furniture in the tradition of Taos and of his own family heritage, which combines the cultures of Mexico, Spain, Native America, and Europe. The classic forms are proportioned for contemporary use and are embellished with Flores's elegant interpretation of historic design motifs. He combines precisely grouped, rhythmically repeated cutout patterns with bright, thin color washes that enhance the basic qualities of the wood. He maintains an extensive line of less common pieces such as coat racks, blanket chests, and mirror frames.

HONORS AND SPECIAL COMMISSIONS: Best of Show awards in three regional art exhibitions. Feature articles, *Taos News* and *New Mexico Magazine.*

PRIMARY PRODUCT: Solid ponderosa pine furniture, sparsely stained and finished only with hand-rubbed wax. Mortise and tenon joinery. Tables, chairs, hutches, sideboards, trasteros, sofas, benches, tables, night-stands, chests of drawers, bed frames, shelves, chests, side cabinets, stools, desks.

PRICE RANGE: $55 to $3,100.

DIRECT SALES: Customers are welcome at the showroom on Bent Street just off the Plaza in Taos. Mail and telephone orders accepted.

CUSTOM ORDERS: As often as necessary.

ONE OF A KIND: Sometimes. Individual inquiries accepted.

CATALOG AVAILABILITY: Send address and check for $6 for color catalog with price list.

RETAIL DISTRIBUTION: At the Taos showroom.

Fourth of July Company

OWNER/DESIGNER: Peter Lynn

ADDRESS: P.O. Box 1060, Dillon, CO 80435

TELEPHONE: (303) 468-6396

Living and working just west of the Continental Divide, on the slopes of Ptarmigan Mountain, Peter Lynn produces a line of pine furniture he characterizes as having a "Mountain Southwest" flavor. His work, which starts by using lodgepole pine as its basic building element, incorporates his own version of the traditional mortise and tenon joinery system used by the region's Spanish settlers and pioneers.

Lynn has, however, improved on this system by crafting his mortise and tenon joinery with a unique, rounded form. The result is a tight-fitting piece of furniture that is extremely durable. Lynn personally selects, peels, and finishes the wood that is incorporated into each Fourth of July furniture piece. The shades of his furniture range from a subtle slate blue to reddish brown and even, on occasion, an orange tone.

Fourth of July Furniture Company furniture has a rugged outdoors appeal. Customers may choose from a variety of wood grades, including Character Grade, which is a bit more expensive but has a finished appearance.

PRIMARY PRODUCT: Lodgepole pine furniture, including coffee tables, artist's easels, benches, porch swings, love seats, rocking cradles, beds of all sizes and configurations, occasional tables, mirrors, picture frames, and kiva ladders.

PRICE RANGE: $135 to $3,500.

DIRECT SALES: Retail and wholesale customers are welcome any time at Lynn's shop in Dillon, Colorado.

CUSTOM ORDERS: Frequently requested and happily filled.

ONE OF A KIND: Much of Lynn's furniture pieces are custom made for installation in large homes built in the Aspen area. He is pleased to do installation work.

CATALOG AVAILABILITY: Brochure is available, as are designer photograph catalogs for a small, refundable deposit.

RETAIL DISTRIBUTION: Great Things West, Breckenridge; Pine and Oak, Vail; The Ranch, Aspen, Colorado.

Free Hand Technique of Wood

OWNER/DESIGNER: David Winblood

ADDRESS: P.O. Box 352-B, Lake City, CO 81235

TELEPHONE: (303) 944-2352

David Winblood has established himself as one of the premier wood craftsmen working in the construction of cabinetry, doors, and windows in central Colorado where he designs his Free Hand line of furniture. He describes his craftsman's education as a combination of "trial, error, and one colorful old carpenter with seven fingers and a hitch in his getalong."

The accent in Free Hand's furniture is on rustic simplicity. Winblood has unlimited access to newly milled and salvaged antique boards and lumber. He enjoys producing furniture pieces that are weathered and aged looking as much as he appreciates filling orders for furniture made from flawless, clear woods of top quality.

The Free Hand line uses a heavy raised-grain wood in the construction process. Mortise and tenon joinery is combined with a series of Southwestern design accents to give the finished pieces a distinctive regional appeal. Winblood is known for his custom-installed bookcases, entertainment centers, stairs, handrails, cedar chests, and cupboards, all of which are designed to order and installed on-site.

PRIMARY PRODUCT: A rustic line of Southwestern/Rocky Mountain weathered spruce and pine furniture, including benches, chairs, dining tables, occasional tables, end tables, hutches, and planters.

PRICE RANGE: $125 to $6,000.

DIRECT SALES: Winblood invites visits from anyone determined enough to drive all the way to Lake City, Colorado to see him at his shop. Once you arrive, he will buy you a cup of coffee at the town's only cafe. Custom installation projects and design challenges are welcome.

CUSTOM ORDERS: The majority of Free Hand's work is done to fill custom orders.

ONE OF A KIND: Winblood has been commissioned throughout Colorado to re-create historic pieces for municipal buildings, museums, and private homes. Travel to out-of-state projects is welcomed.

CATALOG AVAILABILITY: No catalog or brochure, but photographs of specific pieces are available.

RETAIL DISTRIBUTION: Most orders arrive through word of mouth from designers and architects. Once in a while, if the fishing around Lake City isn't too good, Winblood will load up a truckload of his extra pieces and take them to crafts fairs in large Southwestern cities.

WHOLESALE SHOWROOMS AND REPRESENTATIVES: Juniper Tree/Western Slope Crafts, Montrose, Colorado.

HONORS AND SPECIAL COMMISSIONS: Winblood has been commissioned to do numerous historic design and renovation projects throughout central Colorado.

Full House Inc.: Furniture by Jim Wagner & Friends

OWNER/DESIGNER: Diana Whitney, Owner/President
Jim Wagner, Master Designer
ADDRESS: P.O. Box 3257, Taos, NM 87571
TELEPHONE: (505) 758-0045, (505) 751-1231

Jim Wagner is the original creative force behind the brightly painted contemporary furniture that has become a major Southwestern art form. Before his inspired paintbrush paved the way for all sorts of bright, sophisticated furniture, there were only traditional folk painted pieces and naturally finished traditional furnishings. Wagner brought in exuberant swatches of color, bold geometrics, wildly positioned animals, and anything else he could conjure up to increase the liveliness of a piece of furniture. Many jumped on his bandwagon, some with more personal innovation than others. Today the contemporary painted furniture trend is central to Southwest design. It graces the interiors of international stars and of ordinary people with humorous, upbeat lifestyles.

PRIMARY PRODUCT: Handcrafted and hand-painted wooden beds, tables, chairs, benches, and chests. Unique pieces often include handmade tiles or wrought iron hinges and ornamentation.

OTHER LINES: Mirrors, boxes, picture frames. Paintings and monotypes.

PRICE RANGE: $100 to $10,000.

DIRECT SALES: Visitors are welcome at the workshop in Taos, New Mexico. Mail and telephone orders are accepted with 50 percent deposit.

CUSTOM ORDERS: Custom orders are welcome, so long as they allow for artistic freedom.

ONE OF A KIND: Jim Wagner is nationally recognized for his one-of-a-kind pieces for residential and commercial interiors.

CATALOG AVAILABILITY: Inquire about brochure.

RETAIL DISTRIBUTION: La Luna Gallery, Taos, New Mexico. Como No, Santa Fe. TOPS, Malibu, California.

WHOLESALE SHOWROOMS AND REPRESENTATIVES: Full House showroom, Taos, New Mexico.

HONORS AND SPECIAL COMMISSIONS: Mentioned in *House and Garden, House Beautiful, Architectural Digest, Metropolitan Home, Designers West, Vogue, Taxi, Elle, Glamour, New York Times.*

Dan Harshberger Graphic Design

OWNER/DESIGNER: Dan Harshberger

ADDRESS: 1548 East Cheery Lynn Road, Phoenix, AZ 85014

TELEPHONE: (602) 274-9068

FAX: (602) 274-9068

Dan Harshberger's ArizonBack chairs, a blending of Southwestern and Adirondack furniture styles, are a hot item in regional design circles. Constructed of clear, top-grade fir and designed so that no two ever look or are decorated the same, ArizonBack chairs are a strong design statement that can be used indoors or outdoors.

The chairs' backs are decorated with built-in wood figures of prickly pear cactus, six-shooters, chili peppers, cow skulls, horned toads, and just about anything else that comes to Harshberger's mind. Occasionally, smaller designs are sandblasted into the chairs' surfaces in random locations. Each chair is slightly oversized and is finished with a coating of water sealant. Galvanized deck screws secure the chair's wooden components, and all screw holes are concealed by plugs.

PRIMARY PRODUCT: Adirondack-style wooden porch chairs with Southwestern design features. Chairs are fully decorated and painted and are suitable for indoor or outdoor use.

PRICE RANGE: $650 and up.

DIRECT SALES: Yes.

CUSTOM ORDERS: Yes.

ONE OF A KIND: All production is one of a kind.

CATALOG AVAILABILITY: No.

RETAIL DISTRIBUTION: Through production facility.

High Country Workshop

OWNER/DESIGNER: Jim Weatherford and Donna Weatherford

ADDRESS: P.O. Box 1975, Frisco, CO 80443

TELEPHONE: (303) 453-2816

High Country Workshop produces several furniture collections using locally procured woods such as ponderosa pine, white pine, and oak. The designs produced by craftsman/owner Jim Weatherford are especially noted in Colorado furniture circles for their frequent use of the slate blue-colored pine known as "beetle-kill" pine, which brings added richness to any piece of furniture.

Jim and Donna Weatherford previously had a furniture restoration business, so they are familiar with the techniques employed by master furniture craftsman of the past. They like to say that since they have been using some of the old-timers' tricks in making their High Country Workshop line of furniture, they are actually making the antiques of the future.

Working with their associate craftspeople, Roy Long and Mariana Long, the Weatherfords have developed an all-purpose woodcraft shop in their Breckenridge-area production facility. Local ski area owners frequently call on High Country Workshop to restore and refurbish the weatherbeaten and overused cabinetry and wood furniture in ski lodges. Their slate blue furniture line that uses a Southwestern and Mountain West design motif has captured the imagination of local vacation condo owners.

PRIMARY PRODUCT: Complete line of home furnishings and entertainment centers, made from lodgepole pine, beetle-kill pine, and oak.

PRICE RANGE: $350 to $8,000.

DIRECT SALES: High Country Workshop maintains a showroom alongside its production facility three miles north of Breckenridge, Colorado. Retail clients and designers are welcome, as are telephone and fax orders.

CUSTOM ORDERS: Primarily a custom-design shop, High Country Workshop specializes in the on-site design and installation of custom furnishings, both built-in and freestanding, installed in vacation homes throughout central Colorado.

ONE OF A KIND: Yes, with sketches and specific design preferences provided by the customer.

CATALOG AVAILABILITY: Brochure is available at no cost.

RETAIL DISTRIBUTION: Through the High Country Workshop showroom.

HONORS AND SPECIAL COMMISSIONS: Installations in homes throughout Colorado, Texas, New Mexico, and Oklahoma.

Highlander Furniture

OWNER/DESIGNER: James Stepanek

ADDRESS: P.O. Box 1455, Berthoud, CO 80513

TELEPHONE: (303) 532-1455

Highlander Furniture combines the rustic appearance of traditional lodgepole pine furniture with clean, simple design. The furniture is crafted from a selection of Colorado wood, including yellow pine, blue-streaked pine, willow, and aromatic cedar. Emphasis is placed on achieving a substantive, straightforward, fully finished appearance.

Each item produced by Highlander Furniture uses time-honored woodworking techniques including tongue and groove paneling, mortise and tenon joinery, and dovetailed wood drawer joints. Three semi-transparent colored stains and a full range of custom colors are available. Two layers of satin lacquer top coat are applied to each wood surface.

Highlander Furniture also creates carved tabletops made from Colorado red or white sandstone. These tops, which are carved with a selection of Southwestern and Western designs, can be finished in either an etched or a smooth-sanded surface. The stone tops can also be etched to include any type of custom design. Each top receives a final coat of sealant and hand-rubbed wax to preserve its color and beauty.

PRIMARY PRODUCT: Full line of Southwestern and Western furniture made from lodgepole pine, cedar, and willow. Tabletops made from etched sandstone. Individual items include mirrors, lamps, beds, headboards, four-post beds, bunk beds, canopy beds, ottomans, buffets, entertainment centers, armoires, bookcases, end tables, dining tables, console tables, and coffee tables.

PRICE RANGE: $250 to $4,500.

DIRECT SALES: No.

CUSTOM ORDERS: Yes.

CATALOG AVAILABILITY: Yes, through showrooms.

RETAIL DISTRIBUTION: Wholesale only.

WHOLESALE SHOWROOMS AND REPRESENTATIVES: Calger Lighting, New York Design Center, New York City (212) 689-9511. de Aurora, Chicago Design Center, Chicago, Illinois (312) 329-1149. Hoff Miller, Denver Design Center, Denver, Colorado (303) 698-0800. Interiors, Inc., Design Center South, Laguna Niguel, California (714) 643-3487.

John R. Keyser, Inc.

OWNER/DESIGNER: John R. Keyser

ADDRESS: 160 W. Meadowlark, Corrales, NM 87048

TELEPHONE: (505) 897-0468

FAX: (505) 897-2441

John Keyser creates graceful steel furniture with slim, flowing lines. *Newsday* called this design motif "The Wave." His chair backs and legs undulate in tight ripples or in long, tapering Queen Anne lines.

Keyser came to the Southwest with a B.A. from Maryland Institute of Art and continued his education with graduate studies at the University of New Mexico. He was commissioned to do several monumental sculptures and eventually moved into other art forms. His current emphasis is on his furniture, which is actually functional sculpture.

PRIMARY PRODUCT: Polished, lacquered steel chairs, occasional tables, benches, beds. Editions include: Petroglyphic, with cutout designs from ancient rock drawings; Antiquity, with textured and polished heavy steel plate; Equus, integrating horse designs into furniture; Queen Anne, Safari, and Gothic design elements. A wonderful longhorn chair.

OTHER LINES: Painted steel sculptures of masks and animal themes. Rusted steel sculptures of petroglyph images. Sterling silver jewelry of petroglyph images.

PRICE RANGE: $25 (small petroglyph sculpture) to $1,450 (bed).

DIRECT SALES: Retail clients can visit the studio by appointment. Telephone and mail orders accepted.

CUSTOM ORDERS: Keyser frequently fills custom orders. He welcomes clients' input and is challenged to satisfy specific needs.

ONE OF A KIND: Keyser is a sculptor and is experienced in site-specific, one-of-a-kind commissions.

CATALOG AVAILABILITY: $5 or free with purchase.

RETAIL DISTRIBUTION: Neiman-Marcus, New York. Bloomingdale's, New York. Desert Collection, San Francisco, California. Harrod's, London. Billi Bom, Troy, Michigan. Judith McGrann, Minnesota. Melme, New Jersey. Takaraya Co., Ltd., and Mitsui, Japan.

WHOLESALE SHOWROOMS AND REPRESENTATIVES: McNamara & Harris, Phoenix, Arizona. Directional, New York. Permanent showroom, World Trade Center, Design and Craft Gallery. Dallas Market Center. American Craft Showcase, High Point, North Carolina.

HONORS AND SPECIAL COMMISSIONS: Five-page feature article in *Better Homes and Gardens*, July 1990. Commission from Los Angeles designer to do furnishings for an entire home: bedroom, dining room, game room, and so on. Paneola Restaurant, Phoenix, Arizona: twenty-four tables, three large sculptured pineapples. Two six-foot whooping cranes for the entrance of Rio Grande Zoo, Albuquerque, New Mexico.

Kopriva's

OWNER/DESIGNER: Patty Pugh and Doris John

ADDRESS: 2445 East 3rd Avenue, Denver, CO 80302

TELEPHONE: (303) 333-2299

With over twenty years of experience in the interior design and furniture design fields, Patty Pugh and Doris John have been able to create and market their own line of custom furniture under the name of Kopriva's, the interior furnishings store they operate in a Denver suburb.

Their collection, a combination of Western wood and Cowboy steel furniture, features design tidbits such as horseshoe drawer pulls, bucking bronco handles, turquoise inlays, and pony knobs. There is also a line of custom cabinetry that can be finished in any one of thirteen different stains and colors.

The wood finishes range from light and clear to a roughed-out texture that is produced by the rasping of a steel brush.

PRIMARY PRODUCT: Line of custom-designed Western and Cowboy-style furniture, with ironwork attachments in functional roles.

OTHER LINES: Custom cabinetry.

PRICE RANGE: $45 to $3,000.

DIRECT SALES: Retail and wholesale clients may contact Kopriva's retail showroom at (303) 333-2299.

CUSTOM ORDERS: Most of the collection is designed and built for custom orders.

ONE OF A KIND: Yes.

CATALOG AVAILABILITY: Photographs of individual pieces are available at a nominal charge.

RETAIL DISTRIBUTION: Kopriva's, 2445 East 3rd Avenue, Denver, Colorado.

Kozlowski Woodworks

OWNER/DESIGNER: David Kozlowski

ADDRESS: P.O. Box 8316, Santa Fe, NM 87504

TELEPHONE: (505) 989-9189

David Kozlowski's fine art furniture does not at first glance seem Southwestern but rather has echoes of Art Deco and minimalism. Instead of using pine like typical furniture makers of the region, he uses carefully chosen hardwoods whose grains are integrated into each specific design. His tabletops appear to float above their bases.

"Simplicity of line and silhouette is important to me, as are rhythm and negative space," he says. "My challenge to myself is to create a subtle dynamism that is derived from purity of form and surface. Simple furniture need not be boring."

It is this simplicity that relates to the Southwest, where Kozlowski has lived and worked for a decade. He learned woodworking from his father in New England, then earned a B.A. in Comparative Literature from Columbia University. A six-year stint in Europe followed, where he taught English and worked as a translator. The experience broadened his vision so that when he began to design furniture he was not constrained by any regional conventions.

Kozlowski is an innovative artist in the finest tradition of the pioneering West. "I do not restrict my materials to wood," he points out. "I frequently use automotive paints and am experimenting with stone, metal, and leather."

PRIMARY PRODUCT: Museum-quality, one-of-a-kind furniture ranging from simple tables to stereo cabinets to pool tables. Examples of unique designs include a wonderful hexagonal table composed of six three-legged triangular tables that can be arranged in many variations.

PRICE RANGE: $1,000 to $10,000.

DIRECT SALES: Will gladly meet clients by appointment.

CUSTOM ORDERS: All orders are custom.

ONE OF A KIND: All Kozlowski designs are unique.

CATALOG AVAILABILITY: $5 for color laser copies from portfolio.

RETAIL DISTRIBUTION: Kozlowski has a few spec pieces for sale at his workshop as well as some commissions available for viewing in Santa Fe, New Mexico. He crafts a limited number of pieces per year, and a six-month wait should be expected.

Lloyd Kreitz Studio

OWNER/DESIGNER: Lloyd Kreitz

ADDRESS: 1808 Second Street, Studio 4, Santa Fe, NM 87501

TELEPHONE: (505) 984-1841

Lloyd Kreitz's fine steel furniture integrates the multicultural strains of the Southwest into a cosmopolitan style all its own. The sunburst and moon motif, in particular, expresses the mystique of the high desert.

The furniture is thoughtfully crafted, reflecting Kreitz's industrial arts degree and his subsequent graduate work in studio fine arts at the University of Minnesota. The multifaceted Kreitz also is an inventor and holds twelve United States and two Canadian patents.

"Whether I am creating a sculpture or a piece of steel furniture," says Kreitz, "there is an excitement as I see and feel shape and form. I have thoughts about giving each piece life—a personality or a radiance."

PRIMARY PRODUCT: "Functional art" furniture of steel. Fountains, canopied beds, glass-topped tables, chairs, candelabra.

OTHER LINES: Paintings and drawings, steel and bronze sculpture.

PRICE RANGE: $300 to $15,000.

DIRECT SALES: Visitors welcome by appointment at Kreitz's Second Street studio.

CUSTOM ORDERS: Original designs and commissions accepted.

ONE OF A KIND: Most of Kreitz's work is one of a kind.

CATALOG AVAILABILITY: Brochure available at no charge.

RETAIL DISTRIBUTION: Simply Santa Fe and Windsor Betts Gallery, both in Santa Fe, New Mexico.

WHOLESALE SHOWROOMS AND REPRESENTATIVES: Visions Design Studio, Santa Fe, New Mexico.

HONORS AND SPECIAL COMMISSIONS: Furniture and sculpture commission for the new Inn of the Anasazi Hotel in downtown Santa Fe, New Mexico. Several furniture commissions for film and television notables.

Randolph Laub, Designer

OWNER/DESIGNER: Randolph Laub

ADDRESS: 310 Johnson Street, Santa Fe, NM 87501

TELEPHONE: (505) 984-0081, (800) 828-2313

FAX: (505) 983-2230

Randolph Laub's stately, extremely comfortable furniture is modeled after the American Arts and Crafts Movement, also termed Mission or Craftsman furniture, of the late nineteenth and early twentieth centuries. This movement, a reaction against mass-produced furniture of inferior quality, was distinguished by straightforward, honest craftsmanship. Laub carries that tradition forward with massive pieces whose structural features become the focal point of decoration. The furniture is scaled to contemporary standards with an eye toward comfort. "No words can fully describe the pleasure of feeling and sitting in one of our lounge chairs."

Randolph Laub's All-American designs are particularly suited to fine Southwestern-style interiors because of their meticulous construction and natural materials. Such pieces as the Prairie Settle evoke the frontier spirit despite their English heritage. The form of the furniture is complementary to adobe architecture in its absence of gimmicks. Of special interest is Laub's fine hand finishing: much of his furniture can be recognized by the finish alone.

PRIMARY PRODUCT: Substantially scaled tables, chairs, and sofas in white oak. Some cherry, ponderosa pine, and other fine woods. Mortise and tenon joinery.

OTHER LINES: Picture frames for private collections, museum exhibitions, and Fahey/Klein Gallery, Los Angeles. Fine cabinetry for new construction. Mirrors.

PRICE RANGE: $450 to $7,000.

DIRECT SALES: Laub maintains a showroom and workshop at 310 Johnson Street in Santa Fe.

CUSTOM ORDERS: Each client is encouraged to participate in the process of design. The showroom has a full line of furniture pieces, finishes, and upholstery from which to choose.

ONE OF A KIND: Laub frequently travels and visits individuals in their homes to develop furniture from on-site attention to personal specifications. Original design commissions accepted.

CATALOG AVAILABILITY: A brochure describing the designs and showing representative pieces is available at no charge.

RETAIL DISTRIBUTION: The full line is shown in Santa Fe at the 310 Johnson Street showroom.

HONORS AND SPECIAL COMMISSIONS: Exhibition framing for the Los Angeles County Museum and Norton Simon Museum, Los Angeles, California, Smithsonian Institution, Washington, D.C., and others. Residence of Brian Gibson, featured in *Metropolitan Home*. Ranch residence of Henry Singleton, founder of Teledyne. Individual pieces for various film and recording stars.

Frank Leskinen

OWNER/DESIGNER: Frank Leskinen

ADDRESS: 4628 West County Road 56, LaPorte, CO 80535

TELEPHONE: (303) 484-6954

Frank Leskinen has a gopher's knack for finding the hidden treasures under a forest floor and a craftsman's skill that enables him to turn those earthbound clusters into furniture suited for any home. His Rocky Mountain conifer root tables and Rocky Mountain juniper root tables are unique showpieces.

Leskinen searches for roots that have been, in effect, seasoned but not structurally damaged by the flames and heat that once raged above the forest floor. In his Fort Collins-area workshop, he sandblasts and treats these root systems with preservatives, bringing out their individual beauty and allowing them to survive many years after their aboveground appendages were destroyed by the forces of nature.

Leskinen also works with Rocky Mountain juniper stumps and tree trunks, stripping these pieces of their bark, then sanding and polishing them into exquisite table bases and home furnishing accessories.

PRIMARY PRODUCT: Glass-topped tables with sand-blasted root bases made from locally grown juniper and conifers. Table bases made from juniper trunks and stumps.

PRICE RANGE: $150 to $10,000.

DIRECT SALES: Yes, through the workshop for special designs.

CUSTOM ORDERS: Yes. Leskinen wants residential and designer clients to work directly with him.

ONE OF A KIND: Almost all pieces are unique, a result of the variation in the natural materials Leskinen uses.

CATALOG AVAILABILITY: None.

RETAIL DISTRIBUTION: Captured in Colorado, Eckert, Colorado.

HONORS AND SPECIAL COMMISSIONS: None.

Lodgepole Furniture Manufacturing

OWNER/DESIGNER: Larry Jansen and Judy Jansen

ADDRESS: Star Route-Box 15, Jackson, WY 83001

TELEPHONE: (307) 733-3199

For the past fifteen years, Larry and Judy Jansen have been crafting a rustic, semipeeled interpretation of traditional lodgepole pine furniture. While the Jansens are capable of finishing their pieces in a smooth, polished style, their forte is the rugged, hand-hewn look that is possible when the log-peeling process is not carried to completion.

The Jansens use rawhide strips, both light and dark colored, to create webbed, cushioning bases and backs on their chairs, rockers, and sofas. All the materials used in the Lodgepole Furniture Manufacturing line are hand selected and finished by the Jansens.

PRIMARY PRODUCT: Chests of drawers, canopy beds, bedside tables, writing desks, captain's chairs, dining room tables and chairs, chaise lounges, coffee tables, kitchen tables, easy chairs, sofas, and end tables. While lodgepole pine is the main wood material used in these furniture pieces, Lodgepole Furniture Manufacturing is initiating a line of furniture made from aspen logs.

PRICE RANGE: $30 to $3,000.

DIRECT SALES: Orders by mail or telephone are accepted, with a 25 percent deposit required at time of ordering. Visitors are welcome at the company's showrooms in Jackson, Wyoming, (307) 733-3199, and in Ivins, Utah, (801) 628-4045.

CUSTOM ORDERS: Yes, custom orders are welcome.

ONE OF A KIND: Working from customer's own specifications and sketches is possible. On-site work is not accepted.

CATALOG AVAILABILITY: Brochure and price list available at no charge.

RETAIL DISTRIBUTION: Lodgepole Furniture Manufacturing Showrooms in Jackson, Wyoming and Ivins, Utah. Ralph Lauren Polo in Durango, Colorado, Freeport, Maine, and Jackson, Wyoming. Umbrello in Los Angeles, California, and Santa Fe, New Mexico. Portico, New York City. Galisteo, San Francisco, California.

WHOLESALE SHOWROOMS AND REPRESENTATIVES: Contact production facility in Jackson, Wyoming.

HONORS AND SPECIAL COMMISSIONS: Governor's Mansion, Cheyenne, Wyoming.

Ty Loyola Design

OWNER/DESIGNER: Ty Loyola

ADDRESS: 4130 West 1939 South, Suite D, Salt Lake City, UT 84104

TELEPHONE: (801) 977-9317

FAX: (801) 977-9317

Unlike most of the furniture craftsmen of the Rocky Mountain and Southwestern region, Ty Loyola designs and manufactures home furnishings that are not necessarily influenced by cultural or material considerations. "I specialize in re-creating the look, feel, and comfort of furniture that most people associate with the Old World. Most of what I do is made from hardwoods, using traditional designs and fabrication methods."

While much of Loyola's work is generated by orders for French Country or Spanish Colonial furniture, Ty Loyola Design also ventures into Southwestern and Ranch/Cowboy Western styles. Loyola spends as much time crafting a Southwestern furniture piece as he would a French Provincial furniture piece.

Loyola practices Old World craftsmanship. All of his pieces are constructed with mortise and tenon joinery, and he hand mixes his own formulas for stains, lacquers, and waxes. Loyola goes one step further when it comes to accessorizing his furniture pieces, choosing to attach French-manufactured handles, pulls, and other hardware to his finished work.

PRIMARY PRODUCT: Ty Loyola Design manufactures over one hundred different home furnishings products in an assortment of styles. Furniture includes sofas, easy chairs, tables, dining room tables and chairs, armoires, entertainment centers, buffets, and fireplace mantles.

PRICE RANGE: $600 to $8,000.

DIRECT SALES: Clients are welcome at the production facility. Orders are accepted by telephone.

CUSTOM ORDERS: The majority of pieces produced by Ty Loyola Design are built to the specific needs of designers and clients.

ONE OF A KIND: One-of-a-kind installations and designs are welcome. Ty Loyola has completed and installed custom projects in New York, Chicago, and California.

CATALOG AVAILABILITY: Since the focus of Ty Loyola Design is on custom work, no catalog is available, but photographs of individual pieces can be sent on request.

RETAIL DISTRIBUTION: Production facility orders are welcome. Timeless Design Showroom, Park City, Utah. Contract Design, Jackson, Wyoming.

WHOLESALE SHOWROOMS AND REPRESENTATIVES: Design Innovations, Timeless Design, LaVelle Klobes Interiors, and Ontario Design, all located in Park City, Utah.

Maestas Woods

OWNER/DESIGNER: Phillip J. Maestas and David Maestas

ADDRESS: P.O. Box 1352, Taos, NM 87571

TELEPHONE: (505) 758-5731

The Maestas family exemplifies traditional Taos woodworking. Joe Alex Maestas and his two sons, Phillip and David, have a fine workshop on the family property and together produce high-quality furniture in the Taos and Spanish Colonial styles. They are proud of their workmanship and offer to repair or replace any item that is made by Maestas Woods.

"Our furniture advertises itself," says Joe Alex Maestas. "We finish one order and another customer shows up." A descendant of a very old Taos family, he has been in the furniture-making trade for over twenty years. He greatly admires the designs of his son, Phillip, who, although in his early twenties, has already made a name for himself at a private firm in Colorado and has now returned to Taos to spend long hours in the family business.

PRIMARY PRODUCT: Authentic Taos furniture using local woods. Dining room sets, living room sets, bedroom sets, benches, armchairs, and other individual items. Traditional Spanish woodcarving embellishments on most pieces.

OTHER LINES: Doors, windows, screen doors, patio furniture.

PRICE RANGE: From $300 for a chair to $2,500 for a trastero. Custom work priced by the job.

DIRECT SALES: Most of the sales are made in person, but telephone orders will be taken if necessary.

CUSTOM ORDERS: The Maestas family makes just about anything their customers want, including plain pieces with no carving.

CATALOG AVAILABILITY: Photographs of previous work available at the shop. Please call for an appointment.

RETAIL DISTRIBUTION: Most galleries in Taos, New Mexico.

McMillan's Old Santa Fe Furniture Company

OWNER/DESIGNER: Dennis McMillan

WORKSHOP AND OFFICES:

6000 Cerrillos Road, Santa Fe, NM 87505
(505) 471-4934

SHOWROOMS:

2443 N. Campbell Road, #121, Tucson, AZ 85705
(602) 795-2374

1750 S. Rainbow #12, Las Vegas, NV 89102
(702) 258-9933

American Home Furnishings
901 St. Michael's Drive
Santa Fe, NM 87501
(505) 988-4502

Su Casa
1000 E. Camelback Road
Phoenix, AZ 85014
(602) 277-0101

From his earliest years, Dennis McMillan has been involved with furniture making. He assisted his father in special projects and later earned a degree in Industrial Arts (architectural drafting and woodworking) from the University of Northern Colorado, where he also took classes in furniture design and art history. He taught industrial arts in high school before opening his workshop/showroom in Santa Fe in 1976.

McMillan has become known in the business as a pioneer. He has consistently stepped forward to bring excellent Santa Fe and Taos style furniture to clients who appreciate the authenticity and value of his work. (Also see special profile.)

PRIMARY PRODUCT: Home and office furniture of kiln-dried ponderosa pine and Appalachian red oak. Hand carving, hand-fitted mortise and tenon joinery. Some painted finishes and traditional punched tin panels by Streck Family. Santa Fe style, a simpler, lighter version of the classic Taos style with smoother and more elegant lines, reflecting the era of the early Spanish craftsmen who settled in New Mexico.

PRICE RANGE: $229 to $3,000 for regular line.

DIRECT SALES: From the showrooms in Tucson, Arizona, and Las Vegas, Nevada. No direct sales from the production facility in Santa Fe, New Mexico, but visitors are welcome by appointment.

CUSTOM ORDERS: Yes. Custom designs may be viewed at many public sites in the Santa Fe area.

ONE OF A KIND: Dennis McMillan is available by appointment to visit homes or offices of clients and to adapt designs and sizes to their special needs.

CATALOG AVAILABILITY: Catalogs are available by mail or in person from any McMillan showroom.

RETAIL DISTRIBUTION: American Home Furnishings, Santa Fe and Albuquerque, New Mexico. McMillan's Old Santa Fe Furniture Company, Tucson, Arizona, and Las Vegas, Nevada. Su Casa, Phoenix, Arizona. Santa Fe Design, West Vancouver, British Columbia.

WHOLESALE SHOWROOMS AND REPRESENTATIVES: McMillan has exhibited in major furniture shows in Dallas, Texas, San Francisco, California, and High Point, North Carolina.

HONORS AND SPECIAL COMMISSIONS: Member, Better Business Bureau of New Mexico, Santa Fe Chamber of Commerce. Custom furnishings for Vista Del Sol Retirement Village, Santa Fe Public Library and Wadle Gallery in Santa Fe; Los Alamos National Laboratories, Los Alamos; and Glorieta Baptist Assembly, Glorieta, New Mexico.

Rick Montanari – Leathersmith

OWNER/DESIGNER: Rick Montanari

ADDRESS: P.O. Box 65, Englewood, CO 80112-0065

TELEPHONE: (303) 788-1432

Rick's Montanari's leather-crafting abilities make his work a perfect accent or main piece that can be included in a room setting of Molesworth-type or even Southwestern primitive furniture. Like the saddle makers of years ago, he uses underlying wood frames to create solid structural bases for his furniture. Leather is then tooled, colored, stamped, carved, painted, tacked, or gilded before being attached to the surface as a permanent covering.

Montanari's work is unique among Western furniture craftspeople because leatherwork is simply too demanding a craft for most individuals to have the time or patience to master. The process of treating and finishing leather with tooling patterns, dyes, and hand stamps is slow and laborious. Montanari provides an important link to the West's romantic past and does so with meticulous attention to quality and design integrity.

PRIMARY PRODUCT: Leather-covered mirrors, tables, bedroom sets, bookcases, cabinets, desks, and baseboards of tooled and decorated cowhide. Credenzas, both for private homes and commercial projects, have been an important custom order for Montanari.

OTHER LINES: Secondary items include picture frames, architectural millwork, and leather wall treatments.

PRICE RANGE: $800 and up.

DIRECT SALES: Exclusively through Cry Baby Ranch, 1422 Larimer Square, Denver, CO 80202, (303) 623-3979.

CUSTOM ORDERS: Custom orders are a specialty. Collaborative work may be done by telephone and fax.

ONE OF A KIND: Every piece is an original and will never be repeated.

CATALOG AVAILABILITY: Photographs of individual pieces of work will be sent for a nominal charge.

RETAIL DISTRIBUTION: Cry Baby Ranch, Larimer Square, Denver, CO 80202, (303) 623-3979.

WHOLESALE SHOWROOMS AND REPRESENTATIVES: Contact Rick Montanari.

HONORS AND SPECIAL COMMISSIONS: Numerous designer homes in Aspen, Steamboat Springs, and Vail, Colorado.

Mountain Woodcraft

OWNER/DESIGNER: Andy Olsen

ADDRESS: P.O. Box 10, Cloudcroft, NM 88317

TELEPHONE: (505) 682-2620

When Andy Olsen began building custom furniture of his own design in the 1980s, he brought with him ten years of experience in design and manufacturing for a national wholesale company. He located his workshop in the beautiful Sacramento mountain range in southern New Mexico and named it Mountain Woodcraft. There, he produces fine furniture for a steadily growing clientele.

Recently, he has begun logging juniper wood from the surrounding area, milling it himself, and creating rustic furniture that incorporates both smoothly finished wood and the natural bark edge of the juniper tree. The lumber for his pine furniture is also cut locally.

"Our primary goal is not to mass produce furniture but to make each piece an exciting experience for both the maker and the buyer," says Olsen. His attitude and his Southwestern heritage shine through everything he produces, whether it is a massive custom mantelpiece or a simple cowboy hat rack.

PRIMARY PRODUCT: Southwestern-style benches, beds, chairs, and tables made of hardwoods, juniper, and pine. Mortise and tenon construction, reinforced with screws or optional dowels. All hand finished.

OTHER LINES: Mirrors, mantelpieces, coat trees, and other decorative accessories.

PRICE RANGE: $250 to $3,000.

DIRECT SALES: Retail clients are welcome in the showroom and shop. Mail orders accepted. Custom orders require a 50 percent deposit. Mountain Woodcraft is located 13 miles east of Cloudcroft, New Mexico, on Highway 82.

CUSTOM ORDERS: "We specialize in custom orders."

ONE OF A KIND: Original design commissions are accepted. Olsen will visit individuals in their homes and businesses to help lay out and design furniture to the customer's specifications.

CATALOG AVAILABILITY: Brochure available on written request for $2, refundable on first order.

RETAIL DISTRIBUTION: Rio Mercado Furniture, Ruidoso, New Mexico. Wayside Pottery and Swallow Place Artist Studios, Cloudcroft, New Mexico. Mountain Woodcraft Showroom, east of Cloudcroft.

WHOLESALE SHOWROOMS AND REPRESENTATIVES: "All wholesale orders are handled directly through Mountain Woodcraft to keep our production to a level of heirloom quality."

The Naturalist

OWNER/DESIGNER: Jon Clark and Janet Clark

ADDRESS: 1080 South 350 East, P.O. Box 1431, Provo, UT 84603

TELEPHONE: (801) 377-5140

FAX: (801) 377-5158

The Naturalist offers eight different home furnishings collections: Regional Design, American Frontier, Accessories West, American Twig, Logs and Stumps, Homelife, Rocky Mountain Woods, and Designer Accessories. Each collection reflects The Naturalist's efforts at bringing out the best elements of the materials and the design influences of the American West.

From mixed-media tin headboard panels inlaid into the Directions Bed to the dazzlingly colored, art deco-inspired All-American Couch/Day Bed, the home furnishings collections offered by The Naturalist cover a broad range of design themes: from the rusticity of the oak and leather Cowboys and Indians Chair to the timeless elegance of the New Classic Bed.

Jon Clark and Janet Clark have built The Naturalist into one of the nation's premier outlets for American Western interior furnishings. Each year, they exhibit their standard and new furnishings at the International Home Furnishings Show in High Point, North Carolina. They run a sophisticated, international business, yet treat clients like friends.

PRIMARY PRODUCT: The Naturalist collection includes eight home furnishings lines, each with a distinct style. All feature a full range of interior furnishings, including entire room settings, lighting products, custom-designed textiles, tinwork, leather items, and room screens.

PRICE RANGE: $95 to $1,500.

DIRECT SALES: Yes, direct orders are welcome.

CUSTOM ORDERS: The Naturalist carries a strong commitment to custom work; 30 percent of its orders are per designer and client specifications.

ONE OF A KIND: Only on a limited basis.

CATALOG AVAILABILITY: Retail catalogs are $12.50. Wholesale portfolios for designers and store buyers are $75.00.

RETAIL DISTRIBUTION: Call The Naturalist for specific locations of their many retail outlets.

WHOLESALE SHOWROOMS AND REPRESENTATIVES: John Edward Hughes, Dallas, Texas. C. L. McCrae, San Francisco, California. Viewpoint, Atlanta, Georgia. Kemto, Laguna Niguel, California.

Neuvoe Design

OWNER/DESIGNER: Greg Oliver and Debra Oliver

ADDRESS: 5229 Greenview Drive, Fort Collins, CO 80525

TELEPHONE: (303) 223-7418

Using recycled paper products, such as wood pulp, cardboard, and paper, Greg and Debra Oliver assemble home furnishings that are both elegant and structurally sound. They have developed a method for stabilizing and hardening the materials used in their unusual pieces.

Neuvoe Design builds furniture in a range of styles from Southwestern to contemporary to traditional. Each piece is textured to give the appearance that it was crafted from stone, and each comes in a range of colors with a high-quality polymer finish and sealants.

Neuvoe Design lamps feature touch-activated sensors with three brightness levels and porcelain sockets. The Olivers have custom-crafted several pieces of office furniture, including desks and bookcases.

PRIMARY PRODUCT: Home furnishings made from recycled paper products: Entertainment centers, office desks, tables, bookcases, letter trays, lamps, and clocks. Surfaces of each piece textured to duplicate the appearance of stone.

PRICE RANGE: Furniture ranges from $300 to $3,000.

DIRECT SALES: Visitors are welcome, by appointment. Mail and telephone orders are welcome.

CUSTOM ORDERS: Neuvoe Design frequently crafts pieces to the size, shape, and color specified by designers and customers.

ONE OF A KIND: Yes. The Olivers will work on-site to design pieces that fit an individual client's life-style.

CATALOG AVAILABILITY: Brochure is available at no charge.

RETAIL DISTRIBUTION: Complete the Cycle Recycle Center, 3600 East 48th Street, Denver, CO 80209.

WHOLESALE SHOWROOMS AND REPRESENTATIVES: Traditions, Denver Design Center, 595 South Broadway, Suite 111-E, Denver, CO 80209.

HONORS AND SPECIAL COMMISSIONS: Several awards for energy-efficient design, 1991 Boulder, Colorado, Parade of Homes "Best of Show" award.

New West Design

OWNER/DESIGNER: J. Mike Patrick and Virginia Patrick

ADDRESS: New West-Patrick Ranch, 2119 Southfork, Cody, WY 82414

TELEPHONE: (307) 587-2839

FAX: (307) 527-5901

After starting life as a rancher in his native Wyoming, J. Mike Patrick went from building houses to building distinctive, ranch-style furniture. During the past fifteen years, he has become one of the foremost manufacturers of furniture and home furnishings in the style of pioneer furniture craftsman Thomas Molesworth.

Patrick has received extensive coverage in national and international publications. As the largest furniture manufacturer in Cody, Patrick has prospered from the resurgence of interest in Molesworth-style pieces. He is accessible and well organized and is supported by a sophisticated team of craftsmen, designers, and stylists.

The pieces manufactured by New West Design are evocative of America's frontier past. There is a straightforward directness to the New West pieces, an unabashed sense of solidity and permanence.

PRIMARY PRODUCT: Lamps, tables, easy chairs, side chairs, dining chairs, couches, love seats, chandeliers, magazine racks, wastebaskets, bookshelves, desks, bars, dry sinks, buffets, side boards, secretaries, game cabinets, highboys, chests of drawers, beds, blanket boxes, lighting sconces, rockers, benches, cribs, barstools, wardrobes, hall trees, hat racks, curtains, pillows, coverlets, picture frames, and candelabra.

New West uses Douglas fir and ponderosa pine to construct durable, pin-sprayed lacquered home furnishings that are protected from cracking and discoloration. The furniture's construction is complemented by top-quality upholstered coverings made from leathers, blanket weavings, rawhides, and beadwork. Many pieces incorporate hand-wrought steel, carved wood finishes, hand-painted scenes, and custom leather stitchings.

PRICE RANGE: $40 to $4,000.

DIRECT SALES: Clients are always welcome to visit New West's shop and showroom at 2811 Big Horn Avenue, Cody, Wyoming. Calling ahead is appreciated. Mail and telephone orders accepted.

CUSTOM ORDERS: New West's specialty is entire homes and unified roomscapes designed to the customer's needs. The Patricks enjoy the challenge of creating unique pieces and travel extensively for design and installation projects.

ONE OF A KIND: Most of New West's work is one of a kind. Pieces have been designed for many well-known ranch residences.

CATALOG AVAILABILITY: Catalogs are free. Send $10 for a current photo overview or $60 (refundable) for a complete designer portfolio. Designs, drawings, and materials samples are usually provided at no charge.

RETAIL DISTRIBUTION: Ad Hoc, New York City. Rituals and Raffia, both in Los Angeles; Galisteo, San Francisco, California. Yippie-ei-o, Scottsdale, Arizona. Anteks, Dallas, Texas. Squash Blossom, Denver, Colorado. Out-of-the-West, Chicago, Illinois.

Norwegian Wood

OWNER/DESIGNER: Reidar Wahl

ADDRESS: P.O. Box 2425, Telluride, Colorado 81435

TELEPHONE: (303) 728-6222

Norwegian Wood's furniture has an Old World feeling that complements the frontier design tradition of the American West. It is crafted by Reidar Wahl, a self-taught furniture maker who grew up surrounded by Scandinavian antiques in Norway.

Wahl moved to Colorado in the 1980s and began to build furniture that embodies both Southwestern and Scandinavian design. The two influences have in common a respect for materials and a simplicity of line. Wahl produces classic furniture from each style and combines the two in several original designs.

Some of Norwegian Wood's furniture pieces are embellished with accent carving and routed designs. All are meticulously finished with a process that involves many hours of wire brushing. The rich, natural tone of the kiln-dried ponderosa pine is brought out with hand-rubbed waxes. Wahl also uses his own specially formulated stains and paints to create colored finishes that look naturally aged.

PRIMARY PRODUCT: Complete 35-piece line of Southwestern and Scandinavian country furniture. Residential and commercial. Kiln-dried ponderosa pine. Mortise and tenon joinery.

PRICE RANGE: $395 to $4,000.

DIRECT SALES: Norwegian Wood maintains a showroom in Telluride, Colorado, at the Ellison Gallery. Orders may be placed through the showroom or through the production facility in Rico, Colorado. Visitors welcome by appointment. Mail and telephone orders accepted.

CUSTOM ORDERS: Inquiries welcome. Clients can specify designs, dimensions, and finishes.

ONE OF A KIND: Wahl will travel within a limited area to assist with the design and installation of special pieces for homes and offices.

CATALOG AVAILABILITY: Brochure is available at no charge.

RETAIL DISTRIBUTION: Ellison Gallery, Telluride, Colorado.

WHOLESALE SHOWROOMS AND REPRESENTATIVES: No wholesale.

HONORS AND SPECIAL COMMISSIONS: *Snow Country Magazine*, September 1991. *Colorado Homes and Lifestyles*, November 1991, feature article on house furnished by Norwegian Wood.

Distinctly Southwestern/Scandinavian furniture designs

Graham Nugent

OWNER/DESIGNER: Graham Nugent

ADDRESS: Apodaca Road, P.O. Box 265, Dixon, NM 87527

TELEPHONE: (505) 579-4392

A decade ago, Graham Nugent designed the first branch-covered screens, shutters, room dividers, and furniture that have become synonymous with the Southwest look. Those designs were created for The Sombraje Collection and are still available through that company.

Today, Nugent is working independently from his own studio, concentrating on custom and one-of-a-kind furnishings and pursuing his other career as a noted landscape painter. Recent designs incorporate the best elements from each discipline, for instance, a screen with carved and painted landscape forms inlaid with stones and inset with the willow twig panels he originated.

PRIMARY PRODUCT: Contemporary tables, credenzas, and room dividing screens incorporating twigs, rocks, cut stone, and weathered wood, sometimes carved and painted. Nugent personally attends to all design and finishing work.

OTHER LINES: Nugent works with local and out-of-state cabinet and furniture makers in designing and finishing doors and panels for pieces they might build.

PRICE RANGE: $1,500 and up.

DIRECT SALES: All clients are welcome to visit Nugent's workshop/studio by appointment only.

CUSTOM ORDERS: Nugent will discuss clients' requirements.

ONE OF A KIND: All furniture is one of a kind.

CATALOG AVAILABILITY: Photographs available on request.

RETAIL DISTRIBUTION: Shutters at The Sombraje Collection, Santa Fe.

WHOLESALE SHOWROOMS AND REPRESENTATIVES: Works with designers directly.

HONORS AND SPECIAL COMMISSIONS: Shutters, Eldorado Hotel, Santa Fe. Screens, room dividers, and doors for celebrities' residences.

Oblique Design

OWNER/DESIGNER: Jeff Zischke

ADDRESS: 1400 North College, Tempe, AZ 85281

TELEPHONE: (602) 968-2625

The mixed media, stone, and steel tables made by Jeff Zischke, owner of Oblique Design, use a variety of natural materials, including marble, slate, diabase, and sandstone. Ranging in design motif from Southwestern to Neoclassical, the Oblique Design collection evokes a cool, timeless character.

The collection includes coffee tables, dining tables, consoles, pedestals, conference tables, desks, and fireplace facades. The marble pieces are often fabricated from Carrara marble and are solid, carved creations. Hand carving, detailing, and highly polished surfaces are typical of the collection, but rough-hewn, unfinished stone surfaces and sandblasted and other types of glass are also available.

Oblique Design also includes a number of hand-forged, steel frame chairs in its collection. These pieces incorporate symbolic designs, often from Southwestern cultures, into their fabrication. These chairs are available with hand-painted and leather cushions.

PRIMARY PRODUCT: Stone tables made from imported and domestic stone materials, incorporating hand-forged iron bases and stone pedestal bases. Steel chairs, using regional design themes and hand-forged steel.

OTHER LINES: Outdoor furniture made from redwood and designed with a Southwestern contemporary motif. Also manufactures gazebos, which Zischke refers to as being an Egyptian-Southwestern pyramidal outdoor environment.

PRICE RANGE: $500 to $8,000.

DIRECT SALES: Zischke produces and sells his collection through Oblique Gallery, in a historic adobe in Tempe, Arizona. Several local craftspeople are represented. Hours by appointment. Mail and telephone orders are welcome.

CUSTOM ORDERS: A large part of the Oblique Designs business is from custom adaptations of the existing collection.

ONE OF A KIND: Yes. Zischke travels to Italy each summer, learning the latest technological and artistic advances in stone craftsmanship. Any designer or client is encouraged to challenge his imagination and craftsmanship in designing a one-of-a-kind piece.

CATALOG AVAILABILITY: Brochure and color photocopies are available.

RETAIL DISTRIBUTION: Oblique Gallery, Tempe; Beyond Horizons, Scottsdale, Arizona.

WHOLESALE SHOWROOMS AND REPRESENTATIVES: S.C. Smith, Design Center, Phoenix, Arizona.

HONORS AND SPECIAL COMMISSIONS: Arizona Arts Commission project grant, 1990. Oblique Design pieces are included in public and private art and furniture collections around the world.

Pilgrim's Pride

OWNER/DESIGNER: A. Glenn Aaron and Mary Stuckey

ADDRESS: 3440 East 119th Street, Thornton, CO 80233

TELEPHONE: (303) 964-9608

FAX: (303) 457-2838

This Denver-area furniture company produces four completely different furniture collections that cover most of American furnishings history. From the Arts and Crafts designs pioneered by Gustav Stickley to Early American and Shaker furniture designs, Spanish-influenced Southwestern furniture and the high country Western look from Colorado, Pilgrim's Pride seems to specialize in doing nearly everything and doing it well.

Within Colorado furniture circles, Pilgrim's Pride initially developed its reputation for reproductions of Early New England furniture pieces. Using forged cabinet hardware, authentic paint treatments, and elaborate woodwork features that were developed by Pilgrim's Pride designer, Samuel Adams, the company became immediately successful with this traditional type of furniture. Today, while A. Glenn Aaron still produces these popular pieces, Pilgrim's Pride has developed into a multifaceted furniture company.

Pilgrim's Pride feels that its products should be "engineered" and not simply designed. Furniture needs to be structurally sound and make a statement of its owner's values. Aaron believes that great furniture has multiple uses rather than being simply decorative.

PRIMARY PRODUCT: Four complete furniture collections: Shaker/American Primitive, Arts and Crafts, Southwestern/Western, and Early New England. Pieces range from pie safes and dry sinks to mission-style armchairs to trasteros, entertainment centers, beds, and dining tables.

PRICE RANGE: $175 to $8,500.

DIRECT SALES: Pilgrim's Pride prefers working through designers and its retail outlets. Telephone orders are accepted with a deposit.

CUSTOM ORDERS: Custom orders comprise most of the business.

ONE OF A KIND: "This is our forte. New concepts represent a welcome challenge and we will, in certain instances, travel for on-site installations."

CATALOG AVAILABILITY: Catalogs describing each furniture collection are available at no charge. Photographs of individual pieces can be sent on request.

RETAIL DISTRIBUTION: Soho West, Denver; Sedona Designs, Fort Collins, Colorado.

HONORS AND SPECIAL COMMISSIONS: Pieces installed at the Denver Museum.

Frank Lloyd Wright-influenced floor lamp with stained glass inserts

Pinecliffe Design

OWNER/DESIGNER: Jerry Bryant and Sam Clifton

ADDRESS: 12100 Herring, Black Forest, CO 80908

TELEPHONE: (303) 642-3601

The Southwestern furniture designed and manufactured by Pinecliffe Designs has the built-in capacity to be used either indoors or outdoors. Sam Clifton and Jerry Bryant, owners of the business, firmly believe that people are wanting to equip their patios, porches, and backyards with classic Southwestern furniture pieces that are able to withstand the wear and tear of the elements.

The handcrafted Pinecliffe pieces use traditional mortise and tenon joinery combined with a significant amount of hand-carved detail, such as spiral rope carvings, sunbursts, Indian pictograph designs, and Spanish Colonial-style carvings. On some pieces, Pinecliffe incorporates colorful Mexican tilework into the surfaces of tables, especially coffee tables and end tables.

Several stains are available for the Pinecliffe furniture pieces which achieve a rich, aged appearance. There is also a natural finish available, one in which no stains are used and the wood's natural features are emphasized by several coats of hand-rubbed wax.

PRIMARY PRODUCT: Southwestern-style furniture especially intended for indoor or outdoor use. Pieces include picnic tables and benches, chests (also called *harineros*), free-standing benches (also called *bancos*), coffee tables, fireplace benches, and plant stands.

PRICE RANGE: $300 to $1,000.

DIRECT SALES: Yes. Telephone orders are welcome.

CUSTOM ORDERS: Yes.

ONE OF A KIND: Yes.

CATALOG AVAILABILITY: Brochure and photographs are available on request.

RETAIL DISTRIBUTION: Madeiras, 3163 Walnut, Boulder, CO 80301, (303) 443-3078.

Pole Tech, Inc.

OWNER/DESIGNER: Geoffrey C. Whiton

ADDRESS: P.O. Box 1743, Laramie, WY 82070

TELEPHONE: (307) 742-3623

Pole Tech specializes in rustic, lodgepole pine furniture. Geoffrey Whiton brings his experience of more than twenty years in the woodworking and cabinetry fields to the design and manufacture of the Pole Tech line. Whiton's grandfather founded the New York School of Interior Design.

Whiton searches out ponderosa pine, aspen, and Douglas fir that he refers to as "snow load" lodgepole. These pieces, subjected to the stress and strain of Wyoming's winter climate, have been bent and made texturally uneven by drifting snow and blowing winds.

Starting with snow load wood, Whiton uses the natural curvatures and imperfections left in these pieces to create furniture that is full of visual interest yet soundly crafted through its mortise and tenon joinery.

PRIMARY PRODUCT: Beds of all sizes, benches, coffee tables, end tables, dinette sets, hall trees, bar stools, love seats, and bunk beds.

PRICE RANGE: $40 to $700.

DIRECT SALES: With a deposit, orders can be placed directly through the production facility.

CUSTOM ORDERS: Pole Tech frequently designs and builds its pieces to customers' specifications.

CATALOG AVAILABILITY: Information is available in the form of a color photo sheet of the Pole Tech line and an accompanying price list. Detailed photos of individual pieces are available on request.

RETAIL DISTRIBUTION: Pole Tech's showroom, west of Laramie, Wyoming, on Highway 230.

HONORS AND SPECIAL COMMISSIONS: Pole Tech has recently completed a major installation at the Wyoming Territorial Prison Park in Laramie.

Gerald Porter Art Furniture Studio

OWNER/DESIGNER: Gerald Porter and Patricia Porter

ADDRESS: 211 N. Hoff Avenue, Tucson, AZ 85705

TELEPHONE: (602) 628-1411

Gerald Porter refers to his outrageous creations as "Furniture Paintings." Working in collaboration with Gonzalo Espinosa, a talented artist from Guadalajara, Mexico, Porter produces furniture that includes easy chairs, ottomans, tables, dining tables, and dining room sets.

The images on the Furniture Paintings line are whimsical and brilliantly colored. Ranging from quail to cactus to jackrabbits and coyotes, these pieces can be (and have been) commissioned to include interpretive sets of images like creatures on Noah's Ark or even famous scientists. His "Genius Tables" are crafted to replicate the snouts, legs, abdomens, and butts of various types of wildlife and domesticated animals. These pieces are usually made in coffee table and occasional table sizes.

Another of the collections Gerald Porter designs and manufactures is called "Ceramesquite." This furniture combines mesquite wood, using traditional construction techniques, with stoneware and porcelain components (handmade and press-molded). In this collection, the emphasis is on cocktail tables, although case pieces, such as cupboards, are also available.

PRIMARY PRODUCT: Absolutely artistic carved and painted furniture pieces. Using mesquite wood and other media, such as porcelain, leather, and stoneware, Gerald Porter produces furniture that is unlike anything else in the Rocky Mountain or Desert Southwest regions. Brilliant colors, intricate carvings, and surprising design themes dominate.

PRICE RANGE: $450 to $8,000.

DIRECT SALES: Direct sales at the shop are welcome. No telephone orders.

CUSTOM ORDERS: Custom orders are a specialty.

ONE OF A KIND: A regular part of Porter's business. No travel under ordinary circumstances.

CATALOG AVAILABILITY: Brochure is available for a small charge.

RETAIL DISTRIBUTION: Sangin Trading Co., 300 N. 6th Avenue, Tucson; Southwest Arts Portfolio, 3661 N. Campbell Avenue, Suite 313, Tucson, Arizona.

WHOLESALE SHOWROOMS AND REPRESENTATIVES: Sangin Trading Co., 300 N. 6th Avenue, Tucson; Tara, P.O. Box 6, Tucson, AZ 85702; Borderlands, 405 E. 7th Street, Tucson, Arizona.

HONORS AND SPECIAL COMMISSIONS: "Frida Kahlo" chair is currently part of a traveling museum exhibition in the United States and Mexico.

Hillary Riggs, Furniture Designer and Color Consultant

OWNER/DESIGNER: Hillary Riggs

ADDRESS: 544 S. Guadalupe, Santa Fe, NM 87501

TELEPHONE: (505) 988-5567, (505) 455-2351

FAX: (505) 982-5281

Hillary Riggs has a distinguished history as a designer, painter, owner of The Sombraje Collection, and partner in Santa Fe's cooperative venture, Collaboration. She continues to seek new challenges and avenues for her creativity.

Riggs is available to travel for consultations and to conduct workshops or individual training sessions in which she teaches others her color and design techniques. "Happiness comes from right scale," she believes. She also creates special furniture and accessories for individual clients.

Riggs was educated at Instituto Allende and University of Guanajuato in Mexico, where she studied painting and art history. She spent a year visiting museums in Europe on a study course. Her keen color sense was influenced by Mexico and the Earth, and she cites a variety of design inspirations: "Southwestern land and sky masses, French tin roofs/sky/river, washed clothes hung out to dry on rocks and bushes along the roadside in Mexico, driving anywhere, nighttime, and the inner landscape." (Also see special profile with Collaboration.)

PRIMARY PRODUCT: Furniture design, color finishes, and custom color consultations for her own and her partners' furniture businesses. Design and finishes on collaborative art furniture pieces with Peter Gould, including the Iris Bed and the Sunflower Trastero.

OTHER LINES: Accessories, including boxes and mirrors. Paintings.

PRICE RANGE: Will furnish estimate.

DIRECT SALES: Furniture available at Collaboration, Santa Fe.

CUSTOM ORDERS: Most orders are custom.

ONE OF A KIND: Most pieces are one of a kind.

CATALOG AVAILABILITY: Call for photographs.

RETAIL DISTRIBUTION: Collaboration, Santa Fe.

WHOLESALE SHOWROOMS AND REPRESENTATIVES: No.

HONORS AND SPECIAL COMMISSIONS: Extensive coverage in book, *Santa Fe Design*. Absolut Vodka commission. Regional magazine articles.

Rocking "E" Furniture & Design

OWNER/DESIGNER: Ed Young

ADDRESS: P.O. Box 161, Black Hawk, CO 80422

TELEPHONE: (303) 582-3468

Ed Young is a master craftsman who has designed and manufactured Southwestern home furnishings for eight years. He now offers three design motifs in his Rocking "E" Furniture line. He continues to manufacture furniture in his well-known Southwestern style. He also produces a Cowboy Western line and a more traditional aspen log furniture line.

These pieces are available to customers either finished, complete with waxes, stains, and paint washes, or unfinished to order, which allows the customer to make the final decisions.

PRIMARY PRODUCT: Three complete lines of home furnishings, including in aspen log, Southwestern, and cowboy western designs. Pieces include sofas, beds of all configurations, coffee tables, end tables, side tables, easy chairs, and settees.

PRICE RANGE: $100 and up, depending on customer requirements.

DIRECT SALES: Orders are accepted by mail or telephone during weekday business hours.

CUSTOM ORDERS: Custom orders filled recently by Rocking "E" include picture frames designed to match room sets and complete outfitting of retail stores with floor and wall showcases.

ONE OF A KIND: Yes. Young is willing to work with any customer's specific design needs, whether residential or commercial.

CATALOG AVAILABILITY: Available on request.

RETAIL DISTRIBUTION: Country Living Furniture, Boulder, Colorado. Surrisi, Santa Fe, New Mexico. Other locations nationally.

WHOLESALE SHOWROOMS AND REPRESENTATIVES: Blue Mesa Marketing, Denver Merchandise Mart, Denver, Colorado.

Salsa Style

OWNER/DESIGNER: Kristi Allen Hughes

ADDRESS: 2431 East Van Buren, Phoenix, AZ 85202

TELEPHONE: (602) 267-9195

Several lines of home furnishings made from faux stone and various Southwestern woods make up the Salsa Style collection. Starting with their Santa Fe pine line, the Salsa Style collections include Southwest oak, oak with inlaid tile, faux stone, and wrought iron. Furniture pieces are available for outfitting entire homes, from bedrooms to living rooms, family rooms, and dining rooms. All are displayed in the company's Phoenix, Arizona, showroom.

The Salsa Style collections include a complete line of accessory items: original artwork, candelabra, lighting fixtures, sculpture, and custom furniture decorations. Salsa Style also manufactures a collection of Mexican and Spanish colonial furniture replicas. The finishes on these trasteros, *bancos, harineros,* and the like, range from brightly painted to the rustic tones of previous years. Some pieces have cutout design elements, others are elaborately carved, and others are painted with a touch of whimsical Southwestern motifs.

PRIMARY PRODUCT: Southwestern, Spanish Colonial, American West, and regional furniture and accessories for residential and commercial interiors. A selection of hardwoods and softwoods, Mexican tiles, hand-painted finishes and rustic carvings characterize the several lines in the Salsa Style collections.

OTHER LINES: Many accessory items, including original artwork, wrought iron, and lighting fixtures.

PRICE RANGE: $200 to $3,000.

DIRECT SALES: Visitors are encouraged to stop in at the Salsa Style production facility and showroom in Phoenix, Arizona.

CUSTOM ORDERS: Absolutely. Customizing any of the existing Salsa Style lines to suit the needs of a client is a welcome challenge.

ONE OF A KIND: Yes, especially with regard to specific artwork applied to finished pieces.

CATALOG AVAILABILITY: No catalog, but specific product information is available by request.

RETAIL DISTRIBUTION: Salsa Style showroom, 2431 East Van Buren, Phoenix, Arizona.

WHOLESALE SHOWROOMS AND REPRESENTATIVES: Salsa Style Showroom, 2431 East Van Buren, Phoenix, Arizona.

Santos Furniture

OWNER/DESIGNER: Brandon J. Santos

ADDRESS: P.O. Box 61, Dixon, NM 87527

TELEPHONE: (505) 579-4470

"Brandy" Santos's shadowbox table designs feature stylized carved and painted animals inset beneath a framed ¼-inch glass tabletop. No two pieces of furniture are exactly alike because of his handcrafted technique and his use of barn wood and other naturally aged materials. Santos prefers using barn wood as the shadings and marks from weathering and use add character to his furniture pieces.

A degree in anthropology from Notre Dame University did not prepare Santos for a career in woodworking in any obvious way. However, it gave him insight into the culture of New Mexico when it "caught his eye and inspired his hands." He brought a cosmopolitan outlook and an understanding of history to his workshop in a mountain village, and he respectfully transformed a local craft into his own design statement.

Santos's unique contemporary treatment of authentic New Mexico style provides this small family business with a charming but limited line of furniture and accessories. Each carefully crafted piece is a thoughtful expression of a beautiful regional tradition.

PRIMARY PRODUCT: All sizes of tables, chairs, cabinets and desks, including coffee and buffet tables, trasteros, medicine chests, and computer desks.

OTHER LINES: Chip-carved and painted mirror frames. Corbel and repisa-style shelves. Crosses made of painted wood from old houses.

PRICE RANGE: $15 to $2,000.

DIRECT SALES: Telehone orders and workshop visits are welcome.

CUSTOM ORDERS: Special orders are accepted and are individually priced according to labor and materials.

ONE OF A KIND: Santos works closely with clients, usually by telephone.

CATALOG AVAILABILITY: Brochures are available on request.

RETAIL DISTRIBUTION: Dwellings Revisited, Taos; Santa Fe Style, Washington, D.C.

WHOLESALE SHOWROOMS AND REPRESENTATIVES: None.

HONORS AND SPECIAL COMMISSIONS: Private residence, Greenwich, Connecticut: dining room set with eight-foot table and eight chairs, each with a different chip-carved and painted geometric design.

Monte G. Scholten Furniture

OWNER/DESIGNER: Monte G. Scholten

ADDRESS: 2222 East Thomas Road, Phoenix, AZ 85016

TELEPHONE: (602) 954-6271

FAX: (602) 957-4461

Working in an individualistic style that incorporates elements of Territorial and Western Ranch design, Monte Scholten handcrafts furniture that has a weathered appearance. It would be as much at home in a Mexican cantina as in an art gallery.

A member of the Master Artisan's Guild, Scholten has a tremendous array of woodworking and design skills that he draws from in developing his furniture. Occasionally, he will touch on a type of furniture that hints at typical Southwestern design. At other times, he takes regional wood and ironwork into a different dimension, resulting in furniture that looks as if it has been beaten nearly to death by the relentless summer sun of an Arizona desert.

Scholten is mostly self-taught. His artist's touch is the result of studies he undertook with Sioux painter Oscar Howe. He crafts his furniture from several readily available regional materials, including ponderosa pine, oak, ash, copper, hand-wrought steel, and inlaid turquoise.

PRIMARY PRODUCT: Territorial and Western Ranch furniture pieces using various woods and other materials, including copper, turquoise, and wrought steel. Dining tables and chairs, chaise lounges, entertainment centers, trasteros, mirrors, chests, coffee tables, occasional tables, benches, hallway units, bars, and bar stools.

PRICE RANGE: $300 to $10,000.

DIRECT SALES: Retail clients are invited to visit the production facility and shop.

CUSTOM ORDERS: Yes, on a first-come basis.

ONE OF A KIND: Yes. Scholten has created pieces for rural churches and custom residences around the Southwest.

CATALOG AVAILABILITY: Brochure is available at no cost.

RETAIL DISTRIBUTION: Monte Scholten showroom/shop, 2222 East Thomas Road, Phoenix, Arizona. Connections West, Seattle, Washington. Big Horn Gallery, Cody and Jackson Hole, Wyoming. Santa Fe Style, Danville, California.

WHOLESALE SHOWROOMS AND REPRESENTATIVES: Monte sets up his traveling medicine show each spring at the Best of the Southwest show at the Dallas Trade Mart.

HONORS AND SPECIAL COMMISSIONS: 1990 Phoenix Designer's Showcase House (People's Choice Award). 1988 Phoenix Street of Dreams (Designer's Choice Award). Master Artisan's Guild.

Sculptural Forest Furnishings

OWNER/DESIGNER: Steven Rouette

ADDRESS: P.O. Box 882, Williams, AZ 86046

TELEPHONE: (602) 635-2724, (602) 778-1339

Steven Rouette lives and works in the Chino Valley, an oasis of green in the Arizona drylands. There, he pursues a furniture-crafting passion that takes odd-shaped pieces of kiln-dried oak and fashions them into a wide array of home furnishings. Using the gambrel oak that grows throughout Arizona, Rouette crafts his pieces with mortise and tenon joinery, Shaker-style fabric webbing and woven cowhide for seats, and several coatings of hand-rubbed wax. Each piece can take him anywhere from thirty-five to two hundred hours to complete.

"Unlike conventional furnishings, these pieces are built from saplings in either a peeled or unpeeled state. The works that I favor are the more creative pieces that have had their shapes dictated by the harsh natural elements of their mountain environments. This way, chairs look as if they can be blowing away on their top half while their bases desperately cling to the floor," Rouette says.

"These pieces tend to appeal to the individual who can look past a chair as simply being a place to sit or a bed as being a place to get an evening's rest. They may look a bit impractical, but on a structural level they're absolutely sound. I do have a "production line" for the more conservative client, though even in this work the emphasis is on individuality of design. This line is sold on a wholesale basis," Rouette says.

PRIMARY PRODUCT: One-of-a-kind and limited production collection of furniture made from Arizona-grown gambrel oak. Limited production pieces include mirror frames, picture frames, wall shelves, and towel bars. One-of-a-kind pieces include chaise longues, beds of all dimensions, dining chairs, and captain's chairs.

PRICE RANGE: $150 to $8,000.

DIRECT SALES: Visits to the shop, by appointment, are encouraged. Mail and telephone orders are accepted.

CUSTOM ORDERS: All are custom pieces, except for items in the limited production line.

ONE OF A KIND: Art galleries carry Rouette's more unusual pieces. Installations are possible, with adequate terms agreed to by both sides. Rouette has worked as a consultant on several private residences.

CATALOG AVAILABILITY: Catalog is available at a nominal cost.

RETAIL DISTRIBUTION: Offerings, New York. Trompe, Phoenix; Construct, Phoenix, Arizona.

HONORS AND SPECIAL COMMISSIONS: "Arizona Art Forms," a juried PBS production.

Southwest Furniture Sales

OWNER/DESIGNER: Bob Hitt

ADDRESS: P.O. Box 3768, Ogden, UT 84409

TELEPHONE: (801) 392-2625

Bob Hitt's lodgepole pine furniture line features mortise and tenon joinery, light wash finishes, and rich, deep wax coatings. Following a career in furniture retail sales, Hitt began manufacturing his own furniture line under the name "Badlands Southwestern Furniture" in 1988.

PRIMARY PRODUCT: Full line of lodgepole pine furniture, including beds, nightstands, five-drawer dressers, sofas, canopy beds, end tables, coffee tables, easy chairs, love seats, porch gliders, and benches.

PRICE RANGE: $149 to $1,499.

DIRECT SALES: Line is primarily sold through wholesale channels, but retail buyers can be directed by Hitt to one of his many regional outlets.

CUSTOM ORDERS: Southwest Furniture Sales frequently works with commercial and residential accounts to design and manufacture custom pieces.

CATALOG AVAILABILITY: Yes, at no cost.

RETAIL DISTRIBUTION: Habitat, Las Vegas, Nevada. Southwest Shop, Salt Lake City; Coldwater Trading, Ogden, Utah. L & M Design Interiors, Reno, Nevada. Oak-n-Pine, West Yellowstone, Montana. J. Michaels Interiors, Rigby, Idaho. Hansen Floral, Phoenix, Arizona.

WHOLESALE SHOWROOMS AND REPRESENTATIVES: Southwest Furniture Sales, 739 Wall Avenue, Ogden, UT 84404.

HONORS AND SPECIAL COMMISSIONS: Complete renovation of First Class compartments of the Colorado & Wyoming Railroad. Big Sky Resort, Big Sky, Montana. Lost Fork Ranch, West Yellowstone, Montana.

Sparks Brothers Inc. / Peter Gould

OWNER/DESIGNER: Chris Sparks

ADDRESS: P.O. Drawer 1069, Santa Fe, NM 87504-1069

TELEPHONE: (505) 438-7133

FAX: (505) 982-5281

Peter Gould has been well known in Santa Fe furniture design for many years. His robust proportions and attractive details, such as a basketweave chair back, have made his style immediately recognizable. Over the years, he has accepted commissions for large-scale public projects, resulting in high visibility for his furniture.

Recently, he has been joined by Chris Sparks, a Texas Hill Country furniture designer who has introduced a line of native pecan pieces. Sparks's influences range from Shaker to Beidermeyer, which results in a rich, regional feel expressed in clean, elegant lines. (Also see special profile of Collaboration.)

PRIMARY PRODUCT: Handmade furniture. Full lines include beds, cabinets, credenzas, tables, chairs, desks. Blacksmith-forged hinges, pulls, gate-hook shutter latches.

PRICE RANGE: $275 to $7,000.

DIRECT SALES: Retail clients are welcome to visit the workshop at 1541 Center Drive, Santa Fe. A much larger selection is available at the Collaboration showroom at 544 S. Guadalupe, Santa Fe, New Mexico.

CUSTOM ORDERS: Frequently customize designs for homes and offices.

ONE OF A KIND: Large-scale projects such as hotels, restaurants, retail stores. Exclusive private lines for stores looking to have their own line of furniture.

CATALOG AVAILABILITY: Catalog, $5 by mail.

RETAIL DISTRIBUTION: Collaboration, Santa Fe, New Mexico. Hamilton Sparks, Austin, Texas.

WHOLESALE SHOWROOMS AND REPRESENTATIVES: No.

HONORS AND SPECIAL COMMISSIONS: Extensive coverage in book, *Santa Fe Design*. La Quinta Inns of America. Inn at the Old Town, Irvine Ranch, California. Inn at the Citadel; Clarion Inn at McCormick Ranch, Scottsdale. El Dorado Hotel, Bishop's Lodge, La Posada, Hotel Plaza Real, Pink Adobe, Maria's, all Santa Fe, New Mexico.

Spirit Mountain Woodworks

OWNER/DESIGNER: Carlos Luis Medina

ADDRESS: P.O. Box 6386, Taos, NM 87571

TELEPHONE: (505) 758-1624

Carlos Luis Medina has been building quality New Mexican furniture for many years. Over a decade ago, he established Spirit Mountain Woodworks and began creating furnishings for a few interior designers and residential clients in the Taos area, particularly those associated with the famed ski areas of northern New Mexico.

Medina's personal style is distinguished by Queen Anne legs combined with early Spanish Colonial details. He finishes his furniture with smooth, sculptural carving and comfortable, rounded edges. Drawers and side paneling feature grooved designs.

Medina has exhibited his furnishings in galleries but has determined that his rich, substantial designs are best suited to special projects commissioned by interior designers and residential clients.

PRIMARY PRODUCT: Furniture of thick, solid wood including native cedar, ponderosa pine, mahogany, oak, sassafras, and old barn wood. Occasional native sugar pine, which is very rare and grows only at the timberline. Antique finishes include whitewash or blue-stained pine.

OTHER LINES: Spiral architectural columns.

PRICE RANGE: $100 to $3,000.

DIRECT SALES: Sales are usually made through referrals from major commissions. Telephone and mail orders considered; workshop visits arranged by appointment.

CUSTOM ORDERS: Spirit Mountain specializes in dealing with interior designers and building furniture to their specifications.

ONE OF A KIND: Medina works with clients in adapting his own line and incorporating it into their photos and plans.

CATALOG AVAILABILITY: None at this time. Photographs available.

RETAIL DISTRIBUTION: None.

WHOLESALE SHOWROOMS AND REPRESENTATIVES: None.

HONORS AND SPECIAL COMMISSIONS: Furnished ten rooms at Cottam's Alpine and ten rooms at Taos Ski Lodge, both at Taos Ski Valley. Thirty pieces for a Red River, New Mexico, second home and the client's primary residence in Texas.

Streck Family

OWNER/DESIGNER: Clem, Pat, Jim, Mark, Kyle, and Alicia Streck

ADDRESS: 541 Cordova Road, Santa Fe, NM 87501

TELEPHONE: (505) 986-1201

The Streck Family is a veritable Santa Fe institution. Clem and his brood have for years furnished quality resale and antique furniture to the community while developing their distinctive painted folk art furnishings. His sons were helping him restore 18th-century homes before they were old enough to enter school. "With so many personalities involved," Clem Streck points out, "we can draw on individual talents and blend them to form unique pieces." He might add that the resulting furnishings fit beautifully into design plans for any other part of the country.

PRIMARY PRODUCT: Wood and metal painted furniture and lighting with aged and patinated finishes.

OTHER LINES: Chandeliers, sconces, and mirrors. Mailboxes and birdhouses. Folk art objects for home or business.

PRICE RANGE: $50 to $4,000.

DIRECT SALES: The Streck Family maintains a large showroom in Santa Fe. Nearby is a studio/shop where clients may talk directly with designers and production people. Mail and telephone orders are also accepted. A 50 percent deposit is required for custom orders.

CUSTOM ORDERS: Custom work is handled with direct communication between the client and the person responsible for creating the piece, thus ensuring a more fluid interaction with regard to design, color, and timing.

ONE OF A KIND: Members of the family are available to travel and develop basic ideas on site, an important consideration when developing continuity in a project requiring many pieces. In such cases, they can develop furniture, cabinet doors, mirrors, and interior lighting into a uniform theme.

CATALOG AVAILABILITY: Catalog and price lists on request.

RETAIL DISTRIBUTION: Streck Family; Dewey Galleries, Santa Fe, New Mexico. Mongerson Wunderlich Gallery, Chicago, Illinois. Smithsonian Institution Gift Shop, Washington, D.C. Cowboy Hall of Fame, Oklahoma City, Oklahoma. Adam Whitney Gallery, Omaha, Nebraska. Bazaar Del Mundo, San Diego, California. Rituals, Los Angeles, California. Harrod's, London.

HONORS AND SPECIAL COMMISSIONS: Commissions in many private homes across the United States. Published in several national magazines including *Traditional Homes, Phoenix Home & Gardens*, and *Sunset Magazine*, and in *USA Today*.

Sweet Water Ranch

OWNER/DESIGNER: Bryan Taggart and Marc Taggart,
with designer Ric Oliver and master craftsman Lester Santos
ADDRESS: 531 16th Street, P.O. Drawer 398, Cody, WY 82414
TELEPHONE: (307) 527-4044

Using an authentic approach to the re-creation of Thomas Molesworth furniture pieces, Sweet Water Ranch has elaborated on those original pieces by adding stunning, hand-wrought iron artwork and top-quality cushioning to its furniture. Sweet Water Ranch prides itself on its efforts to build furniture that looks exactly the way Thomas Molesworth built his, yet incorporates hidden improvements that allow each piece to function in an updated, comfortable manner.

When the Taggarts take on the task of designing a unique piece, the results are stunning. By using their knowledge of ironwork design and fabrication, they create mixed-media furniture that incorporates exotic woods, like magnolia, with richly colored upholstery and stark yet artistically strong statements in iron.

PRIMARY PRODUCT: Living room pieces such as sofas, love seats, easy chairs, ottomans, freestanding club chairs, cowboy armchairs, coffee tables, burl tables, end tables, and entertainment centers. Dining room tables and chairs and card tables. Accessories include upholstered pillows and cushions, burl floor lamps, ironwork lighting sconces, chandeliers and table lamps with rawhide shades.

PRICE RANGE: $500 to $9,500.

DIRECT SALES: Mail and telephone orders accepted. Swatches and drawings sent for final customer approval. Visitors are welcome at the Sweet Water Ranch production facility, 531 16th Street, Cody, Wyoming.

CUSTOM ORDERS: Craftsman Lester Santos works closely with clients to turn an idea into a custom, one-of-a-kind piece of furniture. Most of Sweet Water Ranch's orders are done on a custom basis. Designer Ric Oliver oversees the on-site installation of pieces that have been custom ordered.

CATALOG AVAILABILITY: Photographs and prices of representative pieces are available at no cost.

RETAIL DISTRIBUTION: Direct sales through Cody, Wyoming, production facility.

WHOLESALE SHOWROOMS AND REPRESENTATIVES: Sweet Water Ranch Showroom at The Ice House, 1801 Wynkoop, Suite 220, Denver, Colorado. Mimi London, Pacific Design Center, 8687 Melrose Avenue, Los Angeles, California.

HONORS AND SPECIAL COMMISSIONS: Major Commissions include the Valley Ranch, Cody, Wyoming, and the Pyle residence in Edwards, Colorado.

Talismans Marble International

OWNER/DESIGNER: Eric Kwong

ADDRESS: 1325 S. Park Drive, Suite 1, Tempe, AZ 85281

TELEPHONE: (602) 829-9455

Talismans' specialty is residential and commercial furnishings made from natural marble, granite, and other stone. Eric Kwong, the company's owner and a trained artist, operates on the principle that there has never existed an interior space for which a complementary stone material cannot be found.

Each piece of furniture crafted by Talismans is made from solid slabs of marble or stone rather than from precut tiles. These slabs, which are ¾-inch thick, range from 4 feet to 5 feet wide and up to 10 feet long. Over three hundred varieties of marble are offered by Talismans, from sleek blacks to classic whites and everything in between. Marble can be ordered polished or unpolished, with the latter finish imparting a rustic, primitive look to an interior space.

PRIMARY PRODUCT: Talismans specializes in reception areas for commercial spaces, conference tables, individual desks, coffee tables, dining tables, occasional tables and picture frames.

OTHER LINES: Countertops, vanities, and fireplace facings.

PRICE RANGE: $500 to $5,000 for furniture; $1000 to $100,000 for commercial installations.

DIRECT SALES: Retail customers are welcome at the production facility, preferably in the company of a professional designer.

CUSTOM ORDERS: Always, including display pieces.

ONE OF A KIND: Once a designer and client inform Kwong of the style and color of the stone material they need, one-of-a-kind pieces can be designed to suit particular interior spaces and built with specific reinforcement qualities.

CATALOG AVAILABILITY: Brochure available at no cost.

RETAIL DISTRIBUTION: Talismans retail showroom, Tempe, Arizona.

WHOLESALE SHOWROOMS AND REPRESENTATIVES: None.

HONORS AND SPECIAL COMMISSIONS: Many installations in custom residences in Arizona and California.

Taos Custom Woodworks

OWNER/DESIGNER: Steve Gomez

ADDRESS: P.O. Box 461, Taos, NM 87571

TELEPHONE: (505) 758-8137

Steve Gomez started out making contemporary hardwood furnishings but eventually found himself influenced by the "Southwest Movement." Educated in the liberal arts, he settled his workshop in Ranchos de Taos, New Mexico, just a block from the fabled St. Francis church that has been so widely photographed and painted. He enjoys the challenge of working with a variety of projects ranging in style from contemporary to Southwestern, including all the possible hybrids.

"I feel that my touch for custom design is our strong point," says Gomez. "I like to work with customers' needs, to find the design solutions, and to transfer that to a high-quality piece of craftsmanship."

PRIMARY PRODUCT: Custom furniture.

OTHER LINES: Doors. "You might say we do whatever comes in the door."

PRICE RANGE: Per commission.

DIRECT SALES: Clients or browsers are always welcome in the shop, where there are a few show pieces as well as works in progress and photographs of previous work. Custom orders can be arranged over the telephone and by mailing drawings and photographs.

CUSTOM ORDERS: Always.

ONE OF A KIND: Taos Custom Woodwork specializes in unique commissions. Will travel to design, deliver, or install.

CATALOG AVAILABILITY: No catalog.

RETAIL DISTRIBUTION: Primary retail outlet is the workshop in Ranchos de Taos, New Mexico, four miles south of Taos.

Taos Furniture

OWNER/DESIGNER: Andy Peterson

ADDRESS: 232 Galisteo Street, Santa Fe, NM 87501

TELEPHONE: (505) 988-1229, (800) 443-3448

FAX: (505) 983-9375

Taos Furniture is one of northern New Mexico's oldest and largest manufacturers of Taos-style furniture. The company offers over eighty standard items for dining room, living room, bedroom, and office. All surfaces are hand planed, and specially developed finishes are applied by hand to give the furniture its distinctive warmth and charm.

The Taos Bed, a traditional design whose popularity was promoted by this company some years ago, is the basis for all of Taos Furniture's upholstered seating, including chairs, love seats, and sectional sofas. The company's designs are extremely flexible, allowing for custom adaptation to any interior setting.

PRIMARY PRODUCT: Furniture for home and office, handcrafted in solid ponderosa pine. Mortise and tenon joinery, hand-planed surfaces, and hand-applied finishes.

PRICE RANGE: $125 to $5,600.

DIRECT SALES: Retail showroom in Santa Fe, but most orders are received by mail or telephone.

CUSTOM ORDERS: About 20 percent of Taos Furniture's work is custom.

ONE OF A KIND: Capable of doing unique pieces or of providing furniture for large commercial projects.

CATALOG AVAILABILITY: Free brochure available on request; 32-page catalog available for $10. Fabric and stain samples on request.

RETAIL DISTRIBUTION: Time-Space, Milan, Italy. Chevignon, Paris, France. NPG Imports, Geneva, Switzerland. Zona, Tokyo, Japan, and New York City; Aspen, Colorado. Futon Design, Chicago, Illinois.

Countries Hurrah, Ft. Myers, Florida. Lifestyle Interiors, Long Island, New York.

HONORS AND SPECIAL COMMISSIONS: "Taos Furniture" is a trademark registered to this company. Special commissions include furniture for Vermejo Park Resort, Raton, New Mexico; Hyatt Regency, Aruba, Netherlands Antilles; and many hotels, bed and breakfasts, country clubs and professional office buildings. Listed with Dun and Bradstreet.

Taos Style

OWNER/DESIGNER: Andrea Rannefeld and James Rannefeld

ADDRESS: P.O. Box 858, Taos, NM 87571

TELEPHONE: (505) 758-8455

Folk furniture is usually bright, cheerful, and crude and fine traditional and contemporary furniture is usually elegant and solid. Taos Style, a business owned and operated by Andrea Rannefeld and James Rannefeld, offers the best of both worlds.

James's solidly crafted furniture is known for its high quality of construction and finish, while Andrea's sprightly but polished paintbrush confers a cheerful, stylish appeal. Her color system, especially, is one of the creamiest, clearest palettes around. The brushwork is fluid and confident.

Both of the Rannefelds studied widely in various design fields before pooling their talents to create Taos Style in 1974. Each is an accomplished artist; together, they have realized a definitive, radiant style all their own.

Taos Style's most popular lines are the Southwestern geometrics they have named "Taos" and "Santa Fe." The most popular color systems have been the strongest ones, like "Salsa," a knockout combination of red, turquoise, yellow, purple, and black.

A new line, Cowboy Country Collection, is hand-painted with silhouettes of bronc busters, ropers, or cowgirls and then branded. Each pieces is distressed and antiqued in a natural finish.

PRIMARY PRODUCT: Handcrafted furniture indigenous to northern New Mexico, in a palette of fifty standard finishes ranging from antique distressed "Museum" to paint-washed solid colors to hand-painted designs from the Southwest.

PRICE RANGE: $150 to $3,000.

DIRECT SALES: Retail sales by visit, mail, or telephone. The display is limited to what is on hand, as there is no showroom at this time. Visits should be arranged by appointment.

CUSTOM ORDERS: Frequently do custom color matching (+15%) and custom sizing (minimum 25% additional). Nonrefundable fee of $150 for new designs that is applied toward purchase.

ONE OF A KIND: The Rannefelds have been creating one-of-a-kind work in Taos since 1974, in both hardwood and native pine.

CATALOG AVAILABILITY: Color brochure of Taos Style. Color flier of Cowboy Country Collection. Price sheets/information.

RETAIL DISTRIBUTION: Yip-Ei-O, Scottsdale, Arizona, and Santa Monica, California. Rituals, Los Angeles; Galisteo, San Francisco, California. Johnson & Benkert, Santa Fe, New Mexico. Blue Corn, Aspen, Colorado. Southwest Designs, Jupiter, Florida. Santa Fe Style, Washington, D.C.

WHOLESALE SHOWROOMS AND REPRESENTATIVES: Time-Space, Milan, Italy.

HONORS AND SPECIAL COMMISSIONS: New Mexico State Capitol Building: oak ribbon benches in main entry through the Halls of History. Sixteen-foot conference tables. Rocking chair for Jimmy Carter.

Teetzel Co.

OWNER/DESIGNER: William Teetzel

ADDRESS: P.O. Box 8649, Santa Fe, NM 87504

TELEPHONE: (505) 471-6853, (505) 986-1726

William Teetzel is noted for his outrageous Art Furniture designs such as the Prickly Pear Table and the Agave Lamp Table. However, his workshop also produces a full line of subtly sophisticated furniture with more sedate decorations including lovely painted and carved motifs.

"My designs are extremely diverse," Teetzel explains. "I produce a style of furniture that is basically desert surrealism. Presently, I'm developing a new style that is an amalgamation of Chinese Chippendale, American Southwest, high tech, and American Indian." Teetzel's previous work indicates that this project will live up to its billing.

"The Teetzels have been designers and producers of finely crafted furniture since 1916," he points out. "I'm just another of them."

PRIMARY PRODUCT: Tables, occasional chairs, secretaries, chests, dressers, and art furniture made of local Southwestern woods including fir, mesquite, cottonwood, pine, and cedar. Other exotic woods include ebony, black heart, and birds-eye maple. Furniture is influenced from many early styles, such as Egyptian, Chinese, and eighteenth- and nineteenth-century English, but features architectural material and historical embellishments from the American Southwest.

PRICE RANGE: $500 to $15,000.

DIRECT SALES: Everyone is welcome at the workshop.

CUSTOM ORDERS: Installations in architectural projects such as Hansen Library and 7th Street Building, Durango, Colorado.

ONE OF A KIND: Specializes in complex and otherwise impossible special orders.

CATALOG AVAILABILITY: Photographs, specifications, and price list on request.

RETAIL DISTRIBUTION: Blue Door, Fort Worth, Texas. C. Hauser Gallery, Scottsdale; Agnisha Gallery, Sedona, Arizona.

HONORS AND SPECIAL COMMISSIONS: Work featured in book, *Santa Fe Design,* and *Dallas Herald Tribune.* Teetzel is included in the Museum of American Folk Art tours from New York.

Ernest Thompson & Co., Inc.

OWNER/DESIGNER: Mike Godwin and Doreen Godwin, Owners
Ernest Thompson and Mike Godwin, Designers

ADDRESS: 2618 Coors S.W., Albuquerque, NM 87121

TELEPHONE: (505) 873-4652

FAX: (505) 877-7185

Ernest Thompson is a fifth-generation northern New Mexican who has been creating fine furniture for two decades. His major influence has been the history and beauty of the region of his heritage, and he is dedicated to maintaining the traditional techniques of Old World master craftsmen. His greatest recognition, however, has come from his unique hand carving, which combines themes from early Spanish Colonial furniture with an expansive contemporary scale and flair.

Thompson's partners, Mike and Doreen Godwin, have taken a hand in the management of the business. This has given him the opportunity to create new designs. (Also see special profile of Collaboration.)

PRIMARY PRODUCT: Full range of residential, office, and commercial furniture of Southwestern/Western regional design. Handcrafted primarily of pine; other woods available. Mortise and tenon joinery. Wide variety of finishes including color washes.

OTHER LINES: Architectural elements such as corbels and doors.

PRICE RANGE: $225 (chairs) to $2,495 (buffets, etc.).

DIRECT SALES: Clients and visitors are always welcome to visit the Ernest Thompson workshop during regular showroom hours. The shop is located ten minutes from Albuquerque International Airport. Orders are also accepted by mail and telephone.

CUSTOM ORDERS: Custom orders are welcome. Custom finishes are available.

ONE OF A KIND: Unique commissions accepted. Can provide on-site installation.

CATALOG AVAILABILITY: Call or write Ernest Thompson for 28-page brochure, $5.

RETAIL DISTRIBUTION: Ernest Thompson, Albuquerque; Collaboration, Santa Fe, New Mexico.

WHOLESALE SHOWROOMS AND REPRESENTATIVES: No.

HONORS AND SPECIAL COMMISSIONS: ASID, ISID. Notable commissions include Disney Dolphin Hotel, Vermejo Park, University of New Mexico, multiple projects for Marriott Corporation, large residential projects.

T-M Cowboy Classics

OWNER/DESIGNER: Tom Bice and Maril Bice

ADDRESS: 444 Main Street, Longmont, CO 80501

TELEPHONE: (303) 776-7142

If you are a cowboy at heart, then Tom and Maril Bice have furniture that will certainly interest you. Whether you are looking for a locking lodgepole pine gun case with glass door panels or a steel and wood wagon wheel coffee table, the collection T-M Cowboy Classics offers is authentically Western.

T-M Cowboy Classics furniture has an antique feeling, which results from the use of elements of older pieces that are incorporated with new wood components to produce newly built furniture. Some of the items the Bices incorporate into their collection, such as clocks, dishes, curtains, chaps, chandeliers, and assorted textiles, are found at flea markets and second-hand shops.

The half-log construction technique used by T-M Cowboy Classics traces its roots to a line of made-in-Colorado furniture from forty years ago. The Bices have made several improvements on these older designs, which they craft completely by hand and finish with several coats of high-quality lacquers.

PRIMARY PRODUCT: Western and Cowboy-style furniture using half-log construction techniques. Wagon wheel coffee tables, gun cases, entertainment centers, easy chairs, end tables, bars and barstools, love seats, sofas, chests of drawers, mirrors, beds, headboards, and china cabinets.

PRICE RANGE: $350 to $3,000.

DIRECT SALES: Yes, through the T-M Cowboy Classics retail outlet and showroom in Longmont, Colorado. A Jackson, Wyoming, retail store is planned for mid-1992.

CUSTOM ORDERS: Yes.

ONE OF A KIND: Maril Bice says that since she has the tools and the truck, anything anybody can dream up can be made and delivered. Residential and commercial custom orders are welcome.

CATALOG AVAILABILITY: Catalog is available at no cost.

RETAIL DISTRIBUTION: T-M Cowboy Classics, 444 Main Street, Longmont, Colorado.

Clint Trafton Furniture

OWNER/DESIGNER: Clint Trafton

ADDRESS: 1223 West Niagara, Tucson, AZ 85745

TELEPHONE: (602) 623-4605

Clint Trafton's furniture collection combines locally grown mesquite wood with copper inlays, copper sheet tabletops, and embossed, hammered copper design elements. In addition, leather is used as both a decorative and a functional element.

PRIMARY PRODUCT: Mesquite, copper, and leather mixed-media furniture in Southwestern designs. Copper inlay and solid copper-top tables in several dining table designs. Several dining chair and easy chair designs in mesquite and leather. Buffets and sideboards in mesquite with copper inlay designs. Coffee tables with copper inlay tops, hammered copper tops with Southwestern designs. Plant stands, children's furniture, beds, headboards in various designs and sizes.

PRICE RANGE: $300 to $4,000.

DIRECT SALES: Through Totally Southwest, Peter Christo, 5575 East River Road, #131, Tucson, AZ 85715, (602) 577-2295.

CUSTOM ORDERS: Yes, to the extent that the item has consistent design features with the rest of Trafton's collection.

ONE OF A KIND: No.

CATALOG AVAILABILITY: No.

RETAIL DISTRIBUTION: Totally Southwest (see above).

HONORS AND SPECIAL COMMISSIONS: President, 1990, Southern Arizona Woodworker's Association.

Triangle Z Ranch Furniture

OWNER/DESIGNER: Kendall Siggins

ADDRESS: P.O. Box 995, Cody, WY 82414

TELEPHONE: (307) 587-3901

The furniture creations of Ken Siggins's Triangle Z Ranch Furniture Company are best characterized as Western renditions of the Adirondack style, tempered by the vision of a craftsman raised in the hometown of Thomas Molesworth-style furniture. Ken Siggins has made a name for himself in Cody, Wyoming, having crafted furniture in this region since 1963. He designs each piece, then brands and numbers it as it leaves his shop.

Triangle Z mixes its furniture styles, producing some pieces that have the straight-rail design of original ranch furniture and other pieces that have Molesworth and traditional Adirondack features. The company produces many interesting accent pieces; a full range of home furnishings is also available. The emphasis here is on craftsmanship, as is evidenced by Siggins's nearly thirty-year tenure as Cody's most established furniture maker.

PRIMARY PRODUCT: Tables, easy chairs, dressers, dining room sets, sofas, bunk beds, toy storage boxes, love seats, benches, nightstands, desks, and assorted chairs.

PRICE RANGE: $350 to $5,000.

DIRECT SALES: Telephone orders can be shipped directly from the Triangle Z production facility. Thirty percent deposit due at time of ordering, with remainder due at time of shipping.

CUSTOM ORDERS: While Triangle Z has a complete line of furniture, each piece is specially branded and numbered by the individual craftsman. Materials, upholsterings, colors, and sizes can be crafted to suit customer's needs.

CATALOG AVAILABILITY: Catalog and price list are available.

RETAIL DISTRIBUTION: The Big Horn Gallery and Home on the Range, both in Cody, Wyoming. Dampierre Studio, New York City.

WHOLESALE SHOWROOMS AND REPRESENTATIVES: Contact production facility.

George Tucker Furniture

OWNER/DESIGNER: George Tucker

ADDRESS: 8230 South Marshall Court, Littleton, CO 80123

TELEPHONE: (303) 978-0999

George Tucker has designed his own line of South-western furniture, which he builds by himself in a small shop on the outskirts of Denver. While the primary building material used for this furniture line is ponderosa pine, Tucker has frequently used other types of wood, depending on the needs of the client.

Tucker's furniture carving work is outstanding. Running the gamut from simple mesa-type cuts to the wildly geometric and spiral designs used on his more elaborate pieces, wood carving is the area in which he shows off the craftsman's skills he applies to the construction of each piece.

Tucker's previous careers were architecture and ownership of a millworking company. He is happy to be in the furniture-making craft and now spends most of his days laboring in his shop, working out the details of each design he produces.

PRIMARY PRODUCT: A full line of Southwestern furniture made from ponderosa pine, including dining tables, dining chairs, china cabinets, buffets, mirrors, armoires, dressers, nightstands, beds of all dimensions, headboards, entertainment centers, coffee tables, couches, easy chairs, and lighting fixtures. Each piece is finished and painted according to customer specifications.

PRICE RANGE: $200 to $3,000.

DIRECT SALES: Customers are invited to visit Tucker's showroom, by appointment, to make arrangements for direct purchase of his furnishings.

CUSTOM ORDERS: Slightly more than half of the volume handled by Tucker comes in from designers and clients requesting pieces to be crafted to specific dimensions and finishes.

ONE OF A KIND: Built-in entertainment centers and cabinetry are a specialty. Each piece is individually designed to fit a specific home setting. Tucker has also produced room settings for corporate and professional offices.

CATALOG AVAILABILITY: No catalog, but photographs of specific pieces are available on request.

RETAIL DISTRIBUTION: Touch of Santa Fe, Littleton, Colorado.

HONORS AND SPECIAL COMMISSIONS: George Tucker has completely furnished several large homes in Colorado and New Mexico.

Universal Concepts Ltd.

OWNER/DESIGNER: Michael J. Besler

ADDRESS: 3334 West McDowell, #18, Phoenix, AZ 85009

TELEPHONE: (602) 269-1889

FAX: (602) 233-1918

Universal Concepts has developed three lines of regionally styled home furnishings. From the heavily distressed appearance of the company's Southwest style to its more traditional Territorial style to its latest European and Southwestern influenced Spanish Colonial line, Michael Besler's designs suit a range of interior environments.

Universal Concepts uses ponderosa pine in most of its production pieces but has worked with oak and a range of hardwoods in producing custom work. Double hardwood dowels and tongue and groove joinery provide structural strength. Distressing treatments are done by hand, using traditional woodworker's tools and rustic-looking oak pegs.

Universal Concepts allows customers to order from a range of finishes and mixed media inlay options. From crackle, casein, and peeled surfaces to leather, tin, and copper design elements, the furniture designed by Universal Concepts has a flexibility and applicability that suit residential design and functional requirements.

PRIMARY PRODUCT: Pine furniture for all residential needs. Three lines are available: Southwestern, Territorial, and Spanish Colonial. Furniture includes trasteros, cabinets, entertainment centers, pie safes, bookcases, coffee tables, end tables, dining tables in round and rectangular shapes, benches, beds of all dimensions, dressers, chests, nightstands, and mirror frames.

PRICE RANGE: $150 to $6,000.

DIRECT SALES: Workshop and showroom visits are by appointment. Telephone and mail orders are accepted.

CUSTOM ORDERS: Drawings and design details must be provided in order for pricing to be determined. Most of Universal's orders are custom work, especially with regard to dimensional changes in the production pieces.

ONE OF A KIND: Can travel to complete on-site installation.

CATALOG AVAILABILITY: Brochure and price list available at no cost.

RETAIL DISTRIBUTION: Universal Concepts Showroom, 3334 West McDowell, #18, Phoenix, AZ 85009.

Ginger Valone

OWNER/DESIGNER: Ginger Valone

ADDRESS: 6650 East Exposition Avenue, Denver, CO 80224

TELEPHONE: (303) 321-5957

Coming from an artistic background, furniture crafts-person and artist Ginger Valone brings Native American, traditional folk art, and twentieth-century contemporary design influences into her work. Her signature design style is one that integrates mixed media such as metals, glass, and stone into painted wood home furnishing pieces of varying styles and dimensions. Her choices run toward the bright and expressive side of the color spectrum, so her finished pieces often have an ersatz, funky appearance that she refers to as being "just plain fun."

Starting with a collection of boxes, cabinets, and wood containers, Valone has gradually developed a range of sizes for her completed pieces, from paperback book size up to room furnishings measuring three feet high by five feet long. She has moved on to working with home furnishing objects of unusual shape, and has produced a unique line of mirrors, tables, and coffee tables. She also makes pieces out of painted animal bones, which she calls "Altars," and crafts votive pieces and spirit boxes.

PRIMARY PRODUCT: Artistic home furnishings in the form of unusually shaped occasional pieces like coffee tables, cabinets, storage boxes, mirrors, and chests. Mixed media and wild colors are dominant, with an emphasis on light-hearted design.

PRICE RANGE: $200 to $1,500.

DIRECT SALES: Visitors and direct sales are welcome through the studio in Denver.

CUSTOM ORDERS: Sometimes.

ONE OF A KIND: Valone prefers to work directly with decorators and clients. She has fashioned numerous pieces to fit the space and/or color scheme requirements of her clients' homes and offices. Travel is limited to nearby regions.

CATALOG AVAILABILITY: No brochure, but will send photographs.

RETAIL DISTRIBUTION: Studio sales from Valone's Denver studio. Heather Gallery, Aspen; The Boulder Co-op, Boulder; Manos Folk Art and Panache Gallery, both in Denver, Colorado.

David P. Vogel

OWNER/DESIGNER: David P. Vogel

ADDRESS: Building B, Old Jerome High School, P.O. Box 153, Jerome, AZ 86331

TELEPHONE: (602) 634-7497

Using native Arizona woods and an assortment of hand tools (gouges, draw knife, adzes, and chisels), David Vogel crafts furniture with a hand-carved surface that exquisitely displays every grain of the wood's natural beauty. Some of the woods that he works with are alligator juniper, oak, mesquite, ironwood, sycamore, cottonwood, and native walnut. His custom-designed dining tables, benches, and chairs as well as his railings, stairways, and built-in wall units have found their way into northern Arizona's finest homes and private offices.

"I carve Southwest folk art animals from any piece of wood I can get my hands on," says the Texas native. "The animals are stylized versions of some of the wildlife in this part of the country, like mountain lions, bears, snakes, horned toads, and turtles." A sculptor at heart, Vogel occasionally turns his considerable talents to mask and totem carving.

PRIMARY PRODUCT: Custom furniture. Vogel crafts just about anything he is given enough time and artistic freedom to design and build. He is known for his outdoor sculpture gardens as well as his furniture and interior installations like wall units, entertainment centers, stairways, bookcases, and railings.

PRICE RANGE: Several hundred dollars to several thousand dollars, depending on the customer's requirements.

DIRECT SALES: Yes, if anybody can find the Old Jerome High School in Jerome, Arizona. Mail and telephone orders are accepted.

CUSTOM ORDERS: Welcome, provided client is willing to work with Vogel's artistic interpretations.

ONE OF A KIND: On-site and one-of-a-kind work make up the bulk of Vogel's business.

CATALOG AVAILABILITY: Transactions are arranged by personal visits, exchange of slides, and portfolio reviews.

RETAIL DISTRIBUTION: Lauren Renee Gallery; Skyfire Gallery; Raspberry Gallery, all in Jerome, Arizona.

HONORS AND SPECIAL COMMISSIONS: Prescott Museum of Fine Art. Verde Valley Art Association. Several articles in regional magazines. Recent installations include a three-story wood staircase in a retail store.

Western Log Furniture

ADDRESS: P.O. Box 1500, Eagle, CO 81631

TELEPHONE: (303) 926-3448, (800) 525-6920

Western Log Furniture's formula for success is the simple acknowledgment that there is an integrity and beauty to time-honored designs and that if one faithfully follows those traditions, quality shines through.

The furniture collection produced by Western Log Furniture has an authentic, rustic feeling that evokes the Colorado wilderness. By choosing to emphasize, rather than disguise, the imperfections and natural growth patterns in each piece of wood it uses, Western Log Furniture imparts a personality to each of its finished pieces.

For variety, Western Log Furniture adds contrasting natural materials such as naturally shed elk antlers, brushed metalwork, and natural hides to its furniture. While most of the company's collection concentrates on all-wood construction, these mixed media pieces are dazzling and would do justice to any country or metropolitan residence.

PRIMARY PRODUCT: Rustic-looking log furniture made from lodgepole pine and, occasionally, white birch logs. Primary products include beds of all dimensions, mirror frames, rocking chairs, sofas, tables, dining tables, ladders, benches, chests, dressers, nightstands, and armoires. Also, mixed media furniture pieces using shed antlers and different metalwork elements.

PRICE RANGE: $240 to $3,000.

DIRECT SALES: Visitors and sales are welcome, by appointment, through the production facility at 385 Ridge Road, West Lake Creek, Edwards, Colorado. Telephone orders are accepted.

CUSTOM ORDERS: Western Log Furniture will custom build any piece of furniture based on its designs to suit a client's dimensional or color requirements.

ONE OF A KIND: Yes.

CATALOG AVAILABILITY: Brochure is available at no charge.

RETAIL DISTRIBUTION: Through the Western Log Furniture showroom and production facility.

James Weller, Furniture Maker

OWNER/DESIGNER: James Weller

ADDRESS: c/o James Reid, Ltd., 114 East Palace Avenue, Santa Fe, NM 87501

TELEPHONE: (505) 988-1147, (800) 545-2056

FAX: (505) 982-6643

James Weller is a furniture artist who makes one-of-a-kind, decorative pieces in styles that draw from the Southwestern tradition without being restricted to it. He does not operate a furniture company with employees, machinery, and a standard line of products. He is, rather, an individual artist-craftsman who works alone, predominantly with hand tools, continually creating fresh designs. His pieces manifest a distinct personality that combines superb craftsmanship with a sensitivity won from many years of a personal, nonmechanized manner of production.

Wood is selected one piece at a time at local lumber yards. All joinery is done with hand saws and chisels, and surfaces are prepared with planes and draw knives for texture. Edges are sculpted with paring chisels and liberally rubbed with smooth stones. Finally, Weller chooses native stain recipes that will approximate colors that the ponderosa pine takes on during its aging process.

Weller is a former teacher who holds a Ph.D. in philosophy. He has been making furniture in Santa Fe for the past twelve years.

PRIMARY PRODUCT: Weller is best known for his chests, trasteros, and dining tables. His pieces sometimes have very massive proportions and liberal carving details.

PRICE RANGE: Despite a time-consuming, labor-intensive manner of construction, Weller's furniture is competitively priced from $2,000 to $6,000.

DIRECT SALES: No.

CUSTOM ORDERS: Weller frequently works directly with clients in creating designs that serve specific purposes or size requirements. Such orders can be arranged by contacting the James Reid, Ltd., gallery.

ONE OF A KIND: All pieces are one of a kind.

CATALOG AVAILABILITY: A brochure/packet of information is available on request from James Reid, Ltd.

RETAIL DISTRIBUTION: Weller's furniture is sold exclusively in Santa Fe at the James Reid, Ltd., gallery.

WHOLESALE SHOWROOMS AND REPRESENTATIVES: No.

HONORS AND SPECIAL COMMISSIONS: First place awards in local arts and crafts exhibits. Featured in *Fine Woodworking, Woodshop News, New Mexico, New Mexico Home Furnishings*, and *Focus/Santa Fe* magazines. Commissions and sales to many prominent personalities.

James Weller's footed chest (above) and trestle desk (below)

Wild Woods

OWNER/DESIGNER: Gregory E. Blanchette

ADDRESS: P.O. Box 8234, Santa Fe, NM 87504

Gregory Blanchette creates the special touches that add a romantic appeal to the functional environment. His kiva ladders are a familiar sight at some of Santa Fe's more stylish compounds. He also creates exquisite adobe-style dollhouses detailed with lintels over windows and doorways and traditional viga rafters. These hand-painted structures are frequently incorporated into glass-topped coffee tables for a decorative accessory that functions as furniture.

Blanchette keeps the organic material in evidence. "My influence is Nature's design," he says. "It has aided me in the evolution of my style. I enjoy leaving Nature's mark in the wood but adding man's structural knowledge to make a functional piece."

PRIMARY PRODUCT: Rustic furniture integrating finished work with native materials such as willow branches.

OTHER LINES: Willow shutters and kiva ladders. Small crafts including birdhouses, oak serving trays, cutting boards.

PRICE RANGE: $40 to $5,000.

DIRECT SALES: Inquiries may be directed to above address.

CUSTOM ORDERS: Willow shutters require custom measurements and installation.

ONE OF A KIND: Most of Blanchette's work is oriented toward making the customers' ideas become reality. "Insight and communication skills may be the strongest asset here."

CATALOG AVAILABILITY: Photographs and descriptions available on request.

RETAIL DISTRIBUTION: Santa Fe Style, Washington, D.C. Americana West, New York. The Ranch, Aspen; Silver Belle Antiques, Telluride, Colorado.

WHOLESALE SHOWROOMS AND REPRESENTATIVES: Ann Ward (505) 988-3836. Wild Woods Showroom, #8 West Side Studios, 2200 W. Alameda, Santa Fe, New Mexico.

HONORS AND SPECIAL COMMISSIONS: Previous exhibits at Goldwater's Department Stores. Pieces shown in *Decorating* and *Remodeling Magazine, Santa Fe Arts*, and *Essentially Santa Fe*. Work in collections nationwide, fron New York to Los Angeles, and in Santa Fe, New Mexico, at Alpha Compound and Betty Stewart Construction homes.

Woodwright, Ltd.

OWNER/DESIGNER: Robin Doughman and Connie Doughman

ADDRESS: P.O. Box 14, Lamy, NM 87540

TELEPHONE: (505) 986-1696, (505) 982-1549

Robin Doughman and Connie Doughman create a wide variety of classically designed furnishings inspired by the Old West. Their workshop in historic Lamy, New Mexico, produces sturdy, comfortable, very durable pieces designed to last for generations.

Both Robin and Connie Doughman graduated from Miami University in Oxford, Ohio. Robin holds an M.F.A. Their university studies covered colonial history as well as eighteenth- and nineteenth-century furniture including Shaker. They are especially interested in western and cowboy history, and it shows in the honest, handsome furniture they produce. Their designs are elegantly simple, influenced by the Appalachian setting in which they were raised.

PRIMARY PRODUCT: Beds, tables, chairs, stools, couches, benches, desks, chests, trunks, wardrobes, blanket racks.

OTHER LINES: Custom cabinetry and architectural components for residential and commercial customers. Custom doors and windows. Store fixtures. Hanging and freestanding cupboards, room dividing screens with punched copper and tinwork, candle chandeliers, towel rails, shelves.

PRICE RANGE: $80 to $3,100 (retail).

DIRECT SALES: Happy to accept mail or telephone orders. Retail clients are welcome to visit the workshop, but please call prior to taking the eighteen-mile scenic trek to Lamy in the historic rural countryside of Santa Fe County, New Mexico.

CUSTOM ORDERS: Frequently accept custom orders and commissions.

ONE OF A KIND: Unique projects welcomed. Open to travel to accomplish the project. Robin Doughman

holds a New Mexico Contractor's License, enabling Woodwright to handle all aspects.

CATALOG AVAILABILITY: Catalog available by sending $5 to Woodwright, Ltd. A $5 coupon is included in the catalog to be applied to the first purchase.

RETAIL DISTRIBUTION: Simply Santa Fe, Rancho, and Johnson & Benkert, Santa Fe, New Mexico. The Arrangement, Dallas, Texas. HOHO Gallery, Washington, D.C. Hoshoni; Umbrello, New York.

WHOLESALE SHOWROOMS AND REPRESENTATIVES: Wholesale showroom at Lamy workshop and studio, Connie Doughman, Director and Sales. Dallas Market Center January Home Furnishings Show. Dallas Market Center "Best of the Southwest" Trade Show.

HONORS AND SPECIAL COMMISSIONS: Connie: Distinguished record of local and national volunteer service. Robin: Long list of national collectors. Commissions: Inn at Loretto (doors and windows); artist Judy Chicago (custom studio furnishings); Frank Croft Gallery (custom gallery furnishings), all in Santa Fe, New Mexico.

Christopher Woolam

OWNER/DESIGNER: Christopher Woolam

ADDRESS: P.O. Box 37, El Rito, NM 87530

TELEPHONE: (505) 581-4703

Christopher Woolam's carved and painted furniture is by turns humorous and romantic. Glossy red chile pepper legs protrude through a tabletop, their bright green stems capping the corners of an otherwise plain, pale surface. A red pickup truck with the requisite stray dog careens across a cloudy, piñon-dotted landscape on the back of a bench crowned with running coyotes. Cabinet door panels offer landscape vignettes that are amplified on their curved pediments, which are often embellished with a miniature carved and painted cow skull.

Woolam lives and works in a rural area of northern New Mexico. He has traveled widely throughout Europe, India, and South America and has studied painting with several notable teachers. But it appears that his major influence is the robust humor and legendary beauty of the American Southwest.

PRIMARY PRODUCT: One-of-a-kind, hand-painted and/or carved benches, tables, trasteros, and armoires. Primarily made of pine, but some cherry and other hardwoods. Mortise and tenon joinery.

OTHER LINES: Hand-carved corbels of various animals. Also well-known watercolor painter.

PRICE RANGE: $350 to $2,000.

DIRECT SALES: Visitors welcome at studio/gallery in El Rito. Mail or telephone orders accepted.

CUSTOM ORDERS: Frequently.

ONE OF A KIND: Always.

CATALOG AVAILABILITY: Send $5 for color photos.

RETAIL DISTRIBUTION: Stewart's Fine Art, Taos, New Mexico.

HONORS AND SPECIAL COMMISSIONS: Taos Arts Association. New Mexico Furniture Guild. Awards of Merit: Taos Art Association, 1989, and Colorado Springs Art Guild, 1991. Special Commission: New Mexico State Capitol, 1991. Listed in *Who's Who in Interior Design*, 1991.

THE STRUCTURE
Architectural Furnishings and Iron

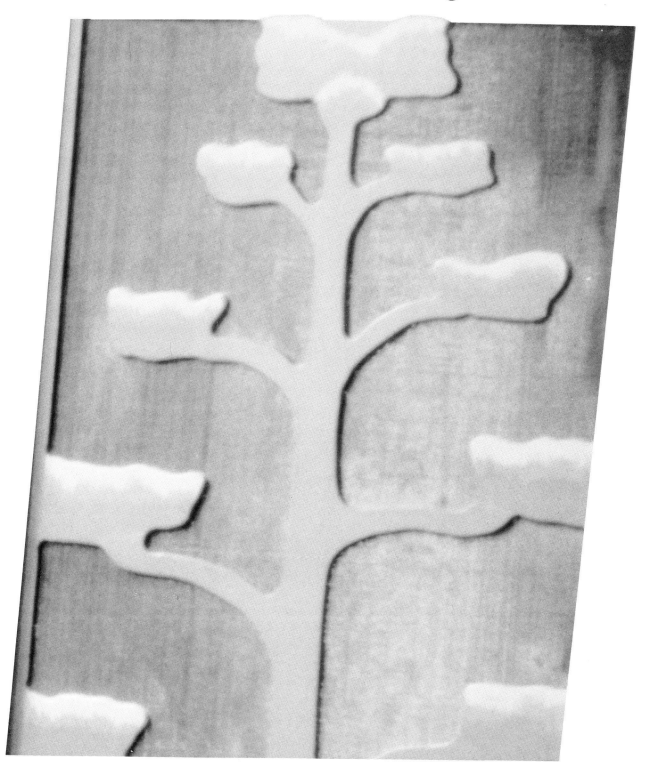

*S*outhwestern craftspeople frequently create embellishments for the framework of a building. The same excellent design that goes into a piece of furniture, for instance, is applied to a door or a kitchen cabinet. The same firing and glaze techniques that produce a beautiful salad bowl are employed in the construction of a wall-sized tile mural.

In this section, *Interior Furnishings Southwest* has listed those whose specialty is architectural furnishings, which include corbels, murals, frames for mirrors, and a few interesting functional art forms that defy categorization.

Southwestern architecture has its own style of detailing whether the basic building is an adobe house or a timbered lodge. Many of these details translate superbly into other traditional buildings. The natural materials and human scale of the hand-carved doors and solid wood cabinets make them classics in any setting. Similarly, the creative interpretation of utilitarian forms results in sculptural plasterwork for walls and stained-glass windows that bring the most starkly minimal contemporary interiors to life.

Ironwork is listed separately in this section of *IFS* because it is such a vigorous field in the Southwest, with activity spanning all five states covered in this directory. Many of these metalsmiths emphasize hardware, but some also create furniture or lighting. Some are primarily furniture designers, and so they appear in the furniture section.

It is not difficult to understand why the current interest in home furnishing objects made from metal has been keeping the western region's iron craftsmen busy. There's no mistaking the heft, symmetry, and permanence of a masterfully made metal object. People appreciate the simple appearance, natural texture, and unadorned ruggedness of a superbly crafted chair, table, lamp, door handle, gate, or window casing made by a metalworker's hands. Whether the material of choice is iron, brass, steel, copper, bronze, or combina-tions of these, the products are stunning accompaniments to any interior scheme.

The days of the village smithy are long past, but most metal furnishings are still hand-forged on vintage machinery. The process involves tremendous amounts of heat, soot, steam, pounding, and bending. Several producers of metal furnishings have begun to use sophisticated machinery in their shops, but for most, the metalsmith's existence harks back to earlier times. The Southwestern heritage of branding irons and other ranching tools as well as fancy Spanish grillwork is alive and well. Today's smith works in solitude as his forebears did but with a world consciousness that is reflected in ageless design.

American Academy of Decorative Finishes

OWNER/DESIGNER: Vonda Jessup

ADDRESS: 14255 N. 79th Street, Suite 10, Scottsdale, AZ 85260

TELEPHONE: (602) 991-8560

FAX: (602) 991-9779

Vonda Jessup's institute, the American Academy of Decorative Finishes, instructs hundreds of craftspeople in the finishing and texturing of furniture that is meant to integrate into specific interior design themes. Classes are run by instructors who number among the world's foremost authorities on decorative styles. They are held not just in Phoenix but also in London and Toronto. Jessup's course catalog reads like a directory of furniture terminology and includes such titles as "Crackle/Painted Peel," "Pickle/Whitewash/Staining With Color," and "Antiquing/Aging/Distressing".

While most of Jessup's time and energy is tied up in the administration of her institute, she has been known to accept certain design challenges for some of the Phoenix area's finest residences.

PRIMARY PRODUCT: Instruction in furniture finishing techniques.

PRICE RANGE: Call for details.

DIRECT SALES: Not applicable.

CUSTOM ORDERS: Call for details.

CATALOG AVAILABILITY: Course catalog is available at no charge.

Architectural Artifacts

OWNER/DESIGNER: Steve Brenna and Melody Brenna

ADDRESS: P.O. Box 638, Abiquiu, NM 87510

TELEPHONE: (505) 685-4546

ADDRESS: P.O. Box 276, Dixon, NM 87527

TELEPHONE: (505) 579-4678

Steve Brenna manufactures amazingly accurate reproductions of antiquities such as Greek or Roman temple ruins and fragments. They look singularly appropriate in the rugged, Mediterranean-like Southwestern landscape with its clear blue light. Using cast pumice and concrete, Brenna creates everything from load-bearing columns to French village square fountains to old Spanish courtyards to dining tables of temple ruin pieces held together with beautifully rusted wrought iron. Always, the patina is ancient, encrusted, worn. He can reproduce any stone finish.

The designs harmonize with Southwestern Territorial adobe buildings, which frequently incorporate Greek Revival porches. Many structures across the country, from Victorians to New England farmhouses, are also embellished with neoclassic, Mediterranean, or Italianate details. Brenna's cast concrete and pumice columns, capitals, cornices, balustrades, fountains, and furniture give any landscape or interior, especially the most minimal contemporary designs, a feeling of sophistication.

Architectural Artifacts appear to have been built on a historical site, for Brenna, a veteran landscape engineer, crafts everything to fit exactly and installs everything himself. His quietly lovely outdoor structures are crafted with a substance and solidity "to last for generations and a classical look that says they already have."

PRIMARY PRODUCT: Cast pumice and concrete architectural elements and furnishings, both load bearing and decorative, of light weight and extreme durability. Wide range of finishes.

PRICE RANGE: From $250 for a pedestal to $25,000 for a small Doric temple.

DIRECT SALES: Retail clients frequently come to the showroom to see work in progress and to discuss the specifics of modifying a piece to fit their site.

CUSTOM ORDERS: Most orders are custom. If you need two aged Roman columns with Corinthian capitals to flank your bathtub at exactly 8 feet 4½ inches, call Architectural Artifacts.

ONE OF A KIND: In their corporate and private work, the Brennas frequently travel and do most of the construction work on-site prior to installation. They recently stayed three months to do interiors and an exterior ruin with pool and landscape.

CATALOG AVAILABILITY: Call for full color catalog ($25) or free brochure.

RETAIL DISTRIBUTION: Civilization Gallery, Dallas, Texas.

Architectural Artifacts' temple ruins against Truchas Peak, New Mexico

Baron Custom Tile

OWNER/DESIGNER: Joan Baron

ADDRESS: 8325 East Monte Vista Road, Scottsdale, AZ 85257

TELEPHONE: (602) 941-5411

FAX: (602) 946-5434

Inspired by her interest in the cultures of Mexico, Africa, and the Mediterranean region, Joan Baron's tile work has transcended many of the traditional limitations of her medium. Textures, creative uses of color, innovative patterns, and unusual forms have become the trademark of her tile applications.

Working primarily in the Phoenix and Scottsdale areas, Baron has received rave reviews for her tile-worked diving board columns, handmade sinks, light fixtures, and murals. The Southwest's indigenous red clay forms the building block for many of her creations, especially those with regional themes such as Desert Critters, Blooming Cactus, Geometrics, and Petroglyphs.

As a custom studio operation, Baron Custom Tile formulates and mixes its own glazes and tiles. By applying her artistic and technical skills, Baron creates myriad unusual washes and other coloration effects.

PRIMARY PRODUCT: Custom tile and glazes. Murals, sinks, lighting, and other installations.

PRICE RANGE: Call for details.

DIRECT SALES: Wholesale only.

CUSTOM ORDERS: Yes. Custom tiles are individually designed for each client. Concept and design consultation, including on-site services, are available.

ONE OF A KIND: Yes, especially with respect to restaurant installations, custom homes, and public buildings.

CATALOG AVAILABILITY: No, but photographs are available.

WHOLESALE SHOWROOMS AND REPRESENTATIVES: Studio is open by appointment.

HONORS AND SPECIAL COMMISSIONS: Over 200 custom home installations in the Southwest. Numerous restaurant and public building commissions.

Lena Bartula

OWNER/DESIGNER: Lena Bartula

ADDRESS: 218 Miramonte, Santa Fe, NM 87501

TELEPHONE: (505) 989-8988

Lena Bartula's architectural murals bring interiors alive. Her most talked-about recent project is Pranzo Portare Via, a Santa Fe restaurant that she transformed with paint into an Italianate courtyard replete with columns and frescoes.

Bartula also makes or buys and reworks furniture. She paints each piece and adds mosaic tiles or painted and carved details such as wings and cars. Her bright, contemporary colors and antic imagination make her work absolutely original. "I am basically an ornamentalist. My eclectic style, which I term Southwest Funk, is influenced by Old Masters, Gaudí, Memphis, Milano, and cartoons. What a combination!"

PRIMARY PRODUCT: Unique wall treatments/murals that are called "space transformations."

OTHER LINES: Vividly colored painted furniture with a humorous Southwestern theme.

PRICE RANGE: $400 to $5,000.

DIRECT SALES: Unique furniture by mail with photographs only.

CUSTOM ORDERS: Bartula likes to work with people to determine their preferences, dimensions, spatial organization, use of the piece, and personal requirements.

ONE OF A KIND: Everything is one of a kind. Bartula will travel, especially for the wall treatments and murals.

CATALOG AVAILABILITY: No production work, but can send photographs.

RETAIL DISTRIBUTION: Works with designers.

HONORS AND SPECIAL COMMISSIONS: Wall mural with world travel theme for Marathon Travel Agency, Florida Keys. Collections: Fountain Valley School, Colorado Springs, Colorado; Fish Films, Dallas, Fox Foto, San Antonio, Texas; Robert Plant, Middlesex, England.

Barbara Burlingame

OWNER/DESIGNER: Barbara Burlingame

ADDRESS: 2027 Keystone Drive, Evergreen, CO 80439

TELEPHONE: (303) 674-5159

Barbara Burlingame is one of those rare individuals who just cannot seem to stop creating. Every piece—hand-painted furniture, birdhouses, collage wall art, and bird boxes—is an example of her artistic genius.

"I'm addicted to my work and love nothing more than experimenting with different materials to see what the results may be," says Burlingame. Her collage artwork literally explodes in a riot of color and dimensional intricacies. Her unique birdhouses are cheerful parodies of human architecture. Her hand-painted furniture evokes images of Oz.

As much a craftsperson as she is an artist, Burlingame builds birdhouses and bird boxes either as interior, decorative objects or as functional homes for your favorite little chickadee. Either way, the art lover and the naturalist benefit from a wondrously creative object.

PRIMARY PRODUCT: Imagination! Artwork birdhouses, collage artworks and wall hangings, functional birdhouses and bird boxes.

PRICE RANGE: $250 to $4,500.

DIRECT SALES: Absolutely.

CUSTOM ORDERS: Absolutely.

ONE OF A KIND: Absolutely, but no travel.

CATALOG AVAILABILITY: Slides and biographical information are available on request.

RETAIL DISTRIBUTION: Galleries in Colorado, Ohio, Indiana, Maryland, and Florida. Call for specifics.

WHOLESALE SHOWROOMS AND REPRESENTATIVES: None.

HONORS AND SPECIAL COMMISSIONS: Many corporate and commercial commissions throughout Colorado, including hospitals and government offices.

Craftsmen in Wood, Mfg.

OWNER/DESIGNER: James P. Schwartz

ADDRESS: 4040 W. Whitton Avenue, Phoenix, AZ 85019

TELEPHONE: (602) 278-8054

FAX: (602) 278-3431

For over 25 years, Craftsmen in Wood has combined traditional construction methods with outstanding design to create a full line of exterior and interior doors, cabinet fronts, and hardware. Each piece is custom crafted to fit the specific design requirements of the homeowner. The company also manufactures main entry pulls, interior door levers and knobs, and cabinet hardware.

Working from a 40,000-square-foot production facility, Craftsmen in Wood produces several lines of doors, including the Santa Fe Series, Arizona Series, and Old Tucson Series. Each has a distinct design flavor, ranging from rustic Spanish Colonial to a geometric-style rail construction to an arched, carved, and mesa-cut style. Two dozen colors and finishes are offered, as are several styles of distressed finishing.

The full line of cabinet fronts is available in styles that echo a range of Southwestern interior design themes. Combined with the company's geometric-patterned hardware line, these cabinets have a strong sense of Southwestern regional style.

PRIMARY PRODUCT: Interior and exterior doors in a full range of Southwestern styles, from traditional to artistic to contemporary.

OTHER LINES: Southwestern-style cabinet fronts and cabinet hardware.

PRICE RANGE: Call for information.

DIRECT SALES: By appointment, at the Craftsmen in Wood showroom, 4040 West Whitton Avenue, Phoenix.

CUSTOM ORDERS: Absolutely. Most orders are custom from start to finish.

ONE OF A KIND: Yes, especially with regard to carved designs, metalwork, and finishes.

CATALOG AVAILABILITY: Complete color brochure of all products is available for $5.

RETAIL DISTRIBUTION: At the Phoenix showroom.

WHOLESALE SHOWROOMS AND REPRESENTATIVES: Call for specific regional representatives.

HONORS AND SPECIAL COMMISSIONS: Street of Dreams commissions in Phoenix and Tucson, Arizona, San Diego, California, and Denver, Colorado.

Created by Carmel

OWNER/DESIGNER: Carmel Rossman-Roeck

ADDRESS: 3838 East Whitney Lane, Phoenix, AZ 85032

TELEPHONE: (602) 788-5990

The handcrafted screen doors created by Carmel Rossman-Roeck are much more than simply a means to allow cooling air into a home. These sculptural, hand-painted doors, made of clear pine or hardwood, are artistic yet fully functional entrances that create a mood for an entire home.

Created by Carmel produces several screen door designs, including the Plantation, which shows orange trees and quail, the Ocotillo, which depicts an elegant cactus and its roots, and the Century Plant, depicting an agave cactus. Two new screen door designs, one influenced by the Florida keys and another by Indian sand paintings, are being introduced.

Starting with a hand-cut core made from birchwood, each design panel is sandwiched onto the birch core, then colored in several layers of oil paints. Wrought iron handles are installed on each screen door. The overall appearance is enhanced by Rossman-Roeck's use of copper and bronze screening in addition to the standard aluminum. French door screens are made so that each half-door completes one-half of an entire design. The effect is that of a framed work of art.

PRIMARY PRODUCT: Handcrafted screen doors in Southwestern artistic designs.

OTHER LINES: Hand-painted furniture line to be introduced in 1992.

PRICE RANGE: $400 to $1,200.

DIRECT SALES: Retail clients are welcome in the Phoenix shop by appointment only. Most business is done by mail.

CUSTOM ORDERS: Yes, Created by Carmel will design doors to fit specific dimensional or design needs.

ONE OF A KIND: Yes, especially doors with family coats of arms or corporate logos.

CATALOG AVAILABILITY: Brochure is available.

RETAIL DISTRIBUTION: Through the production facility.

WHOLESALE SHOWROOMS AND REPRESENTATIVES: Call for information on regional representatives.

HONORS AND SPECIAL COMMISSIONS: Extensive local media coverage.

"Century Plant" screen door

Crystal Glass Studio

OWNER/DESIGNER: Mary Fasanaro Matchael

ADDRESS: 19 Fourth Street, Carbondale, CO 81623

TELEPHONE: (303) 963-3227

Glass craftsperson Mary Matchael is a self-taught artist who works out of a one-time laundromat in Carbondale, Colorado, a small town just a short distance from Aspen. She and her three-woman staff (Kathy Werning, Shannon Gilmore, and Ann Baker) produce a range of architectural glass, lighting pieces, and glass art furnishings that have been installed in the region's finest homes.

Crystal Glass Studio produces high-end glass creations using a variety of stylistic motifs, from contemporary to art deco to Southwestern to realistic landscapes. Matchael often incorporates the metalwork and woodwork of other nearby craftspeople into her own pieces. The results are often stunning, combining her strong artistic talents with her glass fabrication skills, all of which is supported by the harmonious yet distinctly individualistic creations of her collaborators.

Matchael is constantly experimenting with innovative glass fabrication techniques. Fusing glass panels, sandblasting Southwestern designs, adding dimension with layering techniques, and working in iridized glass forms are some of the techniques she is currently employing.

PRIMARY PRODUCT: Architectural glass creations such as door panels, wall displays, and room dividers. Glass home furnishings such as tables, lamps, and lighting fixtures.

PRICE RANGE: $200 and up.

DIRECT SALES: Retail clients are welcome at the Crystal Glass Studio in Carbondale. Mail and telephone orders are accepted.

CUSTOM ORDERS: Most of the studio's orders are built to custom specifications.

ONE OF A KIND: Yes.

CATALOG AVAILABILITY: Catalog will be available by mid-1992.

RETAIL DISTRIBUTION: Crystal Glass Studio, Carbondale, Colorado.

HONORS AND SPECIAL COMMISSIONS: Many designer homes in the Aspen region.

Decorative Materials International

OWNER/DESIGNER: Margot Hampleman

ADDRESS: 1801 Wynkoop Street, Suite 361, Denver, CO 80202

TELEPHONE: (303) 292-5156

FAX: (303) 292-1550

Representing a variety of artists working in ceramic tile, Decorative Materials International (DMI) serves as an entity through which tile artists can create residential and commercial installations using handmade, hand-glazed ceramic tile. Margot Hampleman, the owner of DMI, obtains materials from Europe and Latin America as well as the United States. This gives the artists and their homeowner and designer clients limitless opportunities to create one-of-a-kind tile work masterpieces.

Several lines of tile work are produced by DMI's artisans, including Watercolor Abstract Murals, which are delicate interweavings of color and pattern made to match existing interior fabrics and other appointments, and Southwest Animals, which depict whimsical creatures both realistic and fictional and are made especially for regional architectural styles. African Animals, Contemporary Graphics, and Traditional Florals are among the other lines.

An exciting option offered by DMI is ordering polished and satin-finished cement pavers formed in 60-year-old molds that Hampleman uncovered in her travels. Glazed in a palette of twenty-six color choices, these cement pavers are a unique means of adding Old World charm to contemporary homes.

PRIMARY PRODUCT: Handmade, hand-painted ceramic tiles, tile murals, and custom tile designs for different interior styles.

OTHER LINES: Cement paving blocks made from 60-year-old molds.

PRICE RANGE: $4 to $20 per tile.

DIRECT SALES: Retail clients are welcome in the DMI showroom by appointment. Telephone and mail orders are accepted. Samples are sent before final order is made.

CUSTOM ORDERS: With over a half-dozen artists on her roster, Hampleman finds that custom orders are frequently requested and easily accomplished.

ONE OF A KIND: Yes, especially hotels and other commercial installations.

CATALOG AVAILABILITY: Catalogs and brochures available at no charge. Small charge for sample tiles to be sent.

RETAIL DISTRIBUTION: Wholesale only.

WHOLESALE SHOWROOMS AND REPRESENTATIVES: Design Materials International, 1801 Wynkoop St., Suite 361, Denver, Colorado.

Lily Havey Stained Glass

OWNER/DESIGNER: Lily Havey

ADDRESS: 1449 Browning Avenue, Salt Lake City, UT 84105

TELEPHONE: (801) 583-0509

Taking her artistic inspiration from the pictographs etched into stone cliffs throughout southern Utah, Lily Havey creates Native American motifs on foiled glass panels. She is frequently called on by interior designers and architects in this part of the country, and her work has been installed in high-end homes in Salt Lake City and in the mountains just outside town.

Starting with a foiled glass panel of her own design and fabrication, Havey uses copper foil, gold leaf, sandblasting, fusing, etching, and paint to apply the unique artwork that decorates each of her pieces. She specializes in the creation of glass panels that are sized to fit into doors, windows, room dividers, screens, stand-alone panels, and furniture.

PRIMARY PRODUCT: Glass panels crafted with a foiled glass technique and decorated with assorted Native American and Southwestern motifs. These panels are incorporated into architectural furnishings and furniture and also function as artwork meant to stand alone.

PRICE RANGE: $500 and up.

DIRECT SALES: Contact Havey studio at (801) 583-0509.

CUSTOM ORDERS: Yes. Most orders are created to meet specific needs of designers and other clients.

ONE OF A KIND: Yes. Installation is available within her immediate geographic region.

CATALOG AVAILABILITY: No, but slides can be sent.

RETAIL DISTRIBUTION: None.

HONORS AND SPECIAL COMMISSIONS: First Place Award for Best Window/Panel Design, *Professional Stained Glass Magazine*, 1986.

Hieros Gamos

OWNER/DESIGNER: Jeff Worob

ADDRESS: HC 30, Box 447, Prescott, AZ 86301

TELEPHONE: (602) 445-0008

Jeff Worob creates a broad range of glass items, including windows, lamps, room dividers, and sculpture. He works in both traditional and nontraditional forms. Fairy-tale themes for the windows of a child's room are one example of Worob's traditional forms. His nontraditional forms are three-dimensional pieces in which the design inside the object is not confined by or limited to the borders placed around it.

Hieros Gamos takes three-dimensional forms and fits them into unlikely shapes, often redefining the opening a shape needs to fit into. These create unique atmospheres in which a shape projects out into and moves along the inside of a room. The piece's glass diffuses light in such a way as to add dimensional design solutions to interior spaces.

Worob reaches into his spiritual nature for design inspiration, seeking ideas that suggest art's potential to communicate beyond our worldly limitations.

PRIMARY PRODUCT: Custom-designed glass windows, lamps, room dividers, and other interior items.

PRICE RANGE: Variable. Call for details.

DIRECT SALES: Visits to the studio are welcome, by appointment.

CUSTOM ORDERS: Very few of the Hieros Gamos pieces are produced in a limited production mode. Almost all work is custom.

ONE OF A KIND: Yes, especially commissioned pieces in which the client participates in the design process.

CATALOG AVAILABILITY: No catalog, but photographs are available.

RETAIL DISTRIBUTION: None.

HONORS AND SPECIAL COMMISSIONS: Best of Show, American Craftsman's Council Rhinebeck show.

Integra Cabinets

OWNER/DESIGNER: Thomas Hoag and Gregg Amundson

ADDRESS: 3055 South 44th Street, Suite 2, Phoenix, AZ 85040

TELEPHONE: (602) 921-0550

FAX: (602) 921-2010

Integra Cabinets, which specializes in the design and construction of residential and commercial cabinetry, has established itself over the last twenty years as a leading source for Southwestern interior furnishings. While regional design motifs are an important part of Integra's offerings, the company also produces cabinetry in contemporary, European, and custom designs.

The company also builds custom furniture in oak, cherry, ash, and other hardwoods. Integra's furniture is intended primarily for interiors that use the company's cabinetry, thus offering clients an integrated, single-theme design option. Integra also manufactures a line of built-in entertainment centers, which are offered to both residential and commercial clients.

PRIMARY PRODUCT: Cabinets for home and office, constructed in Southwestern, contemporary, and European designs.

OTHER LINES: Custom furniture and built-in entertainment centers.

PRICE RANGE: Starting at $150 per lineal foot.

DIRECT SALES: Yes, through the company's showroom located in the production facility at 3055 S. 44th Street, Phoenix, by appointment.

CUSTOM ORDERS: Absolutely. The Integra showroom is filled with styles, wood options, hardware selections, and color choices for clients seeking a distinct appearance.

ONE OF A KIND: Yes, especially with respect to working with contractors at job sites to design and install specific projects.

CATALOG AVAILABILITY: Brochure with photos is available at no charge.

RETAIL DISTRIBUTION: Through the company's showroom/production facility.

WHOLESALE SHOWROOMS AND REPRESENTATIVES: None.

HONORS AND SPECIAL COMMISSIONS: Numerous custom residences in the Phoenix area.

JUTTA

OWNER/DESIGNER: Jutta S. Golas

ADDRESS: 6141 Rosewood Circle, Littleton, CO 80121

TELEPHONE: (303) 730-0676

JUTTA's Japanese-influenced ceramic wall sculptures were the direct result of Jutta Golas's studies with Japanese ceramic master craftsman, Setsuko Nagasawa. What began as a line of stoneware and porcelain functional pieces has evolved into JUTTA's distinctive, elegant style that today incorporates several recognizable Japanese aesthetic elements.

All of JUTTA's pieces are fabricated in modular forms, which allows for easier installation and a more integrated composition of large-scale works. These decorative, highly textured pieces depict abstract landscape forms and are colored in a variety of shades, including teal, sand, pinks, and blues. Using glazes and ceramic lusters, Golas airbrushes most of her pieces, giving them subtle, soft underhues and a sensual quality.

Public installations comprise the majority of JUTTA's works. They can be found in hotels and restaurants throughout the country and public buildings both in the United States and Japan. JUTTA pieces are exhibited at art galleries in the United States and Europe.

PRIMARY PRODUCT: Abstract, modular ceramic wall sculpture incorporating Southwest color palettes and metallic lusters.

PRICE RANGE: $150 to $250 per square foot.

DIRECT SALES: Welcome through JUTTA studios.

CUSTOM ORDERS: Frequently.

ONE OF A KIND: Yes, especially commercial installations in hotels, restaurants, and public buildings.

CATALOG AVAILABILITY: Slides and photographs on request.

RETAIL DISTRIBUTION: JUTTA Studio, 6141 Rosewood Circle, Littleton, Colorado.

WHOLESALE SHOWROOMS AND REPRESENTATIVES: Charles Eisen and Associates, Denver; Whitehouse and Bollinger, Denver, Colorado.

HONORS AND SPECIAL COMMISSIONS: Architect's Dozen, Denver, Colorado. National Association of Women Artists, New York. First prize and Amelia Peabody Memorial Award for Sculpture, 1991.

Latka Studios

OWNER/DESIGNER: Tom Latka and Jean Latka

ADDRESS: 229 Midway Avenue, Pueblo, CO 81004

TELEPHONE: (719) 543-0720

Latka Studios creates original, three-dimensional ceramic wall reliefs for architects, designers, and galleries catering to clients seeking to accentuate living and work spaces with innovative design solutions.

These geometric, sculptural wall pieces are pit fired for a natural finish or painted with acrylics for a more contemporary appearance. The modular units are capable of being arranged in myriad combinations, allowing them to be assembled into large wall units or to hang as individual pieces.

Tom and Jean Latka, professional artists for over twenty years, are represented in several corporate art collections, including those of the Digital Corporation, Hewlett-Packard, and McDonnell-Douglas.

PRIMARY PRODUCT: Ceramic wall sculpture and modular, three-dimensional sculptural units.

PRICE RANGE: $125 per modular section.

DIRECT SALES: Sales are made through the Latka Studio in Pueblo, Colorado. Architects and designers are encouraged to send the Latkas photographs of their particular project needs.

CUSTOM ORDERS: Frequently.

ONE OF A KIND: All corporate installations and commercial installations are site specific. Several one-of-a-kind residential projects have also been installed.

CATALOG AVAILABILITY: Photographs are available on request.

RETAIL DISTRIBUTION: American Craft Enterprises, Minneapolis, Minnesota.

HONORS AND SPECIAL COMMISSIONS: Listed in "The Guild 6."

Lay Tuiles

OWNER/DESIGNER: Robert Cao-ba and Pama Peckham

ADDRESS: P.O. Box 13101, Scottsdale, AZ 85267

TELEPHONE: (602) 951-3689

Robert Cao-ba, a craftsman as much at home with steel as he is with ceramic tile and decorative wall sculpture, designs the furniture of Lay Tuiles. He and his partner, Pama Peckham, produce a handcrafted steel furniture line, the Mudejar Collection, that combines Southwestern, Berber, and Japanese design influences.

The primary business of Lay Tuiles has been its tile design and custom ceramic work. Using Southwestern and other hand-painted design themes, Lay Tuiles duplicates complete art scenes and creates colorful, artistic environments for a variety of interior applications. Three-dimensional ceramic surfaces that match elements from nearby materials are a specialty.

The unique lighting fixtures that Cao-ba and Peckham have designed range in style from the Acoma Torchiere, with a verdigris finish and pyramid-shaped reflector, to the Greca Sconce, characterized by a brushed steel and enamel-sealed finish. Another of the Lay Tuiles products is the Clock Rock, featuring petroglyph designs such as Hopi clan symbols and Pueblo animal figures. On these clock faces, the sun, moon, snake, and whorl designs take the place of numerals.

PRIMARY PRODUCT: Furniture line from handwrought steel, including sofas, chairs, tables, coffee tables. Lighting fixtures in hand-wrought steel, including table lamps, torchieres, floor lamps, and sconces. Ceramic tiles, sculptural and painted in custom scenes and Southwestern design motifs.

PRICE RANGE: $50 to $1,500.

DIRECT SALES: Through the production facility/showroom. Retail and trade clients are welcome. Mail and telephone orders accepted with deposits.

CUSTOM ORDERS: Yes. Far more custom tile and murals than stock.

ONE OF A KIND: Yes.

CATALOG AVAILABILITY: Photographs and specs are available. Limited portfolio consignment.

RETAIL DISTRIBUTION: Beyond Horizons, Scottsdale, Arizona. Kern & Co., Encinitas; Brian Flynn & Assoc., Los Angeles, California. Hoshoni, New York.

HONORS AND SPECIAL COMMISSIONS: Construct Gallery, "Art of Furniture," 1989 and 1990. Tile work and furniture installations at airports and retail complexes in Phoenix, Arizona and Albuquerque, New Mexico.

Mattei Glass Studio

OWNER/DESIGNER: Michael Mattei

ADDRESS: 1719 Wazee, Denver, CO 80202

TELEPHONE: (303) 292-0441

As an art glass restoration expert, Denver's Michael Mattei has either studied or actually worked on thousands of antique and contemporary architectural glass pieces. In creating his own architectural glass pieces, Mattei's primary artistic influence is the American art glass movement.

With both a molten glass studio and a glass-cutting studio in his production facility, Mattei is able to create an endless variety of architectural glass pieces that combine elements of both techniques. His sense of color and design are assuredly Southwestern, with many of his patterns reflecting Native American and territorial motifs.

All of the bevel and cut work that goes into his intricate doors, entryways, interior panels, windows, ceilings, and domes is performed in his studio. Whereas lead is the traditional material used to create metal channels that hold glass panels together, Mattei also works in zinc channel, a material that is available in copper-brass, nickel-brass, or black chrome colorations.

PRIMARY PRODUCT: Leaded glass doors in original, Southwestern-influenced designs. Ceiling panels, domes, partitions, room dividers, windows, and other glass specialties combining molten and hand-cut glass panels.

PRICE RANGE: $150 to $2,500 per square foot.

DIRECT SALES: Retail clients are welcome in the Mattei studio/showroom at 1719 Wazee, Denver. Most of the studio's creations are sold to out-of-state designers and architects, and Mattei can work from prints and drawings.

CUSTOM ORDERS: All of the studio's work is made to specific design demands.

ONE OF A KIND: All creations are one-of-a-kind and are frequently delivered and installed by Mattei.

CATALOG AVAILABILITY: None, but pleased to send tear sheets of past work.

RETAIL DISTRIBUTION: Mattei Glass Studio, 1719 Wazee, Denver, Colorado.

WHOLESALE SHOWROOMS AND REPRESENTATIVES: Great Gatsby's, 5070 Peachtree Industrial Boulevard, Atlanta, GA 30341.

HONORS AND SPECIAL COMMISSIONS: Colorado Governor's Mansion and several commercial installations in the Denver area.

Moss Creek Mirrors and Picture Frames

OWNER/DESIGNER: Jeanne Muller

ADDRESS: P.O. Box 1916, Boulder, CO 80306

TELEPHONE: (303) 442-7836

The first thing to keep in mind about Jeanne Muller's exquisite snakeskin picture and mirror frames is that no living creature has had to sacrifice its life to provide the materials for her creations. "I wish everyone would, once and for all, try to remember that snakes naturally shed their skin, much like a deer sheds its antlers, as part of their growth process. I don't kill snakes. I just make use of their shed skin."

Muller may be the only artist who works in this kind of material. Her snakeskin picture frames are astoundingly beautiful. There is also a subtle humor in using these frames for mirrors, because they place the snakeskin in counterpoint to the reflected human skin.

Using the finest available snake skins, including python, rattlesnake, cobra, and water moccasin, Muller chooses skins for their unique characteristics. Since each reptile's appearance is influenced by its particular environment, Muller finds that skins can often be matched to interior design schemes, for example, rattlesnake hide for geometric simplicity and python hide for earthier tones.

PRIMARY PRODUCT: Mirror and picture frames made from snakeskin.

PRICE RANGE: $250 to $3,000.

DIRECT SALES: Contact the Moss Creek studios.

CUSTOM ORDERS: Absolutely. Muller encourages designers and clients to share in the design process.

ONE OF A KIND: Occasionally.

CATALOG AVAILABILITY: Catalog and snakeskin samples are available for a refundable fee of $5.

RETAIL DISTRIBUTION: Designs West, Aspen; Slifer Designs, Vail, Colorado.

WHOLESALE SHOWROOMS AND REPRESENTATIVES: John Edward Hughes, Dallas Design Center, Dallas, Texas. Egg and Dart, Denver Design Center, Denver, Colorado.

HONORS AND SPECIAL COMMISSIONS: Numerous sales to overseas clients, especially in Asian countries.

Kevin Moty

OWNER/DESIGNER: Kevin Moty

ADDRESS: 1572D Center Drive, Santa Fe, NM 87505

TELEPHONE: (505) 471-4146

Kevin Moty, a self-professed "gear head," thrives on impossible challenges such as integrating a state-of-the-art projection room or sound studio into a classic residential interior. He is able to create and install everything from the lighting to the fine finish on his built-in wood furniture for these projects. A highly creative functional artist, he has been the best-kept secret of a few top interior designers until now.

Moty's other design forte is knockdown furniture of an extraordinarily high quality. It is designed for today's mobile society as a practical solution for furnishing yesterday's urban buildings with their narrow windows and staircases. It is eminently practical for the corporate nomad or the technocratic trendsetter.

Moty apprenticed with John McKinney, one of the originators of the Santa Fe look, and studied electronics in San Francisco. His twenty years of experience in creative problem solving has given him the expertise to deal with the realities of antique architecture and the exciting possibilities of tomorrow's technology, blending them into environmental designs that are comfortable and elegant for today's life-style.

PRIMARY PRODUCT: Design, technical consultation, and production supervision of special interior design projects such as nightclubs and custom residences.

OTHER LINES: Quality wood furniture that can be easily folded or disassembled for moving and storage (knockdown furniture). Southwest and contemporary design. Solid lumber: oak, juniper, maple, walnut, etc. Custom cast brass hardware and European hinges. Examples include an armoire with mirrors, dining and side tables, beds, and cedar chests.

PRICE RANGE: $600 to $4,000.

DIRECT SALES: Always welcome. Custom work details by mail or telephone.

CUSTOM ORDERS: All custom.

ONE OF A KIND: Distinguished record of on-site work.

CATALOG AVAILABILITY: Sketches and photos on request.

RETAIL DISTRIBUTION: No.

WHOLESALE SHOWROOMS AND REPRESENTATIVES: Work directly with interior designers.

HONORS AND SPECIAL COMMISSIONS: Technical advisor and production supervisor for Daniel Reeves' video/sculpture installations in San Francisco, Atlanta, Liverpool, and Glasgow.

John W. Moulton

OWNER/DESIGNER: John W. Moulton

ADDRESS: P.O. Box 451, Dixon, NM 87527

TELEPHONE: (505) 579-4492

John Moulton's environment is a study in contrasts. Outside, in his neighborhood in the middle of a small mountain town, there are muddy roads and simple rustic surroundings. Inside his workshop are elegant, beautifully finished cabinets. Though they pay homage to the Southwest in their naturalness and their generosity of proportion, they also function in the most urban, worldly setting. Their refined practicality includes high-tech, damage-resistant work surfaces with complementary colors and textures to enhance any kitchen, bathroom, or workroom.

PRIMARY PRODUCT: Custom cabinetry in hard and soft woods. Countertops and sinks in solid surface: Corian and Avonite. Architectural millwork.

PRICE RANGE: Call for estimate.

DIRECT SALES: No showroom, but commissions accepted.

CUSTOM ORDERS: All are custom orders.

ONE OF A KIND: Frequently works with clients to incorporate unique designs into residential and commercial interiors.

CATALOG AVAILABILITY: Photographs available.

RETAIL DISTRIBUTION: None.

Navarrete Studio

OWNER/DESIGNER: Juan Navarrete and Patricia Navarrete

ADDRESS: P.O. Box 2251, Taos, NM 87581

TELEPHONE: (505) 776-2942

"We are sculptors," says Patricia Navarrete. She and her husband create boldly designed and precisely finished bas relief interior plaster work around fireplaces and windows, as well as cement and plaster exterior designs. They work in "multi-increments of plaster" to achieve such intricate, stylized pieces as a shell shape around a fireplace or an ancient pottery motif on a frieze. The imagery refers to the Southwest but is ultimately universal, carrying echoes of African and Islamic patterns as well as Navajo, Maya, and Zapotec. "Our work is placed in very contemporary homes," explains Patricia. "The art displayed in these interiors crosses the whole spectrum from folk art to abstract to Frederic Remington paintings."

Both Juan and Patricia attended the University of the Americas in Mexico City, where Juan earned a B.F.A. and Patricia earned an M.F.A. Their strongest influence is architecture, from pre-Columbian to Spanish Colonial to contemporary.

PRIMARY PRODUCT: Architectural detailing. Bas relief work in plaster and cement around fireplaces, windows, and other structural elements.

PRICE RANGE: Commissions from $4,000. Prices per square foot.

DIRECT SALES: Direct commissions by fax. Schematics provided.

CUSTOM ORDERS: All custom work.

ONE OF A KIND: The Navarretes travel in the United States and abroad to execute site-specific designs. They collaborate closely with architects and clients and draw their inspiration from the interior and exterior environment of the site itself.

CATALOG AVAILABILITY: Free brochure.

RETAIL DISTRIBUTION: Design Center, Taos, New Mexico.

HONORS AND SPECIAL COMMISSIONS: Allied Member, ASID. *Who's Who of International Design*, Barron's 1991 (Patricia). *Who's Who of the West* (Juan). Petroglyph-design disks on three miles of lamp posts, Central Avenue, Phoenix, Arizona. Published in *Sunset, American Crafts, Designers West*.

Shel Neymark Architectural Ceramics

OWNER/DESIGNER: Shel Neymark

ADDRESS: P.O. Box 125, Embudo, NM 87531

TELEPHONE: (505) 579-4432

Shel Neymark's kaleidoscopic range of glowing, imaginative, impeccably crafted architectural ceramics defy any description save the artist's own. He describes his influences as "Frank Lloyd Wright, Antonio Gaudí, Josef Albers, and the New Mexico sunsets and landscapes." Neymark, who holds a B.F.A. in Ceramics from Washington University in St. Louis, is best known for his non-objective geometric designs and subtle glazes on raku or stoneware tiles that fit together like puzzle pieces on "tile murals, vanity tops and sinks, fireplaces, kitchens, columns, doorways, windowsills, or anywhere else tile could go." He also frequently uses landscapes, botanicals, and animals as themes on his line of decorative tile and on tile murals.

PRIMARY PRODUCT: Custom tile work for public or residential spaces. Sinks, tables, fountains, light fixtures with artist colleagues.

OTHER LINES: Raku bowls in collaboration with Amber Archer. Ceramic wall pieces, hung rather than installed.

PRICE RANGE: $20 to $10,000 or more for major commissions.

DIRECT SALES: "Yes, yes, yes. Call or write for studio appointment." (Note: You may be fortunate enough to accompany Neymark in his canoe across the Rio Grande, which flows between his studio and the main highway.)

CUSTOM ORDERS: Frequently.

ONE OF A KIND: Neymark welcomes commissions and travels to supervise site-specific installations.

CATALOG AVAILABILITY: Write or call for a brochure, $2. Indicate which facet of work you are most interested in.

RETAIL DISTRIBUTION: Counter Point Tile, Santa Fe (tiles). Call for information about galleries that exhibit vessels and fine art pieces.

WHOLESALE SHOWROOMS AND REPRESENTATIVES: Brian Flynn Associates, Los Angeles, California.

HONORS AND SPECIAL COMMISSIONS: Member, Potters for Peace, Tile Heritage Foundation, American Craft Council. Corporate Commissions: AT&T, Holiday Inn, City of White Rock, New Mexico. Numerous private residences throughout the country.

Pacheco's Woodworks

OWNER/DESIGNER: Adonio ("NoNo") Pacheco

ADDRESS: P.O. Box 1525, Taos, NM 87571

TELEPHONE: (505) 758-7874

NoNo Pacheco comes from a family of well-established woodworkers in northern New Mexico. His background is rich in the traditions of Southwestern and Spanish Colonial design. Like many another woodworker, he makes furniture in the local Taos style, but that is not his major achievement.

NoNo Pacheco is best known for his ability to create special designs for customers' requirements, for example, a small space or a certain preference for the way a piece functions. In particular, his pieces that are installed as a part of the architecture of a building are his most noteworthy achievement. Recent commissions include a built-in entertainment center that incorporates stylistic elements from kiva fireplaces and bancos, and a stunning quarter-turn staircase with spindle banisters and matching railings on adjacent arched balconies.

PRIMARY PRODUCT: Cabinets, staircases, built-in entertainment cabinets, custom-designed hand-carved doors, window trimmings, bathroom vanities, fireplace mantels, and much more.

OTHER LINES: Bedroom sets, dining room sets, coffee tables, and more. Cedar, pine, oak, and spruce. Latillas incorporated in selected designs. Mortise and tenon joinery.

PRICE RANGE: All estimates, per commission.

DIRECT SALES: Customers are encouraged to visit the workshop and participate in the construction of their furnishings. Customer satisfaction is top priority. Mail orders and telephone inquiries are welcome.

CUSTOM ORDERS: Custom orders comprise 80 percent of Pacheco's business.

ONE OF A KIND: Pacheco's Woodworks delights in creating one-of-a-kind pieces. They frequently produce furnishings that need to be constructed in a special way or size. Travel to do site-specific installations can be arranged.

CATALOG AVAILABILITY: Brochure.

RETAIL DISTRIBUTION: Granada Furniture, Southwestern Trading Post, Rinconada Trading Company, all in Taos, New Mexico.

HONORS AND SPECIAL COMMISSIONS: NoNo Pacheco is a board member of the Taos Hispanic Art Council, which promotes native Hispanic craftsmen throughout northern New Mexico.

Pettingill & Peare, Ltd.

OWNER/DESIGNER: Shirley W. Prouty, E. W. Butch Walkington,
Summer V. Lawrence

ADDRESS: 2023 West Rose Garden Lane, Phoenix, AZ 85027

TELEPHONE: (602) 483-6296

Working with both hardwoods and softwoods, Pettingill & Peare carries out the traditions of craftsmanship associated with American Country furniture. Whether the product is fireplace surrounds, moldings, cabinetry, doors, or a turn-of-the-century dining table, the craftsmen here know how to take time-honored design concepts and translate them into custom-built home furnishings.

Pettingill & Peare prides itself on its ability to take designer's drawings or a client's verbal descriptions of the kind of piece she or he has in mind, and then turning those concepts into a product that exactly matches the person's needs. The company also installs custom wood floors, completing these with traditional craftsman's flourishes, such as hand-cut nails or pegs.

PRIMARY PRODUCT: Cabinetry, fireplace surrounds, moldings, bookcases, doors for interior or exterior use, and American Country furniture.

PRICE RANGE: Several hundred dollars to several thousand dollars.

DIRECT SALES: Majority of business is to the trade. Individuals should consult with designers to determine the exact type of furniture piece they have in mind before contacting production facility. Telephone, mail, and fax orders accepted. Showroom is located adjacent to the production facility.

CUSTOM ORDERS: Most of Pettingill & Peare's business comes from custom orders.

ONE OF A KIND: Can work from any type description, from a line drawing to a wave of the hand. One-of-a-kind pieces are usually created to replace a single piece in a set of antique furnishings that may have been damaged beyond repair. On-site installation is available.

CATALOG AVAILABILITY: Brochure is available at no charge. Catalog is available for a refundable charge of $15.

RETAIL DISTRIBUTION: Dealer locations are available by request.

WHOLESALE SHOWROOMS AND REPRESENTATIVES: Dealer locations are available by request. Factory showroom is located at 2023 West Rose Garden Lane, Phoenix, Arozona.

HONORS AND SPECIAL COMMISSIONS: Regular exhibitor at Phoenix's annual Showhouse tours. Design students regularly tour the production facility to observe the old-time craftsmanship techniques used by Pettingill & Peare.

Props, Inc.

OWNER/DESIGNER: T. Kevin Douds

ADDRESS: 14255 N. 79th Street, Suite 4, Scottsdale, AZ 85260

TELEPHONE: (602) 991-7577

Props manufactures decorative architectural glass products. Among the items available are leaded glass windows and door panels, epoxy sand-cast faceted glass, beveled and leaded glass framed mirrors, sand-blasted glass panels, copper and glass lighting fixtures and wall sconces, chiseled-edge tabletops in polished or sandblasted finishes, and fused glass tiles.

T. Kevin Douds uses a wide range of colors in his work, with a decided preference for both the brilliant colors of Southwestern cultures and the muted colors of the Southwestern natural environment.

PRIMARY PRODUCT: Architectural glass products.

PRICE RANGE: $500 to $10,000.

DIRECT SALES: Retail clients are welcome, but most production is created for the trade.

CUSTOM ORDERS: Most work is custom.

ONE OF A KIND: Yes, especially for residential installations nationwide.

CATALOG AVAILABILITY: No, but tear sheets are available.

RETAIL DISTRIBUTION: Self-represented through showroom/production facility.

HONORS AND SPECIAL COMMISSIONS: Custom residences in Colorado, Los Angeles, St. Louis, and San Diego. Many commercial installations at country clubs and resorts.

Purpleheart Studios

OWNER/DESIGNER: Yvonne Short and George Blakey

ADDRESS: 618 Aspen Meadows Road, M.S.R., Nederland, CO 80466

TELEPHONE: (303) 938-9658

With over thirty-five color options, a variety of color-intensity choices, and over a dozen different design patterns, the sinks produced by Yvonne Short and George Blakey at their Purpleheart Studios fit the needs of any residential or commercial interior. The finishes on Purpleheart's sinks range from an elegant crackle pattern reminiscent of Oriental vases to Southwestern and Native American influences to abstract and contemporary patterns.

Created in five different sizes, the Purpleheart sinks are all round with self-rimming edges and porcelain construction. Because Purpleheart uses porcelain, the colors are of a high clarity, with bright and bold patterns showing distinctly against colored or white backgrounds.

Purpleheart's sinks are designed and built to accept standard plumbing and drain fittings, and to withstand the standard abuse most residential sinks are subject to. Purpleheart sinks are unique items available as architectural furnishings.

PRIMARY PRODUCT: Porcelain sinks in Southwestern, Oriental, traditional, and contemporary finishes and painted designs.

OTHER LINES: Matching tiles for the border areas in which these sinks are installed.

PRICE RANGE: $225 to $325.

DIRECT SALES: Mail order only. Studio visits are not encouraged.

CUSTOM ORDERS: Yes, as an option in addition to Purpleheart's standard designs and finishes. Additional time is needed to complete custom orders.

ONE OF A KIND: Not at this time.

CATALOG AVAILABILITY: Color brochure of sinks and finishes is available for $4.

RETAIL DISTRIBUTION: Fabian Corporation, Tokyo, Japan.

WHOLESALE SHOWROOMS AND REPRESENTATIVES: Purpleheart exhibits at AIA trade shows in Denver annually.

HONORS AND SPECIAL COMMISSIONS: Architect's Dozen, Denver, Colorado. Included in *Bathroom Design*, by Barry Dean (Simon and Schuster, 1985).

Aliah Sage Studio and Gallery

OWNER/DESIGNER: Aliah Sage

ADDRESS: P.O. Box 2888, Taos, NM 87571

TELEPHONE: (505) 758-9564

Aliah Sage operates on a grand scale. Her tile mural architectural installations, which embellish some of the most interesting residences in the country, are monumental in size. Yet they have an airy grace and jazzy abstraction that is intrinsic to Sage's bold sense of design. She incorporates ancient imagery such as petroglyphs and Mexican masks into her work, but they always emerge looking like tomorrow.

One of her commissions, "Universal Amigos," was a 13½-foot-diameter circle on the bottom of a swimming pool. Another, "The Infinite Dance," was an 11-foot-high mural commissioned by artist R. C. Gorman. Her work has not gone unnoticed nationally, for she recently represented the United States at an International Sculpture Symposium in Yugoslavia.

PRIMARY PRODUCT: Original hand-painted high-fire stoneware tile in many colors. Terra-cotta tile with a contrasting black glaze. Commissions range from kitchens and showers and bathrooms to swimming pools and large-scale murals.

OTHER LINES: Recent work includes freestanding sculptural tile constructions and some cutout work in black metal.

PRICE RANGE: $75 to $25,000. (Large scale commissions: $300/square foot, minimum 20 square feet.)

DIRECT SALES: There is a studio/gallery at 24 Ledoux Street, in the historical district of Taos. The gallery is open every day, and the public is welcome. Many pieces are on display which are available for sale.

CUSTOM ORDERS: Frequent commissions.

ONE OF A KIND: "I will travel to understand the requirements for specific sites and also to spend time with the clients to better design imagery for their particular taste. Clients always have the opportunity to approve final drawings before I paint the tile."

CATALOG AVAILABILITY: Brochure available on request.

RETAIL DISTRIBUTION: Sage represents herself exclusively at her Ledoux Street studio/gallery in Taos.

Samora Woodworks

OWNER/DESIGNER: David Samora

ADDRESS: 2873 All Trades Road, Santa Fe, NM 87501

TELEPHONE: (505) 471-5728

David Samora's fine architectural woodwork combines bold Southwestern style with the clean, pared-down elegance of contemporary furniture design. A carved panel in a cabinet door, for instance, is done in a simple broad basketweave, chaste and flat, with a clear finish.

Samora is a self-taught woodworker who has painstakingly learned the skills necessary to create such exacting work. The attitude behind the apprenticeship comes from his formal education, which includes a B.A. in philosophy and literature from Notre Dame University.

PRIMARY PRODUCT: Architectural woodwork, including carved corbels and beams, custom doors, bookshelves and libraries, TV and entertainment centers. "We work with clear pine and with furniture-grade hardwoods. We also do historic preservation woodwork."

PRICE RANGE: Varies according to commission.

DIRECT SALES: Sells directly from workshop to architects and designers and contractors as well as to the public.

CUSTOM ORDERS: Yes, always.

ONE OF A KIND: Specializes in commissioned woodwork.

CATALOG AVAILABILITY: No.

RETAIL DISTRIBUTION: No.

HONORS AND SPECIAL COMMISSIONS: New Mexico Governor's Mansion and reception bar. Museum of New Mexico/Fine Arts Museum retail store remodel.

Santa Fe Doors

OWNER/DESIGNER: Ed White

ADDRESS: P.O. Box 6322, 3615 High Street N.E., Albuquerque, NM 87197

TELEPHONE: (505) 345-3160

FAX: (505) 345-3730

Doors, doors, and more doors are the stock in trade at Santa Fe Doors. Using well-known Southwestern design motifs such as mesa cuts, arches, spindles, latillas, and punched tin, the shop creates a door that is just right for any application. They also craft lines of window shutters, grills, and cabinet doors. They have added a line of furniture, including the most basic Santa Fe-style pieces such as trasteros, headboards, and benches. "Santa Fe Doors will bring the Southwest to your door."

PRIMARY PRODUCT: Doors. Some thirty different styles that can be adapted to any size or proportion requirement. Cabinet doors, window shutters, grills. Solid kiln-dried wood, usually pine, but some cedar and accents of willow and cactus. Mortise and tenon joinery.

OTHER LINES: Santa Fe-style furniture, including a handsome harvest table and a carved trastero.

PRICE RANGE: $100 to $1,500.

DIRECT SALES: Will accept orders by telephone or mail.

CUSTOM ORDERS: Will do any type of custom woodwork.

CATALOG AVAILABILITY: Brochures available on request.

RETAIL DISTRIBUTION: From showroom address above.

Scottsdale Shutters & Shades

OWNER/DESIGNER: Doug Jones

ADDRESS: 7655 East Redfield Road, Suite 1, Scottsdale, AZ 85260

TELEPHONE: (602) 443-0244

FAX: (602) 443-8868

In the desert regions of the Southwest, year-round sunshine can become as much a headache for homeowners as it is a blessing for golfers and skiers. That is why a business like Scottsdale Shades & Shutters has prospered: it fits the architectural design needs of a specific group of homeowners and office occupants.

The custom wood shutters made by owner Doug Jones's crew are built from both softwoods and hardwoods, depending on the requirements of each interior. Finishes are important here, with offerings as diverse as smooth and contemporary, sandblasted and rustic, satin, and whitewash. The shutters can be configured to fit into any rectangular, square, or semicircular form.

Stained glass arches, made to fit over entryways, and latilla-type shutters, made to suit homes with distinctively Southwestern interior schemes, are the company's newest offerings. Shutter frames use a standard 1½-inch, double-doweled frame. Louvers come in a range of sizes depending on the particular project.

PRIMARY PRODUCT: Louvered shutters made from hardwoods and softwoods. Stained-glass archways.

PRICE RANGE: Call for details.

DIRECT SALES: The company maintains a showroom adjacent to its production facility and invites interested clients and designers to visit.

CUSTOM ORDERS: All orders are custom made to fit individual installation dimensions or design needs.

ONE OF A KIND: Yes.

CATALOG AVAILABILITY: Brochures are available at no cost.

RETAIL DISTRIBUTION: Through the company's showroom in Scottsdale, Arizona.

WHOLESALE SHOWROOMS AND REPRESENTATIVES: Through the company's showroom in Scottsdale, Arizona.

Screen-Play

OWNER/DESIGNER: Ben Eagle and Bruce Thiel

ADDRESS: P.O. Box 1250, Walsenburg, CO 81089

TELEPHONE: (303) 738-3202

FAX: (303) 738-2130

The hinged room dividers made by Screen-Play are dramatic, colorful art pieces that can set the design theme for an entire room. Using Southwest imagery, such as brightly colored saguaro cactus set against geometric landscape backgrounds, the silk-screened artwork on Screen-Play's products evokes a light-hearted feeling that celebrates a whimsical, limitless countryside.

Starting with a translucent, industrial fiberglass material that has the texture and appearance of Japanese rice paper, Ben Eagle and Bruce Thiel use silk screen painting techniques and a variety of woods to create room dividers that have a Southwestern flair and at the same time communicate a playful vision of the inspirational environment of desert landscapes.

PRIMARY PRODUCT: Silk screened room dividers, set into a variety of plain, veneered, and geometrically cut wooden frames.

PRICE RANGE: $600 to $10,000.

DIRECT SALES: Yes, through the production facility in Walsenburg, Colorado.

CUSTOM ORDERS: Yes. Will create dividers to fit specific room sizes and architectural needs.

ONE OF A KIND: Yes, especially with respect to artwork requirements.

CATALOG AVAILABILITY: No, but photographs are available.

RETAIL DISTRIBUTION: Factory direct sales only.

WHOLESALE SHOWROOMS AND REPRESENTATIVES: Topper & Lowell, 392 Fifth Avenue, New York, NY 10018.

Sofia Smith, Inc.

OWNER/DESIGNER: Sofia Smith and Alberta Smith

ADDRESS: 723 Solano Drive, Prescott, AZ 86301

TELEPHONE: (602) 445-0949

FAX: (602) 776-8214

Sofia Smith designs and fabricates large-scale, custom, site-specific art pieces for public spaces. She works in a dimensional collage format, producing artwork that has graced the walls of commercial buildings and hotels throughout the nation.

Sofia's installation at Chicago's luxurious Nikko Hotel is a prime example of the creator's versatility and artistic vision. This 8½-foot-square wall piece takes its design from the form of a Japanese kimono, using acid-etched copper, bamboo, and hand-painted silk to produce a dramatic, theme-setting artwork that is both colorful and sophisticated.

Sofia has constructed collage artworks in series as large as 500 pieces, which are specially designed for the guest rooms of major hotel and resort projects. She strives, she said, to provide clients with an affordable alternative to the art reproductions commonly used in many hotels. "I rely on the power of dimensionality and texture as a basis for my work's appeal," she said. "My materials range from hand-tinted photography to copper, bamboo, raw silk, handmade paper, gold leaf, aluminum, brass, glass, and stucco."

PRIMARY PRODUCT: Custom-designed, dimensional, mixed-media collage wall pieces for large and small public spaces.

PRICE RANGE: $50 to $100,000.

DIRECT SALES: The majority of Smith's work is done through commissioned orders from architects, designers, and developers.

CUSTOM ORDERS: All orders are custom.

ONE OF A KIND: All work is created in response to site, geographic, design, architecture, and budget con-siderations. Smith has designed numerous projects with art consultants and prefers to work from plans, fabrics, color boards, and photographs to determine the needs of each project.

CATALOG AVAILABILITY: A catalog is available for $5.

RETAIL DISTRIBUTION: No.

WHOLESALE SHOWROOMS AND REPRESENTA-TIVES: Margie Armstrong Marketing, Albuquerque, New Mexico (505) 271-8380. Rina Forrest, Phoenix, Arizona (602) 252-8883. Tammy Price, Denver, Colorado (303) 733-5832.

HONORS AND SPECIAL COMMISSIONS: Neiman Marcus and Sheraton Grand Hotel, Los Angeles, California. CBS Corporate Headquarters, New York.

Sombraje

OWNER/DESIGNER: Hillary Riggs

ADDRESS: 544 S. Guadalupe, Santa Fe, NM 87501

TELEPHONE: (505) 988-5567

FAX: (505) 982-5281

The twig shutter and twig panel look in furniture originated with Sombraje in 1982 and has become a hallmark of Southwestern style. The first willow screen was created at that time by Graham Nugent, then a partner in the business that came into being at the same time. He and Hillary Riggs named their enterprise Sombraje, "a branch-covered screen" in Spanish. They began manufacturing window shutters that were immediately recognized as a genuine evolution in Southwestern interior design. Sombraje soon received important commissions.

Riggs created a color system for the shutters and for the twig panel furniture that she had also begun to design and eventually moved into other styles. Always, she concentrated on color as a major element. Today, she operates a business of worldwide stature. Sombraje shutters are sold nationally and in Europe. The style has caught on so dramatically that craftsmen all over the Southwest have incorporated it into their own designs. But the Sombraje pieces still ring truest. (Also see special profile of Sombraje with Collaboration.)

PRIMARY PRODUCT: Shutters: window coverings, doors, cabinet doors, and screens incorporating willow branches and other native twigs. Furniture crafted of solid wood and incorporating panels of willow, salt cedar, and cottonwood twigs. All of the above available in a wide range of colors and finishes, from naturals to any custom color.

PRICE RANGE: Shutters for an average window run about $600.

DIRECT SALES: The showroom at 544 Guadalupe, Santa Fe, is open to the public. Mail and telephone orders are welcome. Will ship anywhere.

CUSTOM ORDERS: Absolutely.

ONE OF A KIND: Sombraje continues to create one-of-a-kind pieces for special applications.

CATALOG AVAILABILITY: Information on shutters and furniture is available. Please send $4.

RETAIL DISTRIBUTION: Sombraje is headquartered at 544 S. Guadalupe in Santa Fe, where the business is showcased along with several others at Collaboration, a major furnishings gallery.

WHOLESALE SHOWROOMS AND REPRESENTATIVES: Sombraje maintains a presence at numerous trade shows.

HONORS AND SPECIAL COMMISSIONS: A steady flow of corporate and private design commissions such as El Dorado Hotel, Santa Fe.

Screens, shutters, tables and chairs with Sombraje's trademark willow twig designs

Southwest Spiral Designs

OWNER/DESIGNER: Norbert Ubechel

ADDRESS: P.O. Box 696, El Prado, NM 87529

TELEPHONE: (505) 758-4974

Southwest Spiral Designs specializes in northern New Mexico architectural details. "Our products are well suited to both interior and exterior locations and are guaranteed to add that classic Southwestern charm to any building project," says Norbert Ubechel. His carved wood structural elements harmonize beautifully with other architectural styles in other locales, perhaps because of Ubechel's cosmopolitan background: he was raised and educated in West Germany and has traveled extensively throughout the Middle East, India, Europe, and North Africa. His architectural studies in these places led him to take up architectural carving in Taos, New Mexico, eight years ago.

PRIMARY PRODUCT: A large selection of spiral columns and corbels, rope carved mantelpieces, and decorative panels.

PRICE RANGE: Spiral columns $90 to $200 each. Corbels $8 to $50 each.

DIRECT SALES: Showroom at 322 Paseo del Pueblo Sur in Taos is open to the public Monday through Friday, 8:00 a.m. to 4:00 p.m. Orders accepted by mail or phone and shipped anywhere in the country. Most orders are shipped UPS.

CUSTOM ORDERS: "We love custom orders and work with our clients on individual design."

ONE OF A KIND: The Southwest Spiral Designs shop is fully equipped to do one-of-a-kind pieces and on-site work.

CATALOG AVAILABILITY: Information sheet and pictures available free of charge through the showroom or post office box.

RETAIL DISTRIBUTION: Southwest Spiral Design, 322 Paseo del Pueblo Sur, Taos. Santa Fe Heritage, Santa Fe, New Mexico.

HONORS AND SPECIAL COMMISSIONS: Twelve spiral columns and carved sunburst panels for Christmas decorations at the Capitol Building, Washington, D.C. All architectural details at the Inn of the Anasazi, Santa Fe, New Mexico.

Starks L.C.

OWNER/DESIGNER: Nancy G. Starks

ADDRESS: 336 South 1100 East, Salt Lake City, UT 84102

TELEPHONE: (801) 359-3008

Utah glass craftsperson Nancy Starks has spent the last twenty years of her life working in glass, using the copper foil technique first developed by Louis Tiffany. Her windows, lamps, cornices, and tables made from welded steel and glass are part of designer homes throughout the Utah and Colorado region. An especially important aspect of Starks's work has been her creations that incorporate Southwestern motifs. These patterns, which take the form of geometric designs and cultural symbols, have been incorporated primarily into variously shaped stained glass windows and glass inserts for doors.

PRIMARY PRODUCT: Stained-glass windows, lamps, and tabletops, using Southwestern designs and cultural motifs.

PRICE RANGE: $200 and up.

DIRECT SALES: Starks surveys clients' offices or residences, deciding on the glass shapes and colors that will best suit their needs. Further selection and design work is done at her studio.

CUSTOM ORDERS: Frequently.

ONE OF A KIND: Frequently.

CATALOG AVAILABILITY: None, but photographs are available.

RETAIL DISTRIBUTION: Only sold directly to clients from studio.

WHOLESALE SHOWROOMS AND REPRESENTATIVES: Ross Howard Designs, Salt Lake City, Utah.

Sunrise Doors of Arizona

OWNER/DESIGNER: Harvey Brodack and Philip G. Roy

ADDRESS: 15023 N. 73rd Street, Suite 102, Scottsdale, AZ 85260

TELEPHONE: (800) 776-7599

FAX: (619) 695-1090

Using several species of wood, including ash, oak, fir, and mahogany, Sunrise Doors manufactures a custom line of exterior entry doors. The company also offers leaded glass side and top windows, including wrap-around transoms, and matching lighting fixtures to accompany its door selections. The result is that Sunrise provides a complete entryway treatment.

Doors range from 1¾ inches to 4 inches thick and are handcrafted using traditional craftsman's joinery techniques, such as mortise and tenon, tongue and groove, and dowel. The company produces doors in a full range of stains and colors, working with builders and designers to match the design and appearance of its doors with any ongoing project.

Sunrise Doors makes several Southwest-influenced door designs, including options such as custom carving, distressing, saguaro cactus ribbing, and wood latillas.

PRIMARY PRODUCT: Custom exterior doors for residential and commercial structures, using a full range of wood for construction.

OTHER LINES: Leaded glass windows and matching lighting fixtures.

PRICE RANGE: $500 and up.

DIRECT SALES: Yes, through the company's showroom and production facility.

CUSTOM ORDERS: Almost all work is custom.

ONE OF A KIND: Sunrise Doors has all the latest manufacturing equipment inside its production facility and is equipped to handle any design needs. On-site consulting with a company representative is frequently arranged.

CATALOG AVAILABILITY: Yes, at no cost.

RETAIL DISTRIBUTION: Sunrise Doors prefers to sell direct, via its 800 number.

WHOLESALE SHOWROOMS AND REPRESENTATIVES: Showroom in Scottsdale, Arizona.

HONORS AND SPECIAL COMMISSIONS: Recently completed a major commission for doors and entry windows for a 21,000-square-foot residence.

Taos Red Cabinet Company

OWNER/DESIGNER: Steve Ninneman

ADDRESS: P.O. Box 5793, Taos, NM 87571

TELEPHONE/FAX: (505) 758-4116

From planning to installation, the artisans of Taos Red Cabinet Company offer a full spectrum of traditional and contemporary home and office furnishings. They emphasize custom built-in cabinetry in a wide range of materials and designs. Taos Red Cabinet Company offers "style to suit your taste and function to suit your needs."

Owner Steve Ninneman is noted for his renovation work on nationally registered historic buildings. He is able to incorporate modern convenience into antique style.

PRIMARY PRODUCT: Focus is on cabinetry ranging from contemporary to distressed Spanish Colonial, from minimalist design to highly carved baroque pieces. Materials include wood, laminates, veneers, metallics, factory-certified Corian, Avonite, and Formica Colorcore. Full range of specialty hardware available.

OTHER LINES: Tables, chairs, complete entries, interior doors.

PRICE RANGE: $400 per piece to $50,000 for large projects.

DIRECT SALES: Retail clients are welcome in the shop by appointment. No mail or telephone orders. Preliminary estimates available by fax or mailed blueprints, subject to on-site verification.

CUSTOM ORDERS: Over 95 percent of the work is custom.

ONE OF A KIND: Accept unique commissions. Can do site-specific installations within reasonable distances. Open to negotiation on expenses associated with long-distance travel.

CATALOG AVAILABILITY: No catalog is available.

However, portfolio and references may be viewed at the shop by appointment.

RETAIL DISTRIBUTION: From the workshop only.

WHOLESALE SHOWROOMS AND REPRESENTATIVES: None.

HONORS AND SPECIAL COMMISSIONS: Numerous large commissions for custom residences.

Vesper Sculpture and Design Studio

OWNER/DESIGNER: Kerry Vesper

ADDRESS: 639 West 2nd Avenue, Mesa, AZ 85210

TELEPHONE: (602) 962-4801

Kerry Vesper uses solid hardwoods and plywood in creating unique functional vessels. He also creates contemporary abstract sculpture in wood, cement compound, and bronze. These one-of-a-kind pieces range in size from a few inches in diameter to larger than life.

Kerry achieves a wide range of textures on his solid and laminated pieces, ranging from a smooth, natural sanded finish to a rough texture that comes from wire brush treatments. He also creates one-of-a-kind wood furniture and handcrafted bowls and other vessels. His style is universal, as is evidenced by his national reputation and client list.

PRIMARY PRODUCT: One-of-a-kind functional vessels made from solid and laminated wood, including plywood.

OTHER LINES: One-of-a-kind wood furniture and wood bowls.

PRICE RANGE: $500 to $5,000.

DIRECT SALES: Telephone orders only.

CUSTOM ORDERS: Yes.

ONE OF A KIND: Commissions are accepted.

CATALOG AVAILABILITY: No, but tear sheets are available.

RETAIL DISTRIBUTION: Call for details.

WHOLESALE SHOWROOMS AND REPRESENTATIVES: JM Gallery, Arizona Design Center, Phoenix, Arizona.

HONORS AND SPECIAL COMMISSIONS: Past president of Arizona Designer Craftsmen.

Waldo Mesa Woodworks

OWNER/DESIGNER: Jim R. Thomas

ADDRESS: P.O. Box 164, Cerrillos, NM 87010

TELEPHONE: (505) 471-1036

Jim Thomas's interest in woodcarving comes from his parents. "In the early 1950s," he recalls, "my father made several pieces of Southwestern-style furniture and my mother carved drawer fronts and corbels." He has since taken several advanced carving classes with Nora Hull at the Anderson Ranch Arts Center in Snowmass Village, Colorado.

Besides his main line of architectural details, he makes carved furniture. For the past several years, he has been making wrought iron hardware pieces, feeling that "this contributes to a continuity of design and helps satisfy my interest in functional art."

PRIMARY PRODUCT: Ornamental carving, primarily architectural details on beams, corbels, lintels, posts, doors, and furniture. Southwest style, based on Pueblo Revival designs. Works in both wood and stone.

OTHER LINES: Dovetailed New Mexico chests, carved signs.

PRICE RANGE: $600 to $4,200. Free estimates on architectural carving projects.

DIRECT SALES: Potential clients are welcome to come to the shop near Madrid, New Mexico, by appointment. Will consider commissions by telephone and mail and will quote prices when possible.

CUSTOM ORDERS: Custom carving and specific furniture and cabinet commissions form the bulk of Waldo Mesa's work. "Will consider any size project."

ONE OF A KIND: Most of the work is one of a kind. Thomas enjoys making his own plans and adapting older designs for a specific carving.

CATALOG AVAILABILITY: Brochure is available.

RETAIL DISTRIBUTION: Santa Fe Heritage, Santa Fe, New Mexico. Thomas/Cutter, Madrid, New Mexico.

HONORS AND SPECIAL COMMISSIONS: Display cabinets in lobby of the Southwest Regional Office of the National Park Service, Santa Fe, New Mexico. E.E. Fogelson Visitor Center at Pecos National Monument, Pecos, New Mexico. Fort Davis Museum, Texas. Teaches woodworking and carving at the Santa Fe Community College and through Elderhostel.

Ann Wolff Glass Design

OWNER/DESIGNER: Ann Wolff

ADDRESS: 1161 St. Paul Street, Denver, CO 81611

TELEPHONE: (303) 388-8350

Ann Wolff's glass and steel creations, whether coffee tables, end tables, columnar stands, windows, or door panels, have a distinct style that blends contemporary high design with a distinctive regional flair. She achieves an effect of signature Frank Lloyd Wright proportions interpreted in Southwestern style.

Wolff has studied glass fabrication techniques at studios around the world. She has also spent many years apprenticing to master glass artists. Her style captures the geometric perfection of squared, cubed, and linear forms. She embellishes her clear glass pieces with a sparing yet well-reasoned amount of glass colored in a Southwestern palette. The result is a stylistic bow toward regional influence tempered by an appreciation and mastery of contemporary form.

The metalwork that frames Wolff's glass creations ranges from a dark, cool iron to a bowed, filigreed light-toned steel. She also produces etched glass panels for her tables and windows in addition to fully colored stained-glass windows.

PRIMARY PRODUCT: Sophisticated glass and steel tables of varying sizes and functions. Southwestern stained-glass windows including full-size commercial stained-glass wall installations.

PRICE RANGE: $800 to $2,200.

DIRECT SALES: Retail and wholesale clients are welcome at the studio.

CUSTOM ORDERS: Frequently.

ONE OF A KIND: Yes, including commercial installations.

CATALOG AVAILABILITY: None, but photographs are sent on request.

RETAIL DISTRIBUTION: Rachael Collection, Aspen, Colorado. PISMO, Denver, Colorado.

WHOLESALE SHOWROOMS AND REPRESENTATIVES: None.

HONORS AND SPECIAL COMMISSIONS: Numerous commercial installations in Miami. Florida. Media profiles in newspapers and magazines from around the country.

Aesthetic Engineering

OWNER/DESIGNER: Ted Woods

ADDRESS: 14602 S. 141st Place, Gilbert, AZ 85234

TELEPHONE: (602) 899-8419

Ted Woods is one of those craftspeople who prefers to live and work outside of the limelight, creating orders for a select group of interior designers and architects who know exactly what he brings onto a jobsite.

He is one of the few ironworkers or metalsmiths to be found anywhere who has achieved a Masters of Fine Arts degree in three-dimensional design. He regularly is called on by national architectural firms to provide site-specific ironwork designs for large commercial projects. The most recent of these challenges was for the interior entryway of One Bell Center, St. Louis, Missouri.

Depending on the needs of a particular project, Woods will design and hand forge everything from driveway gates to doors, lighting fixtures, furniture, and custom accessories. His special touch on a project, he says, is being able to bring an integrated design theme to the selection of metal materials and the fabrication processes of a project and having them fit both their intended form and function.

PRIMARY PRODUCT: Limited production and custom metalwork. All residential and commercial iron and other metals needs.

PRICE RANGE: $200 and up.

DIRECT SALES: Shop visits are by appointment only. Telephone orders accepted.

CUSTOM ORDERS: The mainstay of Aesthetic Engineering's production arises from custom design, site-specific design, and problem-solving design work.

ONE OF A KIND: Frequently.

CATALOG AVAILABILITY: None.

RETAIL DISTRIBUTION: Production is sold directly to retail outlets that place specific orders based on a particular client's needs. Examples of work can be viewed at the shop.

WHOLESALE SHOWROOMS AND REPRESENTATIVES: None.

HONORS AND SPECIAL COMMISSIONS: Listed in *Who's Who in American Art, Who's Who in the West.* Featured in *American Today,* a public television show in Denver, Colorado.

Art Ironworks

OWNER/DESIGNER: Peter Sevin

ADDRESS: 9235 N. 10th Drive, Phoenix, AZ 85021

TELEPHONE: (602) 997-0242

An artist as much as he is a blacksmith, Peter Sevin learned his craft by serving several years as an apprentice to J. E. Hawley, one of the Phoenix area's masters of the blacksmithing trade.

Working exclusively on a custom order basis, Art Ironworks has built a reputation in the Arizona design community as an ironworking shop that produces high-quality, hand-forged work designed with traditional and regional motifs.

PRIMARY PRODUCT: Hand-forged ironwork gates, door hardware, lighting fixtures, fire screens, pot racks, table bases, and chairs.

PRICE RANGE: $200 and up.

DIRECT SALES: Personal visits are welcome, by appointment. Orders are accepted in person.

CUSTOM ORDERS: All work is done to custom order.

ONE OF A KIND: Many gate and door installations are one of a kind, with installation throughout southern Arizona.

CATALOG AVAILABILITY: No.

RETAIL DISTRIBUTION: None.

WHOLESALE SHOWROOMS AND REPRESENTATIVES: L. Mehren/Limited Collections, Scottsdale, Arizona.

HONORS AND SPECIAL COMMISSIONS: Member, Artist Blacksmith Association of North America. Designed and installed entry gates at Arizona Historical Society Museum, Tempe, Arizona.

Dean Crumpacker–Blacksmith

OWNER/DESIGNER: Dean Crumpacker

ADDRESS: Rt. 2, Box 410, Santa Fe, NM 87505

TELEPHONE: (505) 471-6481

Dean Crumpacker produces a truly dazzling array of hand-forged architectural hardware and anything else that can possibly be made of forged iron. He is proficient in many aspects of metalwork and maintains an interest in all of them. He has eighteen years of experience in forge work and currently operates a studio/gallery on the old road to Galisteo, New Mexico, just south of Santa Fe. There, visitors may view all aspects of Crumpacker's ironworking art.

"I do lots of work for architects and builders as well as furniture and door manufacturers," he says. "My best patrons have come to me by word of mouth through my reputation in the business."

PRIMARY PRODUCT: Hand-forged architectural hardware in many styles. Door hardware: knobs, offset handles, escutcheon plates, thumb latches, hinges, slide bolts, dead bolt covers, mortise hardware, and door knockers. Furniture and cabinet hardware: pulls, knobs, hinges, stretchers, and corner brackets. Fireplace screens, tools, andirons, grates, and cranes. Lighting fixtures: chandeliers and wall sconces. Gates, window grills, and railings. Forged furniture: tables, chairs, couches, and beds. Upholstery nails, locks and keys, wind vanes, and cutlery.

PRICE RANGE: $10 to $20,000.

DIRECT SALES: Any customer is welcome to visit the studio/gallery by appointment. There is a large display of primary products and many photographs of custom work.

CUSTOM ORDERS: Much of Crumpacker's work is custom ordered. He likes to meet with customers to discuss design and style and, when necessary, submit drawings for approval.

ONE OF A KIND: One-of-a-kind sculptural wood burning stoves from chrome car bumpers.

CATALOG AVAILABILITY: Write or call directly for information, photographs and prices.

RETAIL DISTRIBUTION: Door and furniture hardware at Southwest Spanish Craftsmen, Santa Fe, New Mexico.

DeLaRonde Forge

OWNER/DESIGNER: Joe DeLaRonde

ADDRESS: P.O. Box 84, Glorieta, NM 87535

TELEPHONE: (505) 757-6725

For almost twenty years, Joe DeLaRonde has operated his own forge in the Pecos River Valley area of New Mexico. He had previously apprenticed under a master blacksmith from Germany for three years and has always maintained a commitment to excellence in traditional design. DeLaRonde teaches workshops on hand-forged iron and produces a range of ironwork for architectural use as well as an interesting group of tools such as knives, axes, and spurs. He works iron to the same level of perfection that he lavishes on his creations in Damascus steel.

PRIMARY PRODUCT: Traditional hand-forged ironwork: fireplace sets, decorative hooks, door hardware, wall and floor sconces. Window treatments: curtain rods, brackets, tiebacks. These are frequently custom made.

OTHER LINES: Knives (including Damascus steel), spurs, axes.

PRICE RANGE: $12 to $900+ for custom orders.

DIRECT SALES: DeLaRonde deals mostly with wholesale buyers and retailers. The shop is not accessible to clients. However, retail orders are accepted over the phone and by mail.

CUSTOM ORDERS: Most of the business is built around availability to do custom hardware.

ONE OF A KIND: Frequently accept commissions and travel to do on-site bids. Currently doing a gate and railing and grill work at the Plaza Mercado in Santa Fe.

CATALOG AVAILABILITY: Architectural design hardware and products brochure. Price lists for wholesale and retail orders. Also, a brochure on knives and spurs.

RETAIL DISTRIBUTION: Johnson & Benkert, Tara Tucker, Ltd., East West Trading Company, Rancho, all in Santa Fe, New Mexico. Common Ground, New York. Mable's, Santa Fe and New York. Rituals, Los Angeles, California. Southwest Design Center, San Juan Capistrano, California.

WHOLESALE SHOWROOMS AND REPRESENTATIVES: Dallas Market (Best of Southwest), Denver Stock Show. Marlis A. Simms, sales representative.

HONORS AND SPECIAL COMMISSIONS: Southwest Association of Blacksmith Artists, Northwest Blacksmith Association. Workshops, lectures and demonstrations at historic sites and museums around the United States, including Palace of the Governors Museum, New Mexico, Bents Fort, Colorado, Cowtown Museum, Kansas, and U.S. Park Service.

Bill Feeley–Steel Artist

OWNER/DESIGNER: Bill Feeley

ADDRESS: P.O. Box 2245, Cody, WY 82414

TELEPHONE: (307) 587-5194

Bill Feeley the sculptor is an accomplished creator of figurative bronzes. His 2,000-pound "The Chadwick Ram," created for the Foundation of North American Wild Sheep, took nine years to complete and is his artistic best. Bill Feeley the architectural metalworker is one of the best-kept secrets in the movement to revive Ranch Western furniture design. From Hollywood, California, to Hungry Horse, Montana, designers, architects, retailers, and homeowners flood Feeley's Wyoming blacksmith shop with pleas for one of his creations.

"Some items, like fireplace screens, andirons, and sconce lamps, I can produce in limited quantity," says Bill. "But customers who order large items tend to want something that's made to suit their particular tastes. On those commissioned pieces, I'll never exactly duplicate a design that I've already made, because that's what I think the customer expects from me. I'm trying to create items with unique, Western motifs that look like they could be products from blacksmith shops of another era. As this takes time, I am not particularly interested in filling volume orders."

Scenes of Rocky Mountain landscapes, foraging wildlife, Indians on a buffalo hunt, firearms, and cowboys roping a runaway steer are just a few of the ways Feeley brings his Wyoming roots into the products he creates. His technique involves both a blacksmith's forge and a modern, electric welder, resulting in items that have a rustic, aged wrought-iron appearance. Since 1976, Feeley has specialized in the fabrication of fireplace screens, sconce lamps, chandeliers, and irons, desk lamps, and floor lamps. In his spare time, he creates tools for other blacksmiths, gates, switch plates, stained glass inserts for his lamps, and an occasional 2,000-pound sculpture.

PRIMARY PRODUCT: Iron and steel architectural furnishings made to look like the products of an 1800s era blacksmith shop. Feeley says he will make anything that can be used in a home or office, as long as it is in iron or steel.

PRICE RANGE: $50 and up.

DIRECT SALES: Yes, but customers must provide precise measurements for items like fireplace screens.

CUSTOM ORDERS: Larger items are almost always custom designed. One customer may prefer scenes with bighorn sheep, while another may want Indian teepees.

ONE OF A KIND: Yes, if that is what is necessary.

CATALOG AVAILABILITY: A brochure will be available by mid-1992. Photographs can be sent, if necessary.

RETAIL DISTRIBUTION: All sold through word of mouth.

WHOLESALE SHOWROOMS AND REPRESENTATIVES: Sweetwater Ranch, Cody, Wyoming.

HONORS AND SPECIAL COMMISSIONS: Many awards as a bronze sculptor. Numerous custom residential installations around the country.

Franzetti Design

OWNER/DESIGNER: Pozzi Franzetti

ADDRESS: P.O. Box 997, Ranchos de Taos, NM 87557

TELEPHONE/FAX: (505) 758-8471

Pozzi Franzetti lives and works in Taos, New Mexico, and draws her inspiration from its tricultural heritage. She imbues these traditional themes with a decidedly contemporary humor, creating a wild range of hardware and ornament. She started out as a sculptor and expanded her repertoire to include architectural pieces with an emphasis on design and function. Her ambition is to "design pieces with functional value and an interactive design quality that includes communication between man and his artifacts."

PRIMARY PRODUCT: Fabricated mild steel, oxidized to a natural rust patina and sealed to discourage further oxidation: light switch plates, outlet plates, light fixtures, candle holders, shelves, tables, weather vanes, fountains, and more.

OTHER LINES: Lawn sculpture, earthquake detectors (whimsical figures mounted on springs).

PRICE RANGE: Catalog items: $18 to $400. Special orders to $10,000.

DIRECT SALES: Telephone and mail orders accepted. Visitors welcome to the studio by appointment.

CUSTOM ORDERS: Franzetti's computerized cutting machine can trace shapes with an electronic eye which makes custom orders a breeze. She welcomes creative input for architectural pieces and just-for-fun projects.

ONE OF A KIND: Franzetti thrives on one-of-a-kind pieces and welcomes the opportunity to be a part of site-specific installations. She can produce uniquely

designed pieces in a timely and economical manner thanks to her creative staff and high tech equipment which lends itself perfectly to shapes cut to drafted specifications.

CATALOG AVAILABILITY: Catalog, $4.

RETAIL DISTRIBUTION: Tara Tucker, Ltd., Johnson & Benkert, Santa Fe, New Mexico. Distant Origins, New York. Galisteo, San Francisco, Folktree Collection, Pasadena, California. Canyon Road, New Canaan, Connecticut. Itchy Fingers, Portland, Oregon. And many more.

WHOLESALE SHOWROOMS AND REPRESENTATIVES: Southwest Exposure, Albuquerque, Stuart Handelsman, Santa Fe, New Mexico; Burke Byrnes, Los Angeles, California; Chuck Chuckovich, Chicago, Illinois; Denver Design Center, Dallas/Best of the Southwest.

HONORS AND SPECIAL COMMISSIONS: Featured in major architectural, home furnishings, and design magazines.

Helios Designer Hardware

OWNER/DESIGNER: Andrew Langmade

ADDRESS: 2645 E. Adams Street, Phoenix, AZ 85034

TELEPHONE/FAX: (602) 244-0644

Helios creates sand cast, hand-finished bronze and brass door and cabinet hardware. The designs offered by Helios are suited for all types of interior and exterior use, from Southwestern to whimsical to contemporary. Standard finishes include polished or satin-finish brass and bronze, antique bronze, and dark, oil-rubbed bronze.

Helios can also create finishes in chrome, aluminum, copper, and verdigris. Another accent feature of the Helios line is the use of several different hardwoods and inlaid stones, such as jade, lapis, coral, turquoise, marble, slate, and granite. Helios also creates custom house numbers in styles that match the composition and design of their door handles.

The passage hardware, cabinet knobs, and entry handles made by Helios have the effect of completely coordinating a home's entry appointments to its Southwestern architecture, no matter which style of Southwestern architecture that home represents.

PRIMARY PRODUCT: Production and custom passage hardware, cabinet knobs, and entry handles for doors and cabinets.

PRICE RANGE: $15 to $2,000.

DIRECT SALES: Retail clients are welcome, by appointment, at the Helios production facility in Phoenix.

CUSTOM ORDERS: Yes, a large portion of the Helios business is dedicated to solving unique design needs of clients.

ONE OF A KIND: Yes, especially for resorts in Arizona and ranches in the Rocky Mountain region.

CATALOG AVAILABILITY: Brochure and price information available at no cost.

RETAIL DISTRIBUTION: Numerous hardware stores throughout the Southwest. Call for details.

WHOLESALE SHOWROOMS AND REPRESENTATIVES: Call for details.

HONORS AND SPECIAL COMMISSIONS: The Boulders, Carefree, Arizona. Custom homes in Arizona and Colorado.

Ross Howard Collection

OWNER/DESIGNER: Steve Powell and Sharon Kindred

ADDRESS: 1105 South 800 East, Salt Lake City, UT 84105

TELEPHONE: (801) 322-5184

Since their initial collaboration in the mid-1980s, Steve Powell and Sharon Kindred, co-owners of Ross Howard Collection, have attained a national reputation in the field of accent furniture, lighting, and room accessories. Working primarily in metal, but also using wood, stone, and leather to complete their pieces, Powell and Kindred have created collections that are are stylistically unique and evocative of the Native American and cowboy spirits of the Southwest.

Their initial signature piece, a table incorporating wooden bows and hand-forged, metal arrows as the table's support elements, brought the couple into contact with Utah sculptor John Prazen. For several years, Prazen had been experimenting with mixed metals to achieve unique coloration patterns on steel sculpture. When he turned his creative efforts to the home furnishings designs drawn up by Powell and Kindred, the marketplace reaction was instantaneous.

Since those early efforts, the Ross Howard Collection has blossomed into a 100-piece grouping of lamps, mirrors, room dividers, tables, lamp stands, andirons, and decorative wall pieces. The Ross Howard Collection is handled under several lines, including Ross Howard II, American Places, Wine Country Collection, and Great Plains Collection. The design influences range from Native American to cowboy western to neoclassical.

PRIMARY PRODUCT: The Ross Howard Collection includes functional and decorative home furnishing items, especially tables, lighting, and room screens. Over 100 individual pieces comprise the several lines offered under the Ross Howard Collection. Most pieces are fabricated from metal, but wood, stone, leather, and glass are occasionally incorporated into a finished piece.

PRICE RANGE: $67 to $4,000.

DIRECT SALES: Yes. Wholesale accounts may contact the production facility.

CUSTOM ORDERS: Over half of Ross Howard Collection's business is performed per customer specifications.

ONE OF A KIND: Most of the Ross Howard Collection pieces are one of a kind.

CATALOG AVAILABILITY: Brochures are free. Designer catalogs are $25.

RETAIL DISTRIBUTION: Sundance Catalog, Utah. Domaine, Seattle, Washington. Great Lakes Designs, Harbor Springs, Michigan. Raffia, Los Angeles, California. Korte Interiors, Ltd., Bismarck, North Dakota.

WHOLESALE SHOWROOMS AND REPRESENTATIVES: Kathy Barrett, Los Angeles Merchandise Mart, Cambridge West, San Diego, Carl Braune, San Francisco, all in California. Past Perfect, Dallas, Texas. Howard Matthew, Denver, Colorado. Pauline Grace, Merchandise Mart, Chicago, Illinois.

HONORS AND SPECIAL COMMISSIONS: Several magazine articles.

Indian Peaks Iron Works

OWNER/DESIGNER: Gary C. Perrett

ADDRESS: 90 Lee Hill Drive, #4-C, Boulder, CO 80302

TELEPHONE: (303) 449-3145

Master blacksmith Gary Perrett produces hand-forged architectural ironwork and home furnishings made from hand-forged iron. An artist and designer as much as he is a craftsman, Perrett combines his outdoorsman's perspective on life in the West with his eye toward classic European design elements. The result is a sophisticated ironwork creation that is as much at home in a mountain cabin as it is in a suburban residence.

In his hand-forged furniture collection, Perrett's most popular item is a glass-topped coffee table in which he uses an organic metalwork design motif to create an object that is both functional and sculptural. His bed frames, especially the four-post models, look as if they would be right at home in the White House of pre-Civil War years. These iron and brass wonders are simple in line, yet tastefully decorated with just the right amount of Greek Revival flourishes.

PRIMARY PRODUCT: Hand-wrought ironwork beds of all dimensions, gates, chandeliers, fireplace doors, pot racks, candelabra, Southwestern wall sculptures, music stands, stair railings, weather vanes, and door frames.

PRICE RANGE: $500 and up.

DIRECT SALES: Customers are welcome in Perrett's shop at any time. It is a regular stop on the Boulder Artist's Studio Annual Tour.

CUSTOM ORDERS: Perrett wants his customers to be absolutely satisfied with their ironwork purchases, so he enjoys hammering out each and every detail on their special projects. "I make unique works of art for each person," he says, "trying to match their needs with their environment and with their particular personality."

ONE OF A KIND: The business is centered on creating one-of-a-kind pieces. Perrett spends a great deal of time traveling to and from job sites across the country.

CATALOG AVAILABILITY: Brochure available.

RETAIL DISTRIBUTION: Through the production facility.

WHOLESALE SHOWROOMS AND REPRESENTATIVES: None.

HONORS AND SPECIAL COMMISSIONS: Perrett's railings were part of the design elements in a home that won a major award from the Chicago chapter of the American Institute of Architects in 1991.

Knobelties–Artware for Doors and Drawers

OWNER/DESIGNER: Allison Leigh Schmidt and Katherine Jones Carmichael

ADDRESS: Fat Chance Ranch, Box 72, Marble Canyon, AZ 86036

TELEPHONE: (602) 355-2215

Knobelties, which co-owner Allison Schmidt says is located about halfway down the road to Nowhere, Arizona, specializes in the production of drawer and cabinet pulls made from hand-cast bronze and overlay-type stamped copper. The forms and images that are captured on these pulls range from definitive Southwestern to cowboy to animal.

The free-form bronze pulls are cast into lazy long-horn, howling coyote, cowboy boot, cowboy hat, jack-rabbit (with an attitude), stout saguaro, slim saguaro, and prickly pear forms. The overlaid, stamped copper pulls are made in several shapes, including rectangular horizontal, rectangular vertical, round, vertical, and horizontal. The images stamped on the overlaid copper pulls are pictograph reindeer, pictograph rams, lost cow, cow in a barbed wire corral, ghost rider, strolling horse, dog cruising for a bone, and dog idea.

Schmidt is a self-taught jeweler who learned silver-smithing, repoussé, and acid etching during thirteen years of managing a Navajo reservation trading post. She colors each pull individually, using a heat process chemical application that builds layer on layer of durable coloration. Each knob is sealed with a matte finish that gives the piece a constant, durable color content. Knobelties pulls are intended to reach the funny bone.

PRIMARY PRODUCT: Door, drawer, and cabinet pulls made from hand-cast bronze and overlaid-type stamped copper.

OTHER LINES: Copper picture frames, light switch covers, candle holders, and sculpture.

PRICE RANGE: $36 to $42 retail.

DIRECT SALES: Absolutely. Anyone traveling near the South Rim of the Grand Canyon is invited to stop by and visit the studio.

CUSTOM ORDERS: Yes. Schmidt and Carmichael enjoy working with designers in creating their production pieces and for custom design needs.

ONE OF A KIND: Yes.

CATALOG AVAILABILITY: Brochure available at no cost.

RETAIL DISTRIBUTION: Sold primarily through art galleries and design stores. Call for specific locations.

WHOLESALE SHOWROOMS AND REPRESENTATIVES: None, but will discount prices for quantity purchases.

Hand-cast bronze and overlay-type stamped copper drawer pulls by Knobelties

Petaja

OWNER/DESIGNER: Dean Petaja

ADDRESS: 335 W. Pierpoint Avenue, #2, Salt Lake City, UT 84101

TELEPHONE: (801) 355-2721

Using a variety of what he refers to as "postindustrial materials," this talented and experienced metalworking artist creates both wall sculptures and freestanding artwork pieces from found objects gathered primarily from Salt Lake City recycling yards.

Petaja's steel creations run the gamut of real and imagined human and animal figures, from "gear ghosts" to animals out of Native American mythology to more contemporary forms like deer and steer skulls. Petaja specializes in creating specific creatures to fit a client's special tastes, from long, twisting snake forms to friendly lizards and fantasy fishes.

PRIMARY PRODUCT: Metal wall and freestanding sculpture made from recycled steel. Fabricated into a variety of animal and humanlike forms, using contemporary and Native American design influences.

OTHER LINES: Functional ironwork such as coat racks and towel bars.

PRICE RANGE: $30 to $1,500.

DIRECT SALES: Retail clients are welcome at Petaja's shop, by appointment.

CUSTOM ORDERS: Welcome.

ONE OF A KIND: Petaja's one-of-a-kind metalwork is collected by art lovers and installed in the homes of Utah's ski country.

CATALOG AVAILABILITY: Catalog/portfolio available for $5.

RETAIL DISTRIBUTION: Masterworks Gallery, Chicago, Illinois; Utah Designer Crafts, Salt Lake City, Utah; Anne Reid Gallery, Ketchum, Idaho.

WHOLESALE SHOWROOMS AND REPRESENTATIVES: Petaja exhibits regularly at the American Craft Collection trade shows in Baltimore and San Francisco.

HONORS AND SPECIAL COMMISSIONS: Exhibited at the Renwick Gallery of the Smithsonian Institution. Member of the American Craft Council.

T. K. Bone Company

OWNER/DESIGNER: T. Kern Hicks

ADDRESS: P.O. Box 737, Tesuque, NM 87574

TELEPHONE: (505) 982-0686

Kern Hicks grew up in the foundry business. A "life-time member" of the noted Hicks family who originated Shidoni Foundry and Gallery near Santa Fe, Kern studied at the University of New Mexico but received his education at the family foundry.

It was only natural, then, that he started a business just for fun (a Hicks family trait) last year and that it became a going concern because of its excellent quality and high good humor. Kern had become well versed in the lost wax process of bronze casting, and he reasoned that a real chile pepper would evaporate as efficiently as wax from the heat of the molten bronze being poured into the casting medium. "It burned out beautifully," he recalls with a smile. "I decided to call it the lost chile process." These door knockers and knobs are prime Southwestern architectural furnishings, and they happen to be a lot of fun, too.

PRIMARY PRODUCT: Bronze chicken bone key rings. Bronze cast chile products: door knockers, door handles, and jalapeño cabinet handles.

OTHER LINES: "Coffee Table Chiles," life-size bronze chiles. Jalapeño bolo ties with the seeds exposed and prominently displayed. ("Where else could you get this kind of detail except with the lost chile process?")

PRICE RANGE: $16 to $300.

DIRECT SALES: Prefers to retail through galleries and shops, but visitors are welcome, by appointment. Likes to barter.

CUSTOM ORDERS: Welcomed and encouraged. Would like to do some chile fireplace tools in bronze.

ONE OF A KIND: A recent commission was a chile hammer for a chile farmer near Las Cruces, New Mexico. Hicks hopes someone will commission him to do an 8-foot standing chile in bronze.

CATALOG AVAILABILITY: Free brochure.

RETAIL DISTRIBUTION: Shidoni Bronze Gallery; The Chile Shop; Southwest Spanish Craftsmen, Santa Fe, New Mexico. The Fired Works, Alamosa, Colorado.

WHOLESALE SHOWROOMS AND REPRESENTATIVES: None. Inquiries invited.

HONORS AND SPECIAL COMMISSIONS: New Mexico Sculptors Guild, founding member.

Christopher Thomson Ironworks

OWNER/DESIGNER: Christopher Thomson and Susan Livermore

ADDRESS: P.O. Box 578, Ribera, NM 87560

TELEPHONE: (505) 421-2645

FAX: (505) 421-2618

Christopher Thomson is creative on a heroic scale. He designs elegant, sculptural forged steel home furnishings and produces them with the help of six apprentices. He spent ten years in a production pottery cooperative that he helped to establish. He has been a carpenter and stonemason and has designed and constructed his present solar adobe home. He has played the flute since childhood and studied it intensely for three years as a music major in college. "I find that ideas first explored playing or listening to music often find their way into my steel work," he observes.

He hammers, stretches, and bends the steel directly, allowing the forming process to add to the design. "Rather than force the hot steel to a preconceived shape," he says, "I strive for an improvised interaction so that each piece comes to life with its own presence and rhythm."

PRIMARY PRODUCT: Transitional and contemporary hand-forged steel in four finishes: pewter black, rust, verde, and rustic. "Simply Santa Fe" and other design lines; optional embellishments. Home furnishings: lamps, tables, candlesticks, fireplace tool sets, chandeliers. Architectural pieces: gates, railings, signs, sculpture.

PRICE RANGE: Production items: $150 to $2,000 retail. Wholesale $75 to $1,000.

DIRECT SALES: Retail clients welcomed by appointment. Mail or telephone orders accepted.

CUSTOM ORDERS: Will consider and quote price.

ONE OF A KIND: Thomson especially enjoys commissions and can travel to the site. He has produced a spiral staircase for a private home in Houston, Texas, and architectural gates and window grills for the luxury Quail Run development in Santa Fe, New Mexico, as well as other large-scale commissions, including Red Sage Restaurant, Washington, D.C.

CATALOG AVAILABILITY: Production home furnishings, $2. Also, photographs of architectural pieces.

RETAIL DISTRIBUTION: La Mesa; Johnson and Benkert; Form + Function; Captain Marble, Santa Fe, New Mexico. Rituals, Los Angeles; Galisteo, San Francisco, California. The Arrangement, Dallas, Texas. And 90 others.

WHOLESALE SHOWROOMS AND REPRESENTATIVES: Has shown twice at Market Hall, Dallas, 1990 and 1991.

HONORS AND SPECIAL COMMISSIONS: Member: Artists-Blacksmiths Association of North America (ABANA) and Southwest Artists-Blacksmiths Association (SWABA).

Christopher Thomson's ironwork lamps with custom shades

Turley Forge and Blacksmithing School

OWNER/DESIGNER: Frank Turley

ADDRESS: Route 10, Box 88C, Santa Fe, NM 87501

TELEPHONE: (505) 471-8608

Turley Forge is a legend in Santa Fe. Not only does the forge produce everything from hinges to branding irons but blacksmith Frank Turley has taught scores of ironworkers their trade and has been involved in numerous historical preservation projects. He has been a visiting artist at most of the major crafts schools in the country, including Penland, Haystack Mountain, and various universities, and runs regularly scheduled intensive workshops at his own forge. He began his ironworking career in 1964 after receiving a B.A. in Sociology and Anthropology from Michigan State University. His name is at the center of every discussion about fine ironwork.

PRIMARY PRODUCT: Door hardware: hand-forged iron latches, hinges, and bolts. Reproduction ironwork and repairs to old ironware for museums, stores, and private parties.

OTHER LINES: Hand-forged, museum-quality hand tools. Bits, spurs, branding irons.

PRICE RANGE: Per job quotation.

DIRECT SALES: Yes.

CUSTOM ORDERS: Always.

ONE OF A KIND: Accepts unique commissions; sometimes travels to site. Existing commissions include reading lamps for the Southwest Room at the Santa Fe Public Library and restoration hardware for Mission San Jose, Fremont, California.

CATALOG AVAILABILITY: No catalog because all jobs are custom. Drawings are generally made. A school brochure is offered: self-addressed, stamped envelope is preferred.

RETAIL DISTRIBUTION: No.

WHOLESALE SHOWROOMS AND REPRESENTATIVES: No.

HONORS AND SPECIAL COMMISSIONS: Co-author (with Simmons) of *Southwestern Colonial Ironwork*, Museum of New Mexico Press (Santa Fe, 1980). State of New Mexico Award of Honor for the above publication, Cultural Properties Review Committee. Alex W. Beeler Award in recognition of outstanding service to the art of blacksmithing, Artist-Blacksmiths' Association of North America (ABANA), 1982, first recipient.

The Village Blacksmith

OWNER/DESIGNER: Jerry W. Harris

ADDRESS: 2967 N. Alverson Way, Tucson, AZ 85712

TELEPHONE: (602) 325-7650

After having spent the last thirty years of his life as a blacksmith, Jerry Harris can sum up his creative direction in two words: Sonoran style. He brings a feeling for the natural beauty of the vast Sonoran desert that surrounds his Tucson workshop into his hand-forged creations.

Desert scenes involving wildlife, plants, cacti, birds, and lizards are what The Village Blacksmith is best known for. These scenes are actually three-dimensional stories and are captured in fireplace screens, patio gates, wall sculptures, chandeliers, coffee tables, and many other home furnishings.

The finished pieces are treated so that each individual animal or plant takes on its own subtle yet discernable coloring. Harris applies his own specially developed patina, called Antique Verde, to everything leaving his shop. He creates these prickly pear, ocotillo, and agave plant and wildlife scenes out of steel, copper, brass, and silver.

PRIMARY PRODUCT: Hand-forged metalwork, using steel, copper, brass, and silver. Doors, gates, lighting, furniture, fireplace screens, hardware, entrances, and wall sculpture.

PRICE RANGE: $35 and up.

DIRECT SALES: Walk-in, telephone, and mail orders are welcome.

CUSTOM ORDERS: Orders are usually custom made to client's specifications, using Harris's artwork and designs. Can also create from rough sketches.

ONE OF A KIND: Numerous pieces in private art collections throughout the Southwest.

CATALOG AVAILABILITY: Brochure is available at no charge.

RETAIL DISTRIBUTION: Several art galleries and Southwestern specialty shops. Call for listings.

WHOLESALE SHOWROOMS AND REPRESENTATIVES: El Mundo Magico, Sedona; Territorial Trends, Tucson; L. Mehren/Limited Editions, Scottsdale, Arizona.

Barry Wenger

OWNER/DESIGNER: Barry Wenger

ADDRESS: P.O. Box 37641, Phoenix, AZ 85069

TELEPHONE: (602) 997-9861

A self-taught artist who proudly cites Frederic Remington, Charles Russell, and Michelangelo as his influences, Barry Wenger creates cast bronze sculpture on a monumental scale. His pieces are installed throughout the Phoenix area, bringing form to Southwestern cultural heritage and folklore legend.

Wenger also creates one-of-a-kind architectural masterpieces for residences and commercial buildings. These functional art items range from doors and door hardware to lighting, lamps, tables, fireplace screens and tool sets, and dining chairs.

"I create Western art using the traditional lost wax method of bronze casting," says Wenger. "I also work by hand-forming, usually in copper, by welding pieces together to form Indian pots, cactus, steer skulls, and just about anything that can possibly be formed by sculpture."

PRIMARY PRODUCT: Hand-formed metalwork architectural pieces, such as gates, doors, tables, lighting fixtures, and sculpture.

PRICE RANGE: $300 and up.

DIRECT SALES: Guests are always welcome in Wenger's open studio. He works primarily through designers, architects, builders, and retail design centers. Orders taken by mail, fax, and telephone.

CUSTOM ORDERS: Almost all of Wenger's work is custom ordered.

ONE OF A KIND: Wenger has created custom, one-of-a-kind pieces for the homes of Hollywood stars and corporate executives throughout the Southwest.

CATALOG AVAILABILITY: Brochures are available at no cost. Video is available to established clients of the designers Wenger already works with.

RETAIL DISTRIBUTION: Beyond Horizons, Scottsdale; Carefree Concepts, Carefree, Arizona.

WHOLESALE SHOWROOMS AND REPRESENTATIVES: Same as above.

HONORS AND SPECIAL COMMISSIONS: Numerous pieces of monumental-size bronze sculpture on display in public spaces throughout Phoenix.

Wild West Designs

OWNER/DESIGNER: Peter Fillerup

ADDRESS: P.O. Box 286, Heber Valley, UT 84032

TELEPHONE: (801) 654-4151

Peter Fillerup's sculpture is found in public parks, on college campuses, outside of churches, and in front of libraries throughout the West. A product of Cody, Wyoming, the West's emerging center of cowboy culture, Fillerup travels the world from his Utah home, opening exhibitions of his work and learning the latest tricks of his trade.

While most of Fillerup's sculpture is done in the monumental size suitable to public artworks, he also creates a limited line of architectural ironwork, lighting fixtures, chandeliers, and fireplace screens made from hand-forged iron. Working in collaboration with Jimmy Covert, one of Cody's leading re-creators of the furniture designs pioneered by Thomas Molesworth, Fillerup creates relief inlay panels for some of Covert's custom-designed pieces.

Fillerup's chandeliers are especially innovative, with his most popular design depicting a band of Indians, complete with feather headdresses and mounted on horseback, circling a large ceremonial teepee.

PRIMARY PRODUCT: Cast iron ornamental pieces, ironwork chandeliers and lighting sconces, fireplace screens.

PRICE RANGE: Depends on the difficulty of the order.

DIRECT SALES: Clients are welcome to visit the showroom, which is also Fillerup's home, in Heber Valley, Utah.

CUSTOM ORDERS: Yes, comprises most of Fillerup's work.

ONE OF A KIND: Yes. These one-of-a-kind pieces may or may not require on-site installation.

CATALOG AVAILABILITY: Yes, for $10.

RETAIL DISTRIBUTION: Wild West Designs Showroom, Heber Valley, Utah.

WHOLESALE SHOWROOMS AND REPRESENTATIVES: Jimmy Covert, Cody, Wyoming. (307) 527-6761.

HONORS AND SPECIAL COMMISSIONS: Custom homes throughout Utah, Wyoming, and Colorado.

THE FINISHING TOUCH

Ceramics, Glass, Lighting, and Textiles

*N*owhere is the sheer complexity and variety of the Southwestern life-style more apparent than in the smaller functional furnishings that complete an interior. The complexity is expressed as an attention to detail; the variety shows up in the exuberant creativity that infuses each piece. This section of *Interior Furnishings Southwest* focuses on objects that work as tableware, lighting devices, and floor or window coverings. And not just incidentally, each piece is a hand-crafted work of art as well.

Ceramics are a natural craft for the desert, a region of earth and fire. Many tribes of Pueblo Indians have evolved pottery styles for which they have become famous. As the contemporary art scene has mushroomed, many excellent potters from all over the world have been drawn to the area and have developed styles that interpret the natural beauty of the Southwestern landscape and cultural traditions.

The same influences are at work on the strong glasswork production in this region. Air, earth, and fire are the elements used to produce glass, and the luminosity of the stones and skies furnish inspiration. Southwestern architectural glass craftspeople (see Architectural Furnishings) and glassblowers create windows, goblets, bowls, and many other glass objects that reflect the brilliant skies and radiant heat of the Rocky Mountains and the high Sonoran desert.

The region's craftspeople have a special affinity for lighting. They produce a wide variety of lamps, sconces, chandeliers, and outdoor lighting. They work in a great many mediums, from adobe-look ceramics to punched metals to wrought iron to complex chandeliers made from naturally shed antlers. The unifying element is a frontier-style imagination that combines form with function.

Weaving has ancient precedents in the Southwest, where the Pueblo Indians and the sixteenth-century Spanish settlers each established styles based on cultural symbolism. They used wool from native sheep and dyed it with locally available plant substances. Even today, these textiles are treasured heirlooms with strong value as antiques. Today's textile artists are frequently descended from these early weavers. There are also contemporary mainstream artists who take the medium straight into the future with bold designs and innovative techniques.

All these functional furnishings put the finishing touch on a carefully constructed interior. In their utilitarian role, they make the environment livable. In their artistic role, they create stable underpinnings for a changing array of paintings, sculpture, folk art, and accent pieces.

Amber Archer

OWNER/DESIGNER: Amber Archer

ADDRESS: Route 6, Box 165A Agua Fria, Santa Fe, NM 87501

TELEPHONE: (505) 471-8728

Amber Archer is a nationally active professional artist and craftsperson who moves easily from unique sculptures to fine production work, distinguishing herself in both fields. She is a graduate of Goddard College and attends at least one conference or workshop each year.

PRIMARY PRODUCT: A full range of contemporary hand-thrown ceramic ware: (1) One-of-a-kind decorator pieces; vases, jars, lamps, sculpture, wall work with a high-tech approach, mainly black and white. $50 to $2,000. (2) Raku bowls, in collaboration with Shel Neymark (see Architectural Furnishings). Southwest colors on hand-thrown bowls, lamps, candleholders. $36 to $300. (3) Hand-thrown sinks, in collaboration with Counter Point Tile (see Sources). $180 to $300. (4) A full line of handcrafted hotel ware: soap dishes, amenities, ashtrays, accessories. $3 to $25.

DIRECT SALES: Yes, by telephone or letter. Hotel orders in Arizona: CM Supply Co., 7127 E. Bedershite 85, Scottsdale, AZ 85254. Raku Bowls: Shel Neymark Studio, P.O. Box 125, Embudo, NM 87531. Sinks: Direct or through Counter Point Tile, 1519 Paseo de Peralta, Santa Fe, NM 87501

CUSTOM ORDERS: Frequently.

ONE OF A KIND: Enjoys one-of-a-kind pieces. Has worked with designers such as Loyd-Paxton of Dallas on a specific house, which was later featured in *Architectural Digest*. Has also worked with hotel interior decorators for specific sites: the El Dorado Hotel in Santa Fe, New Mexico, and Mountain Shadows and Inn at McCormick Ranch in Scottsdale, Arizona.

CATALOG AVAILABILITY: Raku brochure at no charge. Hotel samples available free to hotel representatives.

RETAIL DISTRIBUTION: Gallery 3, Phoenix, and Beyond Horizons, Scottsdale, Arizona. Spider Woman, Santa Fe; Mariposa, Albuquerque; and The Taos Company, Taos, all in New Mexico. Este Es, La Jolla, California. Designs West, Aspen, Colorado. Santa Fe Styles, Washington, D.C.

WHOLESALE SHOWROOMS AND REPRESENTATIVES: CM Supply Co., Scottsdale, Arizona, for hotel work. Counter Point Tile, Santa Fe, New Mexico.

HONORS AND SPECIAL COMMISSIONS: New Mexico Artists in Residence Program–NEA/NMAD Grant. Very Special Arts artist.

Blue Heron Pottery

OWNER/DESIGNER: Janet Lever

ADDRESS: 11753 N. 85th, Longmont, CO 80503

TELEPHONE: (303) 772-4554

Blue Heron Pottery specializes in a full line of functional stoneware tableware and also produces lamps, decorative vessels, sculptural forms, and custom tile. They will also inlay tiles into custom furniture pieces. Janet Lever, owner of Blue Heron, is an accomplished artist and archaeological fieldworker. She has exhibited her creations and has worked on field digs throughout the West. The pictograph images from which she takes her inspiration are found on cave walls, boulder surfaces, and sandstone cliff walls. Lever uses these simple, sticklike forms and more complicated painted and textured forms as a starting point for her own designs.

"The quest for rock art leads me back into a sacred geography, where mountains, springs, and other landscape features emanate supernatural powers," Lever says. "The mystery and power of these places connects one to the land as well as the magic of drawings left behind by those ancient artists."

PRIMARY PRODUCT: Hand-painted functional stoneware pottery with pictograph designs and sculpted animal forms. Airbrushed design features with rich, glazed surfaces.

OTHER LINES: Lamps, decorative vessels, sculptural forms, tiles, and inlaid tile for furniture.

PRICE RANGE: $10 to $250.

DIRECT SALES: Orders can be taken at studio/showroom. Welcomes special orders by mail or telephone.

CUSTOM ORDERS: Sometimes.

CATALOG AVAILABILITY: Illustrated price list available.

RETAIL DISTRIBUTION: Boulder Arts and Crafts Cooperative, Boulder, Colorado. City Wood, Highland Park, Illinois. 10 Arrow Gallery, Cambridge, Massachusetts.

Carlson Clayworks

OWNER/DESIGNER: Lisa G. Carlson

ADDRESS: P.O. Box 596, Peñasco, NM 87553

TELEPHONE: (505) 587-2030

Lisa Carlson uses red clay as a canvas and hand paints layers of colored slips to create each piece. The work is then shaped by drying on molds. Her well-known platters incorporate bold, semiabstract geometric, spiral, fish, and leaf designs as well as Escher-like dancing figures. A contrasting palette is chosen to complement the main color of each piece.

PRIMARY PRODUCT: Earthenware designed for dual use as tableware and decoration. Each piece has been finished with a lead-free, food-safe glaze. The earthenware is dishwasher and microwave safe but is not recommended for baking.

OTHER LINES: Ceramic vases and unglazed decorative pieces.

PRICE RANGE: $50 to $500.

DIRECT SALES: By mail and telephone. Retail clients by appointment only.

CUSTOM ORDERS: Sometimes, via portfolio.

ONE OF A KIND: Unique sculptures.

CATALOG AVAILABILITY: By mail, no charge.

RETAIL DISTRIBUTION: Adesso, Highland Park, Illinois. Steve, Beverly Hills, California. Nantucket Looms, Nantucket, Massachusetts. Objects by Design, Bethesda, Maryland.

WHOLESALE SHOWROOMS AND REPRESENTATIVES: Atlantic City Buyers Market, National Juried Exhibition, February 1990. Miami Buyers Market, National Juried Exhibition, January 1990. Boston Buyers Market, National Juried Exhibition, June 1987, 1988, 1990, 1991.

HONORS AND SPECIAL COMMISSIONS: Penland Craft School Scholarship, 1988.

Coal Creek Mountain Potters

OWNER/DESIGNER: Ruth Briggs and Steve Briggs

ADDRESS: P.O. Box 7278, Golden, CO 80403

TELEPHONE: (303) 642-3019

These artists share a studio space and their last names, but the work each produces is highly distinctive. In fact, this Golden, Colorado, couple takes extra measures to make it known that Steve's wheel-thrown pottery is worlds apart from Ruth's colorfully decorated dinnerware.

Ruth Briggs calls herself a "folk potter." She uses traditional decorating techniques to create sponge-ware, sliptrailed redware, and Western ranch dinnerware in her studio. Each of her Western-style creations, made of white stoneware clay, is built for durability and beauty. Ruth creates specialized designs for ranches throughout the West and Southwest and is known as one of the few individuals capable of customizing a dinnerware line to suit the identity of a working ranch dining room.

Steve works with the iron-rich clay of southern Colorado, which turns a rich sienna after firing. Utilizing slips made from locally found elements, he uses brush patterns and metallic oxides to produce unique finishes on his Native Redware creations. He tries to make his pottery suggestive of Southwestern natural elements without resorting to overt design schemes. Steve's functional dinnerware has thick, no-nonsense rims and comes in numerous natural colorations.

PRIMARY PRODUCT: Dinnerware and pottery products in various styles, including Spongeware, Redware, and Western ranch dinnerware.

PRICE RANGE: Steve: $15 to $150. Ruth: $6 to $800.

DIRECT SALES: Studio sales are made by both Ruth and Steve at their Golden studio. Mail and telephone orders are accepted.

CUSTOM ORDERS: The branding patterns on Ruth's Western ranch dinnerware are custom designs. Steve uses his patterns to create custom dinnerware sets.

ONE OF A KIND: Steve: No. Ruth: Ranch patterns and sets are all one-of-a-kind commissions.

CATALOG AVAILABILITY: Steve: Descriptive rack sheets and price list available. Ruth: Brochure available.

RETAIL DISTRIBUTION: Ruth and Steve: Galleries and craft stores throughout Colorado, including Spectrum Gallery, Estes Park, and Two Potters, Littleton.

HONORS AND SPECIAL COMMISSIONS: Ruth Briggs and Steve Briggs are frequently found at high-end craft shows throughout the Intermountain West.

Crosshatch Clay

OWNER/DESIGNER: Jeannie Cornelius

ADDRESS: P.O. Box 96, Dixon, NM 87527

TELEPHONE: (505) 579-4608

Jeannie Cornelius has lived and studied all over the world, from the American South to Indonesia and Holland, and has acquired a cosmopolitan education and aesthetic. While studying traditional Santa Clara black pottery and Taos mica pottery techniques with Rose Naranjo of Santa Clara Pueblo, she became fascinated with the rock formations of New Mexico. Her discovery of the colors and textures of this seemingly monochromatic landscape opened up new ideas, culminating in her "Landscape Pots," which are vases, bowls, and wall pieces. These pieces, in turn, have influenced her functional tableware.

Cornelius lives and works in Dixon, a mountain village in northern New Mexico. She participates in the annual Dixon Studio Tour in addition to shipping out orders for her functional dinnerware to all points and maintaining a busy production schedule.

PRIMARY PRODUCT: Functional stoneware, sturdy kitchen and dinnerware: $81 to $500. Unglazed stoneware vases and lamps ("Rock Pots") of brown textured clay colored with a multitude of stains and oxides: $35 to $250.

OTHER LINES: "Landscape Pots," which are mostly decorative pieces depicting the New Mexico sky and landscape: $35 to $200.

DIRECT SALES: By mail or telephone. Clients welcome in studio.

CUSTOM ORDERS: Frequently.

RETAIL DISTRIBUTION: Open Space Cooperative and Variant Gallery, Taos; Galleria Ortega, Chimayo; and Craft Collection, Santa Fe, all in New Mexico. Spring Wind Gallery, Eureka Springs, Arkansas.

Fish Creek Pottery

OWNER/DESIGNER: Larry McCool and Pam McCool

ADDRESS: P.O. Box 218, Wilson, WY 83014

TELEPHONE: (307) 733-9181

Taking their creative cues from the natural environs of their Wyoming home, potters Larry and Pam McCool have developed an extensive line of Fish Creek Pottery items that are sold through their Jackson, Wyoming, River Rock Gallery.

Using the bisque firing process, the Fish Creek Pottery items feature Larry's specially formulated glazes and, on occasion, Pam's hand-glazing with sumi brushes. About half of the pottery they produce is made to fill custom orders, while the rest is sold exclusively through their gallery. The McCools will ship anywhere in the country, which has become especially important since Jackson has attracted hordes of visitors who make River Rock Gallery one of their favorite stops.

Larry and Pam McCool characterize their work as having both Asian and European design influences. Their items are crafted so as to be completely functional, and only functional items are made by Fish Creek Pottery. The McCools have developed lines of dinnerware that reflect regional influences, such as Chaco Canyon, Montana Dust, Wyoming Wildflower, Stream Bottom, and Log Cabin.

PRIMARY PRODUCT: Functional pottery items of all kinds, including tableware, sinks, communion sets, bird feeders, platters, candlesticks, cookware, teapots, and pie plates.

PRICE RANGE: $15 to $300.

DIRECT SALES: Yes, through the River Rock Gallery, (307) 733-9181.

CUSTOM ORDERS: Yes, about half of the Fish Creek Pottery production is for custom orders.

ONE OF A KIND: Yes, and Larry is happy to provide installation information for items like sinks.

CATALOG AVAILABILITY: Brochure available at no cost.

RETAIL DISTRIBUTION: Only through River Rock Gallery.

Functional Stoneware by Sonja Templeton

OWNER/DESIGNER: Sonja Templeton

ADDRESS: 1547 E. Caroline Lane, Tempe, AZ 85284

TELEPHONE: (602) 839-8183

Sonja Templeton specializes in producing custom, one-of-a-kind dinnerware. Each of her stoneware pieces is either hand-thrown on a potter's wheel or hand press molded, with richly colored slips and decorations applied to assure the piece's uniqueness. Designs and colors are influenced by Southwestern culture, such as petroglyphs and indigenous animals.

Templeton also creates sculptural animal figures decorated with various fetishes. These pieces are produced from molds, which helps keep prices affordable. Pieces such as buffalo and lizards range from just over a foot to 2 feet in length and are painted with Southwestern-inspired designs in metallic and earth colors.

PRIMARY PRODUCT: Stoneware dinner settings in one-of-a-kind glazes and finishes.

OTHER LINES: Sculptural Southwestern animal figures.

PRICE RANGE: $15 to $900.

DIRECT SALES: Retail clients are welcome to visit the studio by appointment.

CUSTOM ORDERS: Specializes in custom colors and forms.

ONE OF A KIND: Many unique specifications have been applied to Templeton's commissioned work.

CATALOG AVAILABILITY: Tear sheets are available at no charge.

RETAIL DISTRIBUTION: Numerous galleries and craft stores in the Southwest and on the West Coast. Call for specific areas.

WHOLESALE SHOWROOMS AND REPRESENTATIVES: Best of the Southwest, Dallas, Texas.

HONORS AND SPECIAL COMMISSIONS: Member, ACC and Master Craftsman's Guild.

Gaustad Pottery

OWNER/DESIGNER: Peggy Gaustad

ADDRESS: 323 S. Guadalupe, Santa Fe, NM 87501

TELEPHONE: (505) 988-7687

After receiving a B.A. degree from the University of California at Riverside, Peggy Gaustad continued her education in Mexico, earning an M.F.A. from the University of Guanajuato. While living in Mexico, Gaustad was exposed to the beauty, simplicity, and playfulness of the local earthenware pottery—features she has incorporated into her own work. Borrowing from the Mexican tradition of using handcrafted pottery for everyday use, Peggy has created a line of dinnerware and accessory pieces that will enliven any table. It is her belief that functional need not be ordinary, that handmade objects can both enhance and enrich one's daily life.

PRIMARY PRODUCT: Earthenware pottery: dinnerware, platters, and serving bowls in a variety of bright festive colors. All items are oven, dishwasher, and microwave safe and lead-free.

PRICE RANGE: Place settings begin at $104. Large serving pieces range from $64 to $140.

DIRECT SALES: Gaustad works out of Santa Fe Pottery, a studio and showroom of several local potters. Wholesale and retail customers are welcome. Orders are also accepted by telephone or mail.

CUSTOM ORDERS: Custom orders are accepted.

CATALOG AVAILABILITY: Slides and price list available on request.

RETAIL DISTRIBUTION: Gaustad's primary outlet is her studio and showroom located at Santa Fe Pottery, 323 S. Guadalupe, Santa Fe, New Mexico. Her work may also be seen at La Mesa of Santa Fe, Santa Fe, New Mexico, Santa Fe Style, Washington, D.C., and Dean & Deluca, New York.

Joshua Tree Pottery / Hazelton Jones Studio Pottery

OWNER/DESIGNER: Nan Hazelton and Alan Jones

ADDRESS: 3126 West Madison, Phoenix, AZ 85009

TELEPHONE: (602) 272-3023

Alan Jones and Nan Hazelton are a husband and wife team who create Southwestern-inspired functional pottery from a small studio. Their Joshua Tree Pottery creations are manufactured in a high fire process, with the result that these items are completely safe for all kitchen uses. Their stoneware lines include kitchenware, cookware, and tableware in a "Sonoran Desert" color palette.

PRIMARY PRODUCT: Functional stoneware.

PRICE RANGE: $10 to $120.

DIRECT SALES: No, except through mail or telephone orders.

CUSTOM ORDERS: Sometimes.

ONE OF A KIND: Sometimes.

CATALOG AVAILABILITY: Photographs and price sheet are available.

RETAIL DISTRIBUTION: Gourmet shops and craft galleries throughout the Southwest. Call for specific locations.

WHOLESALE SHOWROOMS AND REPRESENTATIVES: Businesses should contact Hauser & Associates at (602) 581-3724.

La Chiripada Pottery

OWNER/DESIGNER: Pat Johnson and Michelle Johnson

ADDRESS: P.O. Box 192, Dixon, NM 87527

TELEPHONE: (505) 579-4675

One of the most unusual pottery showrooms anywhere is located in the tiny village of Dixon, in the mountains of northern New Mexico. There, Pat and Michelle Johnson exhibit lovely functional stoneware and their own highly regarded wines. Both of these products originate on the premises: grapevines are just outside the door, and kilns, wheels, and winemaking equipment are adjacent to the retail space.

PRIMARY PRODUCT: Functional stoneware pottery glazed in earth tones accented with deep blue decoration.

OTHER LINES: Wine.

PRICE RANGE: $7 to $350.

DIRECT SALES AND RETAIL DISTRIBUTION: Yes, from the winery in Dixon and from the La Chiripada Pottery and Winery shop in Taos.

CUSTOM ORDERS: No.

CATALOG AVAILABILITY: None. Suggest attending the Dixon Studio Tour, first weekend in November each year.

Pamela Messer

OWNER/DESIGNER: Pamela Messer

ADDRESS: P.O. Box 14, Santa Fe, NM 87504

TELEPHONE: (505) 982-9563

Pamela Messer is a fine artist whose platters and bread plates make a statement when hung on the wall and an occasion when placed on the table and filled with food. She holds a Master's degree from Columbia University and a B.S. in Ceramic Engineering from Rutgers University.

PRIMARY PRODUCT: Ceramic platters and bread plates that also hang on the wall.

OTHER LINES: Ceramic pins and earrings in a variety of abstract, geometric, and animal designs.

PRICE RANGE: Platters $75 to $150. Bread plates $35.

DIRECT SALES: Yes. Retail clients are welcome in the studio. Please call ahead for an appointment.

CUSTOM ORDERS: Frequently.

ONE OF A KIND: Mostly unique pieces. Frequently do special orders on platters and groups of platters. Work with interior designers.

CATALOG AVAILABILITY: Some information available on mostly one-of-a-kind pieces.

RETAIL DISTRIBUTION: Mariposa Gallery, Santa Fe and Albuquerque, New Mexico. Sheila Nussbaum Gallery, Millburn, New Jersey. P. R. Coonley, Palo Alto, Handworks, Carmel, and Freehand, Los Angeles, all in California.

HONORS AND SPECIAL COMMISSIONS: Series of ten platters for the AT&T Building in Kansas City. Teaches pottery to children at the Children's Museum in Santa Fe, New Mexico.

Raku Gallery

OWNER/DESIGNER: Tracy Weisel

ADDRESS: P.O. Box 965, 250 Hull Avenue, Jerome, AZ 86331

TELEPHONE: (602) 639-0239

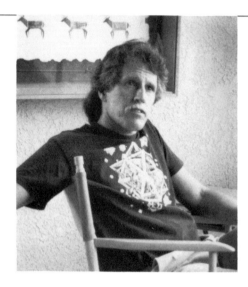

Tracy Weisel produces a full line of functional pottery and a limited line of raku vessels. All products are sold through his gallery in Jerome, Arizona.

PRIMARY PRODUCT: Functional pottery and raku vessels.

PRICE RANGE: $6 to $250.

DIRECT SALES: Yes, through the gallery.

CUSTOM ORDERS: No.

ONE OF A KIND: No.

CATALOG AVAILABILITY: No.

RETAIL DISTRIBUTION: Through the gallery.

WHOLESALE SHOWROOMS AND REPRESENTATIVES: None.

Stoneware Designs

OWNER/DESIGNER: John Burt

ADDRESS: 1107 Windsor Street, Salt Lake City, UT 84105

TELEPHONE: (801) 467-0679

Many creative individuals have incorporated a measure of Southwestern artistic feeling into their work, but few have managed to so thoroughly master so many different interpretations of this region's underlying texture and color as John Burt has done. His vases, orbs, plates, covered containers, and hand-painted tiles seem to flow directly from the craggy, red-hued southern Utah landscape and into the beholder's home.

The pigments used in Stoneware Designs' collection suggest the rust reds, muted yellows, oranges, and blacks one sees in the desert. Tall, slender vessels are edge broken with an elongated "V" shape, suggestive of the face of a rock wall. Petroglyph figures are often used to decorate the vessels' sides. Orbs have wavy, horizontal striations and darkened upper and lower portions, suggestive of a landscape. Tiles have monochromatic petroglyph designs done on reddish-brown or yellowish-brown backgrounds and can be used as wall decoration or as tile installations.

PRIMARY PRODUCT: Tiles, vessels, orbs, bowls, plates, and containers from clay. Southwestern desert colors and rock wall forms. Petroglyph and landscape designs, using muted desert colors.

PRICE RANGE: $40 to $600.

DIRECT SALES: Telephone and mail orders are accepted.

CUSTOM ORDERS: On occasion.

ONE OF A KIND: Special commissions in tile have been installed in custom homes in Salt Lake City and Park City, Utah.

CATALOG AVAILABILITY: None, but photographs can be sent.

RETAIL DISTRIBUTION: U.D.C. Gallery, Salt Lake City, Kimball Art Center, Park City, Utah. Zonies Gallery, Sedona, Arizona.

WHOLESALE SHOWROOMS AND REPRESENTATIVES: None.

HONORS AND SPECIAL COMMISSIONS: Member of Utah Designer Craftsmen Gallery. Numerous exhibitions and museum shows in the Utah region.

Alan Tyrrell Pottery

OWNER/DESIGNER: Alan Tyrrell

ADDRESS: Box 254, Dixon, NM 87527

TELEPHONE: (505) 579-4627

(505) 758-8216 (after 6:00 p.m., Nov. 25 to Apr. 15)

Alan Tyrrell shows his high-quality line of production pottery in the picturesque setting of Dixon, New Mexico, where he lives and works. He originally came to the area to attend a pottery workshop taught by Santa Clara Pueblo potter Rose Naranjo. He has been in New Mexico since 1975.

PRIMARY PRODUCT: Place settings: 10-inch dinner plate, 7-inch salad plate, 12-ounce bowl, 10-ounce cup. High fired stoneware, ovenproof and microwave safe. No lead glazes. All handmade on a potter's wheel and individually formed. Each one is trimmed to form a foot on the bottom, which raises the piece off the table. Colors include deep cobalt blue, daylight blue, peach bloom, buttermilk white, and a pale emerald green.

OTHER LINES: Vases with unusual glazes that have been described as "frozen fireworks."

PRICE RANGE: Place setting (4-piece) $32. Most range from $15 to $35 per piece.

DIRECT SALES: Direct sales are welcome. Studio and home can be found in Dixon, New Mexico, at the first left turn north of Dixon Elementary School. Call ahead for directions.

CUSTOM ORDERS: Most place settings are treated as custom orders and take about six weeks to complete and ship.

ONE OF A KIND: Each piece is individual. One-of-a-kind pieces sometimes come out of the firing that way, not necessarily by design.

RETAIL DISTRIBUTION: Bryan's Gallery on the Plaza and Taos Cookery, Bent Street, Taos, New Mexico. Smithsonian Institution Gift Shop, Washington, D.C.

HONORS AND SPECIAL COMMISSIONS: Member of Dixon Artists Association. Has shown for ten years at the Dixon Annual Studio Tour, held the first weekend of November.

Wayside Pottery

OWNER/DESIGNER: Patti Fish

ADDRESS: P.O. Box 643, Cloudcroft, NM 88317

TELEPHONE: (505) 682-2081

Wayside Pottery is a working studio and retail outlet in the mountains of southern New Mexico. Artist Patti Fish produces a full line of functional stoneware and decorative terra-cotta. Customers are welcome to watch Fish work and become familiar with the complete process of making pottery.

She studied ceramics at New Mexico State University and has worked in relative isolation as an independent artist from 1981 to the present. She has developed many original techniques, glazes, designs, and concepts during this time. For example, she has recently begun creating stoneware and earthenware baskets that are woven with strips of clay and has carried this idea into other pieces that incorporate the basket motif.

PRIMARY PRODUCT: Hand-thrown functional stoneware. Complete line in a selection of four different glaze patterns. Dinnerware on a special order basis. Serving pieces for Southwest style cooking: tortillas, nachos, salsa, and so on. Woven clay baskets in stoneware and terra-cotta: large to small fruit bowls and bread baskets woven with strips of clay. Glazed rims with natural clay woven bottoms.

OTHER LINES: Decorative terra-cotta with basketry. A blending of two vessels: the pot and the basket. A basket is woven on the pot in vivid colors on terra-cotta. Each piece is unique.

PRICE RANGE: $5 to $125.

DIRECT SALES: Wayside Pottery's separate showroom displays finished products. Orders are also accepted by telephone or mail.

CUSTOM ORDERS: Yes, keeping within the glaze color and items normally produced.

ONE OF A KIND: See above for pottery/basketry. Has worked with several interior designers to produce lamps, planters, and accent pieces.

CATALOG AVAILABILITY: Fish chooses not to limit the scope of her work, therefore a catalog is not available. Snapshots of work can be sent on request.

RETAIL DISTRIBUTION: Wayside Pottery artist studio and showrooms, Cloudcroft, Canyon Gallery at Carrizo Lodge, Ruidoso, New Mexico.

WHOLESALE SHOWROOMS AND REPRESENTATIVES: None.

White Oaks Pottery

OWNER/DESIGNER: Ivy Heymann and Gary Vogel

ADDRESS: White Oaks Route, Carrizozo, NM 88301

TELEPHONE: (505) 648-2985

White Oaks Pottery is located in a scenic rural area of southern New Mexico. Owners Ivy Heymann and Gary Vogel produce a line of fine-quality handmade stoneware. Both wheel-thrown and slab-built techniques are used to produce tableware and lighting.

Major influences are Professor Christine Federighe of the University of Miami (Florida) and Vernon Owens, fourth-generation master folk potter, Jugtown, North Carolina. "Living in the Southwest, building my own adobe studio, understanding form and function in architecture—the simplicity of line and curve is so much like making pots."

PRIMARY PRODUCT: A wide variety of functional vessels, dinnerware, and serving pieces in handmade stoneware. Also produces a variety of lighting fixtures in Southwestern style, including wall sconces and table lights.

PRICE RANGE: $12 to $200.

DIRECT SALES: Clients are welcome, by appointment. Orders via mail with deposit.

CUSTOM ORDERS: Yes.

ONE OF A KIND: Yes. Lighting commissions.

CATALOG AVAILABILITY: Yes.

RETAIL DISTRIBUTION: 31 Burro Alley, Santa Fe; Taos Cookery and Murray's Deli, Taos; Hondo Lodge, Taos Ski Valley; Hearts Delight, Ruidoso; and Teiraonias, Las Cruces, all in New Mexico.

HONORS AND SPECIAL COMMISSIONS: Lighting designs for custom adobe home, Scottsdale, Arizona, and for Dave McGary Studio, Nogal, New Mexico. Member, New Mexico Potters Guild.

Waine Archer, Glass Designer

OWNER/DESIGNER: Waine Archer

ADDRESS: 1603 4th Street N.W., Albuquerque, NM 87102

TELEPHONE: (505) 242-5582

Waine Archer specializes in one-of-a-kind and hard-to-find glasswork. He produces architectural glass sculptures as well as tableware. He has been a glass-worker for fifteen years and during that time has acquired a reputation for excellent contemporary design and for the wide variety of glassmaking techniques he employs. These include hot glass, lampworking, fusing and slumping, casting, etching, and precision glasswork.

PRIMARY PRODUCT: Functional and decorative glassware in production and on commission.

PRICE RANGE: $140 to $1,200.

DIRECT SALES: Studio visits at 1603 4th Street N.W., Albuquerque, by appointment only.

CUSTOM ORDERS: Commission work is encouraged.

ONE OF A KIND: Yes, both functional and architectural pieces.

CATALOG AVAILABILITY: None.

RETAIL DISTRIBUTION: Mariposa Gallery, Albuquerque, New Mexico. Tesuque Glassworks, Tesuque, New Mexico. Garland Gallery, Santa Fe, New Mexico. White Bird Gallery, Cannon Beach, Oregon.

HONORS AND SPECIAL COMMISSIONS: American Scientific Glassblowers Society. Board of Directors, New Mexico Glass Artists Association.

Robison Glassworks

OWNER/DESIGNER: Peet Robison

ADDRESS: 412 Barton Road, Santa Fe, NM 87505

TELEPHONE: (505) 471-4864

Peet Robison is a favorite among collectors of Southwestern glass because of his handsome, simple, and highly original designs that incorporate the colors of the desert landscape with the special fluidity of glass. Examples include his metallic, raku-like glazes and his goblets with raised concentric rings.

He earned a B.F.A. from Kansas City Art Institute and an M.A. from Kent State University and studied at the renowned Pilchuck Glass Center.

PRIMARY PRODUCT: Handblown (furnace worked) glass specializing in functional forms. Bowls utilizing contemporary Italian glassblowing techniques and influenced by Pueblo pottery forms.

OTHER LINES: Vases with landscape motif inspired by Southwest colors. Paperweights, using Robison's own crystal formula developed over a period of years, encasing various abstract forms.

PRICE RANGE: $50 and up.

DIRECT SALES: Yes, by mail or telephone.

CUSTOM ORDERS: No.

CATALOG AVAILABILITY: No.

RETAIL DISTRIBUTION: Tesuque Glassworks, Tesuque, New Mexico. La Mesa, Santa Fe, New Mexico.

HONORS AND SPECIAL COMMISSIONS: Member, Glass Art Society.

Salusa Glassworks

OWNER/DESIGNER: Bandhu Scott Dunham

ADDRESS: P.O. Box 703, Clarkdale, AZ 86324

TELEPHONE: (602) 639-1049

Bandhu Scott Dunham creates lampworked glass stemware of uncommon wit. His one-of-a-kind individual pieces and glassware sets are crafted from borosilicate (Pyrex) glass and are infused with brilliant colors.

Dunham's Salusa Glassworks offers clients a range of designs, from whimsical to contemporary and abstract. Cactus motifs, including prickly pear and saguaro, are among the designs favored by his customers.

As an accomplished glass artist, Dunham's work has been collected by other artists, including Dale Chihuly, Fritz Scholder, and Ginny Ruffner. Native American ritualistic objects provide the inspirational basis for many of Dunham's most popular pieces. In his spare moments, he finds time to create an unconventional line of neon sculpture.

PRIMARY PRODUCT: Glass goblets, made in Southwestern, contemporary, and abstract designs. Colorful pieces produced by the traditional lampworking technique.

OTHER LINES: Neon sculpture.

PRICE RANGE: $50 to $150 per stemware piece.

DIRECT SALES: Customers may visit Dunham's studio by appointment.

CUSTOM ORDERS: Custom orders are a specialty.

ONE OF A KIND: Many of the Salusa Glassworks pieces are one of a kind. Numerous collections of one-of-a-kind stemware sets have been commissioned by Dunham's collectors.

CATALOG AVAILABILITY: Brochure available at no cost.

RETAIL DISTRIBUTION: Del Mano Gallery, Los Angeles, California. Adam Whitney Gallery, Omaha, Nebraska. Garland Gallery, Santa Fe, New Mexico.

HONORS AND SPECIAL COMMISSIONS: First Place, 1991, Sedona Arts Center Annual Guild Show. Best of Show, 1989, Arizona Glass Competition.

Santa Fe Glassworks

OWNER/DESIGNER: Chris Heimerl, Glass Artist
Heather Heimerl, Business Manager
ADDRESS: 1807 Second Street, Studio 14, Santa Fe, NM 87501
TELEPHONE: (505) 471-8903

Chris Heimerl is known for his innovative, dynamic, and abstract use of color and the strength of his forms, which suggest the Southwestern landscape and cultures. Often, his designs reflect the high desert and mountains, traditional Native American pottery, and classical Japanese forms. His work is suitable for a wide range of traditional to minimal/modern 1990s interiors.

Heimerl majored in glassblowing at the University of Wisconsin at Madison, where he received a B.S. in Fine Arts. He has fifteen years of experience in glassblowing, including seven years as an independent, self-employed craftsman.

PRIMARY PRODUCT: Traditionally handblown glass with desert colors and designs, including serving platters, salad plates, dessert plates, fruit bowls, and other tableware. Lighting, including sconces and one-of-a-kind lamp bases.

OTHER LINES: Handblown art glass vessels: ornamental rondeles, vases, and bowls. Paperweights, perfume bottles, Christmas ornaments.

PRICE RANGE: $8 to $150, wholesale.

DIRECT SALES: Visits to the studio for glassblowing demonstrations and special orders are welcome. By appointment only, please. Mail and telephone orders accepted.

CUSTOM ORDERS: Sometimes.

ONE OF A KIND: All of Heimerl's blown glass work has the one-of-a-kind character of fine handcrafted work. Commissions are somewhat limited to color and form combinations existing within our product line, or similar. A wide range of color is available.

CATALOG AVAILABILITY: Wholesale price lists and photo tear sheets available on request. Please specify area of interest: production glassware, lamps, one-of-a-kind vases and rondeles, etc.

RETAIL DISTRIBUTION: Frank Howell Gallery, Santa Fe, New Mexico. Jaymes Gallery, Kansas City, Missouri.

WHOLESALE SHOWROOMS AND REPRESENTATIVES: Heather Heimerl, Representative, Business Manager, Wife/Partner.

HONORS AND SPECIAL COMMISSIONS: Glass Artists Society of America. First Artist of the Month Award, Santa Fe Arts Board. New Mexico Glass Artists Association Best Sculpture Award.

Tesuque Glassworks

OWNER/DESIGNER: Charles Miner

ADDRESS: P.O. Box 146, Tesuque, NM 87574

TELEPHONE: (505) 988-2165

Tesuque Glassworks is a glassblowing studio and retail store in Tesuque, New Mexico, just north of Santa Fe. In the shop, customers may acquire the work of Charles Miner and other top glass artists. The studio is on the premises, and there is a large window where one can watch this fascinating process. Miner is a self-taught artist who has been blowing glass for eighteen years.

PRIMARY PRODUCT: Handblown glass, primarily functional pieces such as elegant wine goblets and a new group of large shallow bowls with stratified, almost geological forms encased in glass.

OTHER LINES: Vases, perfume bottles.

PRICE RANGE: $50 to $1500.

DIRECT SALES: Tesuque Glassworks is open to the public six days a week. Mail and telephone orders are welcomed.

CUSTOM ORDERS: Sometimes.

ONE OF A KIND: Tesuque Glassworks will accept commissions.

CATALOG AVAILABILITY: Most all of the work is one of a kind.

RETAIL DISTRIBUTION: Tesuque Glassworks, Bishops Lodge Road, Tesuque, New Mexico.

Ulrich Art Glass

OWNER/DESIGNER: Jeffrey A. Ulrich

ADDRESS: 226 Regal Street, Louisville, CO 80027

TELEPHONE: (303) 666-9490

An accomplished artist in the handblown glass medium, Jeff Ulrich creates a limited production line of exquisite, and affordable, functional art glass pieces. His snakeskin-pattern vases, delicate mushroom bowls, optique and trophy vases exhibit design influences ranging from the Southwest landscape to contemporary, avant-garde motifs. His resume is filled with references to prestigious art and craft shows in which he won top prizes, including shows in the Southwest and Pacific Northwest. Ulrich has had more than ten years of experience in the field of handblown glass. He is an accomplished, yet affordable, creator of functional glass items.

PRIMARY PRODUCT: Functional, handblown glass creations, such as bowls, vases, and other vessels.

PRICE RANGE: $10 to $175 wholesale.

DIRECT SALES: Mail and telephone orders are accepted.

CUSTOM ORDERS: Yes.

ONE OF A KIND: Yes, including liturgical pieces for churches.

CATALOG AVAILABILITY: Slides are available by request; new pieces are being produced regularly.

RETAIL DISTRIBUTION: Garland Gallery, Santa Fe, New Mexico. Joan Hodgell Gallery, Sarasota, Florida. Evergreen Gallery, Evergreen; Handmade in Colorado, Boulder, Colorado.

WHOLESALE SHOWROOMS AND REPRESENTATIVES: None.

HONORS AND SPECIAL COMMISSIONS: Many awards at art and craft shows throughout the West.

Chapman Studio Lighting

OWNER/DESIGNER: Sally Chapman

ADDRESS: 2133 Yarmouth Avenue, Boulder, CO 80301

TELEPHONE: (303) 449-2165

The architectural ceramic lighting fixtures made by Sally Chapman have the style and elegance of sculptural pieces. These pieces are functional and also add the finishing touch to any interior setting. More than simply a sconce, the Chapman Studio Lighting fixture has a versatility of shape, color, texture, and feeling. Chapman uses a variety of finishes, such as mother-of-pearl, bisque, terra-cotta, and a sophisticated black on gold combination. Color selections include taupe, rose, peach, teal, and white.

Chapman has developed a wide range of shapes and size variations for her architectural ceramic lighting pieces: a fractured heart form, flower shapes, pendant forms, swirls, ziggurats, and torches. Southwestern, contemporary and even ranch-style residential and commercial settings are perfect for Chapman's sculptural lighting fixtures.

PRIMARY PRODUCT: Ceramic lighting fixtures in various finishes and colors. Sophisticated shapes and a full range of sizes. All components are UL approved; all sockets are porcelain and accept a standard medium base "A" lamp up to 100-watt intensity.

PRICE RANGE: $65 to $225.

DIRECT SALES: From Chapman's studio and by mail or telephone.

CUSTOM ORDERS: Frequently, including lighting fixtures to fit curved surfaces such as log beams.

ONE OF A KIND: Yes.

CATALOG AVAILABILITY: A complete brochure is available for $3 which includes a list of distributors.

RETAIL DISTRIBUTION: Dahl Inc., Santa Fe, New Mexico. Foothills Lighting, Lakewood, Colorado. Lighting Plus, Boulder, Colorado. Fan Shack, Miami, Florida.

WHOLESALE SHOWROOMS AND REPRESENTATIVES: Dan Kuhl, Portland, Oregon. Light Solutions, Los Angeles, California. M & H Lighting, San Diego, California. Cronin Mason, Denver, Colorado. Yadgaroff & Assoc., Miami, Florida.

HONORS AND SPECIAL COMMISSIONS: Numerous museum shows and gallery shows in Colorado. Extensive regional media attention as a leading craftsperson. Architect's Dozen Association, Denver, Colorado.

Crystal Farm Antler Chandeliers

OWNER/DESIGNER: Stephen C. Kent and Joan L. Benson

ADDRESS: 18 Antelope Road, Redstone, CO 81623

TELEPHONE: (303) 963-2350, (303) 963-0709

Although Stephen Kent and Joan Benson made their reputation in the lighting fixture field, they have since branched out into furniture pieces, mirror and picture frames, and other art furnishings. Because Crystal Farm Antler Chandeliers produces such an outstanding lighting product, however, they will probably always be known as the "antler chandelier people." The naturally shed moose, elk, deer, and fallow deer horns used in Crystal Farm's collections are gathered through a network of Western forest-floor scavengers.

From massive hotel lobby installations to a simple pair of candelabra, Crystal Farm makes just about anything that can be fabricated from antlers. Their upholstered furniture uses animal hides, leathers, Navajo rugs, and antique rugs to create unique exterior coverings. Kent and Benson also design residential and commercial buildings, an endeavor that combines their experience in the construction and interior design fields.

PRIMARY PRODUCT: Chandeliers made from naturally shed moose, deer, elk, and fallow deer antlers. Residential and commercial installations. Furniture, such as dining tables, coffee tables, chairs, sofas, coat trees, wall sconces, and floor lamps made from antlers, leathers, tapestries, and animal hides.

PRICE RANGE: $2,250 to $7,850.

DIRECT SALES: Most business is conducted over the telephone and from industry referrals.

CUSTOM ORDERS: Working with designers and for specific client design requests is a large part of Crystal Farm's business.

ONE OF A KIND: Yes, especially the large-scale commercial installations that have been commissioned.

CATALOG AVAILABILITY: Yes, for $3.

RETAIL DISTRIBUTION: Crystal Farm Antler Chandelier showrooms in Aspen and Redstone, Colorado, and Santa Fe, New Mexico.

WHOLESALE SHOWROOMS AND REPRESENTATIVES: Crystal Farm Antler Chandelier showrooms in Aspen and Redstone, Colorado; Santa Fe, New Mexico; David Sutherland, Dallas, Texas; Callard and Osgoode, Chicago, Illinois.

HONORS AND SPECIAL COMMISSIONS: Ralph Lauren residence and commercial stores throughout the Western region. Residence of the Duke of Bedford, Woburn Abbey. Caribou Club, Aspen, Colorado. Numerous celebrity residences throughout the country.

Those Gringos

OWNER/DESIGNER: Larry Virtue and Buel Wetmore

ADDRESS: 3133 East Sheridan, Phoenix, AZ 85008

TELEPHONE: (602) 956-4958

Larry Virtue and Buel Wetmore, a couple of gringos if there ever were such a pair, manufacture a line of lighting fixtures made from stone and other materials imported from Mexico. They use Cantera stone, thick glass, tin shades, and other components to produce a unique line of products that proclaim originality as well as regional design influence.

Styles range from very contemporary to traditional variations on Southwest themes. Their secondary line includes lamps made from functional stoneware pieces such as fountains and candlesticks.

Those Gringos also imports Talavera ceramic pieces, some of which they craft into lamps, as well as Mexican ironwork, tinwork, and antique Charro items. These guys are hard-core Southwestern traders.

PRIMARY PRODUCT: Lighting fixtures made from imported stone and glass.

OTHER LINES: Mexican ironwork and tin products.

PRICE RANGE: $200 to $700 retail.

DIRECT SALES: Yes, contact the studio.

CUSTOM ORDERS: Sometimes.

ONE OF A KIND: No.

CATALOG AVAILABILITY: Brochures for lighting products are available at no cost. Ironwork catalog is available for $3.

RETAIL DISTRIBUTION: Barrows, Phoenix, Arizona.

Santa Fe Lights, Inc.

OWNER/DESIGNER: Frank Willett and Louise Baldinger

ADDRESS: Rt. 10, Box 88-Y, Santa Fe, NM 87501

TELEPHONE: (505) 471-0076 (with fax switch)

Santa Fe Lights are designed by ceramic artists Frank Willett and Louise Baldinger and produced in their studio in Santa Fe. The pieces are individually formed by hand and reflect the handmade feel of adobe. The indirect light cast from these fixtures is soft and subtle, accented by the light dancing from the pierced holes used as a border treatment. They are designed to coordinate with Pueblo and Territorial as well as Contemporary architectural styles.

Willett and Baldinger bring to Santa Fe Lights over thirty years of experience as designer-craftspeople, producing light fixtures that reflect their concern with function, elegant form, and quality craftsmanship. Their beautifully made stoneware and porcelain pottery is widely collected throughout the Southwest. Their work has been used by designers, architects, builders, and electrical contractors in commercial and residential installations nationally and internationally.

PRIMARY PRODUCT: Handcrafted ceramic architectural lighting fixtures: indoor and outdoor wall lights, hanging lights, garden lights, and chandeliers made of stoneware clay fired to 2250° F. They are vitreous and impervious and will withstand harsh outdoor weather conditions. They are equipped with a superior quality porcelain socket and hardware ready for mounting. They fit standard electrical boxes and are UL listed. The fired colors are adobe tan and off-white.

PRICE RANGE: $68 to $2,500.

DIRECT SALES: Mail or telephone orders may be made directly to Santa Fe Lights.

CUSTOM ORDERS: Custom orders are gladly taken. Santa Fe Lights has full design capabilities and can work with individual clients on specific needs. Custom orders can vary from simple alterations to our standard fixtures to completely new designs and large-scale commissions.

ONE OF A KIND: Yes.

CATALOG AVAILABILITY: Yes. Write or call.

RETAIL DISTRIBUTION: Full line is available for purchase at The Santa Fe Pottery, 323 South Guadalupe, Santa Fe, New Mexico. Representative pieces at Talavera, Albuquerque, New Mexico, and The Clay Pigeon and Whittaker's Furniture and Lighting, Sedona, Arizona.

Adobe wall reflecting ceramic fixture by Santa Fe Lights

Santa Fe Lightscapes

OWNER/DESIGNER: William E. Szczech

ADDRESS: P.O. Box 5693, Santa Fe, NM 87502

TELEPHONE: (505) 986-9657 (with Fax switch)

Santa Fe Lightscapes, a collection of lovely brass light covers with hand drawn and cut landscapes, originated in a very simple way: from William Szczech's desire to create beautiful touches for the custom homes he has been building for the past fourteen years in Santa Fe.

Szczech's background is anything but simple. He designs and constructs luxury dwellings in a contemporary interpretation of traditional adobe architecture. He brings to this task diverse experiences such as being a gallery owner, serving as a VISTA and Peace Corps volunteer, and doing graduate work in urban planning at the University of New Mexico.

He began experimenting with the "Lightscape" form as a sculptor, starting with sheets of heavy brass that were formed to the size and shape of the projected light cover. Various steps have since evolved. The surface is sanded to various degrees to create patterns within the brass, then desertscapes are drawn directly on the surface. With a plasma torch, he cuts the design into the metal so that the light outlines it at night. Finally, chemical patinas are "painted" on the brass, as on a piece of bronze sculpture, resulting in a work of art.

Today, Szczech continues to build custom homes while producing his handcrafted Lightscapes. His inspiration comes from the beauty of the high desert that surrounds his workshop. By day, these brass pieces are generously scaled, wall-mounted artworks. At night, they "just happen to create soft, warm images that double as functional lighting."

PRIMARY PRODUCT: Light fixtures fabricated from sixteen-gauge brass, with landscapes sanded, drawn, and cut into the formed light cover. Custom sizes up to 6 feet high × 4 feet wide. Layers of patina, as in any brass sculpture, include turquoise blue, emerald green, pewter, black, brown, and gray. This process of "painting" with chemicals creates a surface of depth and beauty that is then sealed with a protective lacquer finish. Lightscapes are suitable for interior or exterior use, residential or commercial applications.

PRICE RANGE: $200 to $1,200 and up for commissions.

DIRECT SALES: Mail or telephone orders accepted, with an agreed upon down payment for custom work. Clients are welcome in the workshop for a private showing.

CUSTOM ORDERS: "We frequently do custom orders for clients who have a certain theme or feeling they are trying to create."

ONE OF A KIND: "We work with clients in design development."

CATALOG AVAILABILITY: Yes, on request, at no cost.

RETAIL DISTRIBUTION: Through the workshop.

HONORS AND SPECIAL COMMISSIONS: Collection, Traulsen Vineyard and Winery, Napa, California. Private residence designed by Gordon Rogers, AIA.

As different as night and day: Above, Santa Fe Lightscapes glow against a wall with starlike perforations. Below, day, they are richly colored metal artworks.

Chimayo Weavings and Gift Shop

OWNER/DESIGNER: Marcella Garduno and Sammy Garduno

ADDRESS: P.O. Box 427, Chimayo, NM 87522

TELEPHONE: (505) 351-4751 (evenings)

Marcella Garduno's grandmother, Benita Ortiz, and her mother, Beatrice O. Martinez are the major influences on her weaving. They were weavers, and so were her great-grandmother and her great-great-grandmother. Marcella's ancestral home is Chimayo, New Mexico, a mountain village noted for its authentic Spanish colonial crafts, particularly weaving. The wool comes from sheep raised in the area, and some of the dyes are local also. Designs are traditional geometrics.

Marcella and Sammy Garduno operate a shop that displays crafts of the area such as woodcarving and other folk arts.

PRIMARY PRODUCT: Traditional Chimayo weavings, mostly rugs, crafted of hand dyed 100 percent wool.

OTHER LINES: Vests and jackets.

PRICE RANGE: $5 to $1,500.

DIRECT SALES: Chimayo Weavings and Gift Shop, on Highway 76 between the Chimayo Post Office and O. M. Martinez General Store.

CUSTOM ORDERS: Sometimes.

CATALOG AVAILABILITY: No.

RETAIL DISTRIBUTION: See above.

Cinnabar 'N Celadon Studios

OWNER/DESIGNER: Willow Connery and Sharon Brown

ADDRESS: 1944 Hudson Street, Denver, CO 80220

TELEPHONE: (303) 333-4932

Cinnabar 'N Celadon Studios produces a range of textile and fabric art items that have design influences ranging from Southwestern to Asian to Contemporary.

While Willow Connery and Sharon Brown occasionally venture into the creation of throw robes and wall hangings, their primary focus has been the creation of custom bed coverings, which include quilted spreads, comforter covers, dust ruffles, pillow shams, and throw pillows. Their fabric selections range from designer cottons with satinlike finishes to imported silks. All of their fabrication work is done on machine.

Final design impressions can range from the appearance of an Oriental rug to an African tribal textile to a Native American blanket. Coverings are often styled to resemble floral or geometric shapes.

PRIMARY PRODUCT: Custom designed and fabricated bed linens.

OTHER LINES: Fabric wall hangings and furniture throws.

PRICE RANGE: Fabric prices vary.

DIRECT SALES: Business is primarily limited to the design trade. Exchanging photographs and fabric swatches by mail is the preferred way of ordering.

CUSTOM ORDERS: All custom work.

ONE OF A KIND: All orders are one of a kind.

CATALOG AVAILABILITY: Catalog and photographs are available on request.

Cottage Weaving

OWNER/DESIGNER: Patricia Marshall

ADDRESS: P.O. Box 39, High Rolls, NM 88325

TELEPHONE: (505) 682-2455

Patricia Marshall operates a busy weaving studio as a cottage industry in High Rolls, New Mexico, whose inhabitants cheerfully refer to themselves as High Rollers. (The name actually comes from the surrounding hills.) "Triti" Marshall, a self-taught weaver, welcomes retail clients to her workshop at #19 Terrace Circle Drive, but you might want to call ahead for directions to High Rolls itself.

PRIMARY PRODUCT: Hand-woven throws (lap blankets) in wool or acrylic yarns: 30″ to 32″ width and 70″ to 72″ length including fringe. Twill weave with plaids, stripes, or solids. Weaver's color choice or custom order. Linen, cotton, or acrylic table runners, twill, huck, or plain. Unique cotton rag rugs, 30″ to 32″ width and 60″ to 65″ length or custom order.

OTHER LINES: Large and small market baskets, heart shape and wall baskets.

PRICE RANGE: $20 to $300.

DIRECT SALES: Retail clients are welcome by appointment.

CUSTOM ORDERS: Custom orders are welcome.

CATALOG AVAILABILITY: Sample color photographs available by request.

RETAIL DISTRIBUTION: Swallow Place Artists Studio through Shades of Sara, Chipmunk and Swallow, all in Cloudcroft, New Mexico.

Estelle Gracer, Inc.

OWNER/DESIGNER: Estelle Gracer and Lea Gracer

ADDRESS: 950 West Hatcher Road, Phoenix, AZ 85014

TELEPHONE: (602) 944-2658

FAX: (602) 944-2650

Estelle Gracer established herself as a nationally known designer of knit sweaters during the 1970s and 1980s. Now, with her daughter Lea Gracer, she has extended her design capabilities into the field of interior design accessories.

Using a wide range of fabrics, Estelle and Lea Gracer prefer to work with colorful swatches that reflect the brilliant color of the Southwest. They create wall hangings, throw pillows, and assorted textiles for interior use. Lea's wall hangings combine primitive and natural themes with contemporary colors and materials. Pieces are woven from refined and unrefined natural fibers, ribboned fabrics, and nettings. Paints, sands, metals, and glass are among the materials used to complete the wall hangings' textural treatments.

Throws and pillows are created out of a collection of hand-dyed threads and ribbons, assembled into unique color combinations. Weaving and hand-crocheting are among the techniques used to assemble these items.

PRIMARY PRODUCT: Wall sculpture, pillows, throws, and textiles made from Southwestern-colored fibers and ribbons.

OTHER LINES: Knit designer clothing.

PRICE RANGE: Wall hangings start at $250. Throws start at $500.

DIRECT SALES: Showroom is adjacent to the company's production facility in Phoenix.

CUSTOM ORDERS: Custom orders are welcome. Estelle and Lea maintain a wide selection of fabrics and materials in their 5,000-square-foot production facility.

ONE OF A KIND: Yes, especially in terms of a commission's size and color requirements.

CATALOG AVAILABILITY: Photographs and tear sheets are available to designers at no cost.

RETAIL DISTRIBUTION: Through the Phoenix showroom.

WHOLESALE SHOWROOMS AND REPRESENTATIVES: Marge Carson Showrooms in Dallas, Texas, Los Angeles and San Francisco, California, and High Point, North Carolina. Hoffmiller's in Denver, Colorado. Pillow Finery in New York City. Call for others.

Marla Hattabaugh

OWNER/DESIGNER: Marla Hattabaugh

ADDRESS: 6339 East Mitchell, Scottsdale, AZ 85251

TELEPHONE: (602) 947-8900

Marla Hattabaugh is a quilt maker with a large following in Arizona craft circles. She creates quilts from 100 percent cotton. Each is designed and built through machine-piecing and hand-quilting techniques. Hattabaugh refers to her quilts as being one-of-a-kind art pieces.

PRIMARY PRODUCT: Handmade quilts in unique designs.

PRICE RANGE: Call for details.

DIRECT SALES: Visitors to Hattabaugh's home/studio are welcome, especially for the purpose of selecting specific colors and patterns.

CUSTOM ORDERS: Yes.

ONE OF A KIND: Commissions are accepted with a 50 percent down payment.

CATALOG AVAILABILITY: None.

RETAIL DISTRIBUTION: Craftsman's Gallery, Phoenix, Arizona. (602) 253-7770

HONORS AND SPECIAL COMMISSIONS: Has served on many boards and commissions for Arizona arts organizations. In 1990, Hattabaugh won Best Original Design at the Quilt Quest in Iowa.

Mitchell John Designs

OWNER/DESIGNER: Mitchell John

ADDRESS: P.O. Box 44583, Phoenix, AZ 85064

TELEPHONE: (602) 947-3815

Stopping at the limits of any medium has no appeal for Phoenix textile artist Mitchell John. His colorful, hand-painted fabrics have brought national recognition, as he has designed Southwestern and African-influenced fabrics for the Westgate and Quadrille textile corporations. He has also created designs that were inspired by Australian and Alaskan native cultural elements.

But the design and hand-painting of his own line of textiles is what brought Mitchell John to prominence in Southwestern design circles. He has expanded his talents and influences into many other areas, including custom painting and the design of wall finishes, set design for theater and other public events, public art sculpture, and the manufacture of interior accessory items such as pillows, drapery, bedcovers, and floor covers on canvas.

Mitchell John has been commissioned to create kinetic fabric sculpture for places like football stadiums and arts centers. He calls himself an artisan of mixed media and a purveyor of dreams, seeking to elevate man's spiritual condition. His work has been featured in the nation's leading interior design publications, and his list of major installations reads like a road map to notable structures in and around the Southwest.

PRIMARY PRODUCT: Fabric design, both hand-painted yardage and for major textile firms.

OTHER LINES: Kinetic public art, sculpture, custom painting and wall finishes, theater set design, interior accessories such as pillows, drapes, bed coverings, and floor coverings.

PRICE RANGE: $5 to $20 per square foot for walls. Fabrics start at $50 per square yard, with a 10-yard minimum.

DIRECT SALES: All work is custom to the trade.

CUSTOM ORDERS: John collaborates with designers and clients. All work is done on-site. Clients allowed into studio only for approvals.

ONE OF A KIND: All pieces are custom, one of a kind. Travel to national sites is a frequent part of John's business.

CATALOG AVAILABILITY: Portfolio review by appointment. Tear sheets are available. Catalog available for $120.

RETAIL DISTRIBUTION: Only through interior designers.

WHOLESALE SHOWROOMS AND REPRESENTATIVES: Self-represented.

HONORS AND SPECIAL COMMISSIONS: Public installations throughout the Southwest. Music festivals, public celebrations, department stores, museums, and stage productions are a specialty.

JON CO–Fiber Arts Surface Design

OWNER/DESIGNER: Jon Drayson

ADDRESS: 1642 East Minton Drive, Tempe, AZ 85282

TELEPHONE: (602) 820-5546

JON CO specializes in the interior use of natural fabrics, colored with the same tones found in Arizona's wilderness areas. Using silk, wool, cotton, and linen, Jon Drayson creates window treatments, upholstery, bed and table linens, pillows, floor cloths, wall coverings, and a new line of napkins that when folded resemble Southwestern desert flowers.

Drayson says that her window treatments do as well as, if not better than, stained glass in bringing color and light variation into an interior area. "Besides, you can take the window treatments down to clean them or even change them all for a lot less money than glass requires."

Silks are her preferred medium for room dividers, throws, and bed coverings. Cotton is used for table and bed linens. Drayson uses floral designs as a means for expressing the individuality of her clients; depth can be explored in overlapping leaves and branches, the stages of a plant's growth, and the colorful flowerings that plant produces.

PRIMARY PRODUCT: Bed coverings, wall hangings, pillows, table linens, bed sheets, napkins, and other interior fabric accessory items, made from hand-colored natural fibers.

PRICE RANGE: $50 to $400 a square yard; $250 to $5,000 for individual works.

DIRECT SALES: Studio visits and trips into the Arizona wilderness are available, by appointment.

CUSTOM ORDERS: Frequently. Clients give final approval on design and color but are welcome to participate in the creative process.

ONE OF A KIND: Drayson enjoys travelling to sites and creating specific designs to suit a project. Commercial and residential one-of-a-kind projects form a large part of the work.

CATALOG AVAILABILITY: No catalog, but a tear sheet is available at no cost. Slides are available for a deposit fee.

RETAIL DISTRIBUTION: Mind's Eye, Scottsdale, Arizona. Dee Morris Phase II, Sedona, Arizona. Tiziana's, Los Angeles, California.

WHOLESALE SHOWROOMS AND REPRESENTATIVES: McNamarra & Harris, Phoenix, Arizona. Kriska, Salt Lake City, Utah.

Kathy Kankainen Fiber Arts

OWNER/DESIGNER: Kathy Kankainen

ADDRESS: 1174 Harrison Avenue, Salt Lake City, UT 84105

TELEPHONE: (801) 485-9464

Kathy Kankainen has spent the better part of her career studying and working with the intricate weavings made by Native American people of the Southwest. She is an acknowledged expert on the subject of Navajo rug restoration and is regularly called on by museums, galleries, and private collectors to evaluate and restore priceless weavings contained in their collections.

Kankainen is a faculty member at Weber State University and also an established artist. Her recent weavings reflect her deep commitment to the Native American cultures and traditions of the Southwest. The intriguing designs of petroglyph figures and other rock art forms inspire the designs contained in her painted-warp wall pieces, scarves, shawls, wraps, table mats, and runners.

These unique, functional pieces are created by painting the vertical, or warp, threads that make up a design, then expertly weaving those threads into a distinct pattern on the loom. "Painting warps allows me to manipulate the fibers and to decorate them with artistic elements," she says. Kankainen frequently creates large pieces, which are framed and hung as independent artworks. The beauty of the Southwest permeates her work.

PRIMARY PRODUCT: Weavings of Southwestern scenes and Native American-influenced designs. Created as artwork and also as functional pieces.

PRICE RANGE: $100 to $1,500.

DIRECT SALES: Clients are welcome at the studio. Mail and telephone orders are accepted.

CUSTOM ORDERS: Sometimes.

ONE OF A KIND: Commissioned pieces are created as one-of-a-kind items.

CATALOG AVAILABILITY: No brochure, but photographs are available.

RETAIL DISTRIBUTION: Utah Designer Crafts Gallery, 38 West 200 South, Salt Lake City, UT 84104.

HONORS AND SPECIAL COMMISSIONS: "A tribute to the Nature World," Best of Show Award, Salt Lake City, 1989.

La Lanzadera Weaving Shop

OWNER/DESIGNER: Teresa Cordelia Coronado

ADDRESS: P.O. Box 756, Medanales, NM 87548

TELEPHONE: (505) 685-4678

La Lanzadera Weaving Shop is the home of a remarkable weaver, Teresa Cordelia Coronado, whose parents were Chimayo weavers from a seven-generation tradition. (Chimayo is a mountain village in northern New Mexico that is celebrated for its long history of fine weaving by descendants of the original Spanish settlers.) Coronado now teaches Southwestern design and weaving techniques and continues to produce her notable weavings.

PRIMARY PRODUCT: Traditional and semicontemporary Southwest weavings in all sizes and colors, all in 100 percent wool. These include rugs, hallway runners, drapes, and New Mexico table settings: table runners, placemats, and coasters.

OTHER LINES: Navajo style wall hangings, belts, vests, coats.

PRICE RANGE: $3.75 to $1,200.

DIRECT SALES: The studio has an open door policy. The public is welcome to our studio to watch the weaving or teaching and to see the shop's inventory.

CUSTOM ORDERS: Yes.

ONE OF A KIND: Coronado has been weaving commission pieces for over 15 years, for example, chair cushions and other functional pieces as well as religious stoles, vests, and other pieces.

CATALOG AVAILABILITY: No.

RETAIL DISTRIBUTION: Spanish Market, Santa Fe, in summer and winter. Ghost Ranch Presbyterian Conference Center, above Abiquiu, New Mexico, in summer. Española (New Mexico) Tri-Cultural Festival, in fall. Full line shown year-round at La Lanzadera Weaving Shop.

HONORS AND SPECIAL COMMISSIONS: Teresa Cordelia Coronada has a permanent exhibit in Madrid, Spain. She has exhibited at the Museum of International Folk Art in Santa Fe. She has been nominated a Living Treasure in New Mexico.

Mackender Designs

OWNER/DESIGNER: Gary Mackender

ADDRESS: 168 West Kennedy, Tucson, AZ 85701

TELEPHONE: (602) 623-5092

Gary Mackender, a painter, sculptor, and creator of wearable art, has found a way to use his artistic talents in the production of one-of-a-kind floor coverings and wall hangings. These hand-painted canvas creations are done with acrylic paints on a primed #10 canvas sheet, all of which is then sealed with an acrylic varnish. The result is a durable work of art that is meant to be used on the floor.

Floor coverings are an early-twentieth-century American art form that fell out of favor after the use of linoleum and carpeting became widespread. But these designs resonate with bold colors and geometric patterns that are distinctly modern, and they bring a distinctive element to the brick, tile, and sealed mud floors that are common throughout the Southwest.

Mackender's floor coverings are available in a range of sizes and can be custom ordered in practically any size. Mackender also creates upholstery designs, placemats, room dividers, and picture frames out of similar materials and colors for complete room decor theme.

PRIMARY PRODUCT: Floor coverings of sealed, painted canvas. Contemporary and Southwestern designs.

OTHER LINES: Matching placemats, room dividers, picture frames, and upholstery.

PRICE RANGE: $150 to $1,500.

DIRECT SALES: Yes, through the studio, which is open by appointment.

CUSTOM ORDERS: Custom orders are encouraged. Designers and other clients are advised to become familiar with Mackender's product and color choices before ordering.

ONE OF A KIND: All floor coverings are one of a kind.

CATALOG AVAILABILITY: Color photocopies are available.

RETAIL DISTRIBUTION: La Mesa, Santa Fe, New Mexico. Contents, Tucson, Arizona. Silverworks and More, Lawrence, Kansas.

HONORS AND SPECIAL COMMISSIONS: Mackender is the lead artist on an interstate highway design team, in which capacity he determines the aesthetic quality of overpass treatments and decides on mural installations.

Carolyn McClain, Fiberartist

OWNER/DESIGNER: Carolyn McClain

ADDRESS: 3150 Raindrop Drive, Colorado Springs, CO 80917

TELEPHONE: (719) 591-9580

Carolyn McClain's creations, which are known as both studio quilts and traditional quilts, are works of art by an accomplished craftsperson.

McClain's studio quilts are meant to be hung on a wall and appreciated as the kind of artwork that can set a dramatic, Southwestern tone within a room area. These quilts range in size from smallish pieces that are best displayed within a frame to massive artworks that hang on wooden dowels. Carolyn uses a variety of techniques on these pieces, including appliqué, hand painting, beadwork, and embroidery.

The design motifs may be simple, such as a few Anasazi petroglyph figures arrayed on a desert landscape, or highly complex, geometric creations that bring elements of Southwestern design and traditional quilting patterns together into a unified whole. McClain's work is always thought-provoking as well as beautiful.

PRIMARY PRODUCT: Studio quilts and traditional quilts. Southwestern design wall hangings that use the quilt form. Intricate hand-painting, stitching, and beading are a few of this craftsperson's many techniques.

PRICE RANGE: $500 to $2,000.

DIRECT SALES: Retail clients are welcome at the studio. Mail and telephone orders are accepted.

CUSTOM ORDERS: Frequently.

ONE OF A KIND: Only one-of-a-kind pieces are created. No specific pattern is repeated on traditional quilts, and there is no repetition of studio quilt designs.

CATALOG AVAILABILITY: Slide packet is available at no charge.

RETAIL DISTRIBUTION: SoHo West, Denver, Colorado. Quilts, Ltd., Santa Fe, New Mexico. Rising Phoenix Gallery, Cripple Creek, Colorado.

HONORS AND SPECIAL COMMISSIONS: Several exhibitions at art galleries and museums in Colorado.

Sara McCook Textiles

OWNER/DESIGNER: Sara McCook

ADDRESS: 1218 Escalante, Santa Fe, NM 87501

TELEPHONE: (505) 982-6224

Sara McCook's vibrant fabrics have a distinctive look that comes from her long experience in the exacting dye medium of paste resist. She studied this technique in Tokyo after receiving her B.S. in Textile Design from the University of California at Davis. She has worked consistently with paste resist since 1976, concentrating at first on wearable art and then evolving a mixed medium that combined the paste resist dye method with paper collage to produce exquisite wall-hung artworks. She still creates some of these and also teaches others her techniques at formal workshops and as a community service at a small college. Her greatest recognition, however, is for her elegant hand-printed fabrics that have become an integral part of the Southwest look.

PRIMARY PRODUCT: A full repertoire of designer fabrics for upholstery and draperies, hand printed using paste resist process. Major themes, each incorporating a selection of colors and designs, include Classic, an abstract collection in white on white; Botanies, in which leaves and other plant forms are printed on a range of monochromatic colors; Motifs, such as a swirl pattern, in a selection of colors; Chromatic, a group of designs such as Carnival and Mardi Gras, in bright, vivid colors; Desert, a softer, more landscape-influenced color range with Southwestern design themes.

OTHER LINES: Paper collage.

PRICE RANGE: $80 to $150 per yard.

DIRECT SALES: Yes.

CUSTOM ORDERS: Yes. Can match dyes to existing elements and help with the selection of fabrics for custom work.

ONE OF A KIND: Yes. McCook has created designs for individuals.

CATALOG AVAILABILITY: No. Will send photos of fabrics. Swatch book available at Collaboration in Santa Fe, New Mexico.

RETAIL DISTRIBUTION: Collaboration, Santa Fe, New Mexico.

HONORS AND SPECIAL COMMISSIONS: New Mexico representative for Surface Design Association, a worldwide organization. Fabrics commissioned for Zona Rosa Condominiums, a luxury development in Santa Fe.

Peck Taylor Designs

OWNER/DESIGNER: Harriet Peck Taylor

ADDRESS: 329 29th Street, Boulder, CO 80303

TELEPHONE: (303) 499-9914

Textile artist Harriet Peck Taylor cites both artist Georgia O'Keeffe and textile designer William Morris as among her most important influences. Peck Taylor's love of Southwest design and nature is exceeded only by her knowledge and mastery over her materials.

"My work has been described as whimsical, mystical, vibrant, playful, and bold. I try to entice the viewer with my imagery and hope people can find something to relate to," she says. An increasing number of individual and commercial clients are feeling the same way. Her commissions range from custom homes at mountain resorts to hotel and theater lobby installations to restaurants and public buildings.

Using hand-painted batik, a fabric that is dyed using wax, the banners, wall hangings, and fabric installations of Peck Taylor Designs may be displayed framed or unframed. From whimsical and figurative to realistic landscape, these textile creations range in color from bright and startling to subdued and relaxing.

PRIMARY PRODUCT: Hand-dyed batik fabric artwork in Southwestern designs and patterns. Wall hangings, framed pieces, and banners depicting Southwestern legend, nature tales, and landscape scenes.

PRICE RANGE: $100 to $10,000.

DIRECT SALES: Interested clients are invited to visit the studio, by appointment. Mail and telephone orders are accepted.

CUSTOM ORDERS: Frequently taken and always enjoyed, from the perspective of the order's design challenge. Enjoys client input.

ONE OF A KIND: Site-specific installations are a common part of Peck Taylor's business, especially in regard to commercial projects.

CATALOG AVAILABILITY: Photographs and prices are available on request.

RETAIL DISTRIBUTION: Boulder Arts and Crafts Cooperative, Boulder; Spectrum Art Gallery, Breckenridge; Boselli of Vail, Vail, all in Colorado.

HONORS AND SPECIAL COMMISSIONS: Numerous greeting card designs for national corporate clients.

Ramah Navajo Weavers Association

OWNER/DESIGNER: Forty traditional women weavers from the Ramah Navajo community

ADDRESS: P.O. Box 153, Pine Hill, NM 87321

TELEPHONE: (505) 775-3253

Ramah Navajo Weavers Association is the first group in the Navajo Nation to work on land-based self-reliance from weaving, sheep, and related traditions. Each member raises her own sheep, creates her own designs, spins her own yarn, hand dyes the yarn using vegetal dyes from local plants, and works on traditional Navajo upright looms. The wool comes from either fine Rambouillet or traditional Navajo-Churro sheep, a rare breed that is the sacred ancestral sheep of the Navajo people.

Each weaver has her own distinctive weaving designs, passed on to her through generations by family members. "We weave, expressing the beauty and order of life. We pray, we sing for our own survival and for the survival of this land and people."

PRIMARY PRODUCT: Traditional Navajo weavings, ranging in size from 5″ × 6″ miniature art pieces to 5′ × 6′ area rugs. Pillows: 16″ × 16″, 14″ × 18″, and 18″ × 18″.

OTHER LINES: Raw, washed fine and Navajo-Churro wool; Navajo-Churro breeding sheep.

PRICE RANGE: $60 and up.

DIRECT SALES: Ramah is a cooperative. Call to inquire about visits with the weavers. Ramah welcomes special orders as well as wholesale/retail orders. Delivery time and costs depend on each order. Mailing costs additional.

CUSTOM ORDERS: Custom orders available.

ONE OF A KIND: All pieces are one of a kind. Commissioned pieces are also welcomed.

CATALOG AVAILABILITY: Photographs.

RETAIL DISTRIBUTION: Call for information.

WHOLESALE SHOWROOMS AND REPRESENTATIVES: Wholesale inquiries invited.

HONORS AND SPECIAL COMMISSIONS: Collaborative weaving done with N. Kozikowski to commemorate the Centennial celebration of the Statue of Liberty; weaving now hangs in the Statue of Liberty Museum. Weaving awards at Santa Fe Indian Market's competition, 1989-1991. Awards for wool at National Wool Show and New Mexico State Fair competitions, including grand champion awards, 1989-1991.

Southwest Quiltworks

OWNER/DESIGNER: Terri Edwards

ADDRESS: 7370 E. Florida, Suite 1030, Denver, CO 80231

TELEPHONE: (303) 654-3485, (800) 441-2829

A broad range of quilts, all sizes, shapes, and designs, is Terri Edwards's specialty. From Southwest to American Country to Contemporary patterns, Southwest Quiltworks has quilted designs to suit the interior schemes of any residence.

Edwards is adept at running the business side of her successful craft venture. Her 800 number, her demanding regimen of regional and national trade shows, and her ability to supervise a crew of dozens of employees are testimony to her managerial skills.

On the design side, her signed and numbered limited edition quilts are artistic masterpieces, and her production quilts, couch covers, and mini-quilts are equally attractive. From Southwest landscape scenes to mythical figures from Native American legends and Navajo rug pattern-inspired quilts, Edwards has developed an ability to respond to limitless interior design needs.

PRIMARY PRODUCT: Machine-sewn and hand-quilted quilts, from king size to miniature, and couch coverings and wall quilts with painted and penciled detailings.

PRICE RANGE: $10 to $2,000.

DIRECT SALES: Sold through trade shows throughout the West and Southwest or through her studio, by appointment.

CUSTOM ORDERS: Absolutely. Edwards enjoys responding to the specific design needs of customers.

ONE OF A KIND: Yes, and Edwards's travel schedule allows her to visit and work directly with clients, if necessary.

CATALOG AVAILABILITY: Color brochure is available for $2 through her toll-free number.

RETAIL DISTRIBUTION: Colorado Sampler, Denver, Colorado; Country Interiors, Broomfield, Colorado.

WHOLESALE SHOWROOMS AND REPRESENTATIVES: Call for specific regional representatives.

HONORS AND SPECIAL COMMISSIONS: Numerous magazine articles and regional media attention.

Spark of Soul

OWNER/DESIGNER: Theodora J. Ladnya

ADDRESS: 4214 Bonita Way, Prescott Valley, AZ 86314

TELEPHONE: (602) 775-5225

Artist Theodora Ladnya creates contemporary fabrics that are decorated with patterns used by Mimbres Indians, a tribal group that lived in New Mexico over 1,000 years ago. Ladnya draws her inspiration not only from the aesthetic qualities of Mimbres designs but also from their humanistic and spiritual meanings.

She uses a widely colored palette in developing her designs and fabrics, with each bold, sophisticated form having a personal symbolic meaning. The fabric designs she sells as part of her Mimbres Mythmaker Collection use a plane-implied line to suggest dimensionality and emotionally charged lines.

Ladnya says that she "creates strong, clear, concise patterns that reflect the balance between man and his environment and affirm the immortality of the human spirit."

PRIMARY PRODUCT: Designer fabrics using Southwestern, Mimbres Indian imagery.

PRICE RANGE: $33 to $48 per yard.

DIRECT SALES: Yes.

CUSTOM ORDERS: Yes.

CATALOG AVAILABILITY: Brochure is available at no charge.

RETAIL DISTRIBUTION: Thomas & Co., 3600 E. University, Phoenix, AZ 85034.

HONORS AND SPECIAL COMMISSIONS: Exhibitions both national and international. Twenty one-person shows. Museum awards.

Gail Szpatura

OWNER/DESIGNER: Gail Szpatura

ADDRESS: Rt. 14, Box 199-B, Santa Fe, NM 87505

TELEPHONE: (505) 471-4496

Gail Szpatura studied weaving formally for two years and has broad exposure to its various aspects. She attended Goddard College in Plainfield, Vermont. Her emphasis is on rug weaving, and her main interest is natural dyes. "I use many of the historic dyes such as indigo, cochineal, and madder. I prefer the colors derived from natural sources. Technically defined, they are multifaceted colors, meaning they possess depth and life. To my eye, they are superior, as they have a subtle hue and vibrant quality."

Szpatura uses a shaft-switched block weave, which is two interlocking layers woven simultaneously with an opposite design on either surface. It produces a heavy-weight rug that lies well.

PRIMARY PRODUCT: Handwoven all-wool rugs. They are designed to function well as floor rugs but may be hung on a wall.

PRICE RANGE: $975 and up; $65 per square foot, 3′ × 5′ minimum.

DIRECT SALES: Encouraged. Orders accepted by mail or telephone. Clients may visit by appointment.

CUSTOM ORDERS: Yes. An on-site visit may be arranged. Yarn samples available to establish color choices; paint chips, fabric swatches, wallpaper samples, photographs may be sent.

ONE OF A KIND: Yes. Unique commissions are considered a challenge and generously accepted within the nature of rug weaving.

CATALOG AVAILABILITY: Packet containing information sheet and biographical information and prints or slides of current rugs available free of charge.

RETAIL DISTRIBUTION: Oleg Stavrowski Gallery, Santa Fe, New Mexico. Tomlinson Craft Collection, Baltimore, Maryland. Telephone for others.

HONORS AND SPECIAL COMMISSIONS: National juried exhibition: "Fiber Celebrated '89," Salt Lake City, Utah.

Twining Weavers

OWNER/DESIGNER: Sally Bachman

ADDRESS: 135 Paseo del Pueblo Norte, P.O. Box 2434, Taos, NM 87571

TELEPHONE: (505) 758-9000

Sally Bachman has long specialized in custom hand weaving for private and corporate clients. For ten years prior to her purchase of Twining Weavers, her finely crafted tapestries had been exhibited in invitational juried shows throughout the country. As owner and chief designer of Twining Weavers, she says, "The excellence in the quality of our weaving is attributable to master weaver Tomasita Varos Martinez."

Bachman now introduces twelve new production designs a year at Twining Weavers as well as doing the design work for all special commission pieces. Under her supervision, the shop is one of the most exciting places in the West. It affords not only an excellent line of handwoven interior furnishings but also a wealth of handspun yarns whose strikingly vivid colors are named after native plants, among them Alpine Lily, Fireweed, and Thistle.

PRIMARY PRODUCT: Rugs, pillows, throws, blankets, placemats, table runners, and handloomed designer fabric, all in hand-dyed domestic wool.

PRICE RANGE: $35 to $285.

DIRECT SALES: Twining Weavers is open to the public six days a week. Mail and telephone orders also accepted.

CUSTOM ORDERS: A specialty. The shop works closely with the client to design textile furnishings compatible with wall covering samples, paint chips, and interior photographs.

ONE OF A KIND: Special commissions gladly accepted.

CATALOG AVAILABILITY: Photographs, brochure, price lists on request.

RETAIL DISTRIBUTION: At Twining Weavers shop in Taos plus forty other retail outlets nationwide and in Italy and Japan.

HONORS AND SPECIAL COMMISSIONS: Bachman is a member of the American Crafts Council and the Handweavers Guild of America. Photographs of her work have appeared on the covers of four textbooks. She has exhibited her work in juried shows at the Dallas Museum of Fine Arts, at the Philbrook Art Center in Tulsa and many others. Her own tapestries are in the corporate collections of Phillips Petroleum, IBM, Ingersoll Rand, and numerous banks and private collections.

Weaving/Southwest

OWNER/DESIGNER: Rachel Brown

ADDRESS: 216-B Paseo del Pueblo Norte, Taos, NM 87571

TELEPHONE: (505) 758-0433

Rachel Brown has lived and worked in Taos for thirty-five years and has been a major influence on contemporary weaving in New Mexico. Since she completed her formal education at Radcliffe, Cooper Union, and the Art Students League, her work has been most influenced by the art of Navajo and Hispanic weavers of the eighteenth- and nineteenth-century Southwest. This influence shows in every color, shape, and line of the rugs and pillows designed by Brown and the weavers at the Weaving/Southwest studio.

Brown has gathered a dozen of the finest textile artists in the Southwest to show their own work at Weaving/Southwest. The shop has a studio adjacent to the exhibit space. Several looms are used for weaving projects that the public may watch.

PRIMARY PRODUCT: Handwoven tapestries for wall or floor. Hand-dyed pillows. Moki and banded blankets.

PRICE RANGE: Rugs and blankets $20 and up per square foot. Pillows $75 each.

DIRECT SALES: Studio/shop is open to the public 6 days a week. Mail and telephone orders accepted.

CUSTOM ORDERS: On commission.

ONE OF A KIND: Yes. Exhibit space is noted for its unique tapestries.

CATALOG AVAILABILITY: Photographs and price lists on request.

RETAIL DISTRIBUTION: Weaving/Southwest, Taos, New Mexico.

HONORS AND SPECIAL COMMISSIONS: Numerous awards in juried exhibitions. Private collections, United States and Canada. Public collections: University of New Mexico Library, Albuquerque, and Harwood Library, Taos, both in New Mexico. Member, American Crafts Council.

Charlotte Ziebarth Tapestries

OWNER/DESIGNER: Charlotte Ziebarth

ADDRESS: 3070 Ash Avenue, Boulder, CO 80303

TELEPHONE: (303) 494-2601

The pictoral weavings of Charlotte Ziebarth have a recognizable imagery that ranges from Native American-influenced to nearly Middle Eastern. Creating tapestries, rugs, and pillows in her Boulder studio, she fills orders from clients ranging from New York corporations to individuals she meets at regional crafts shows.

Whether crafting a wool tapestry made up of colorful, geometric forms or weaving silks to fashion a sofa pillow, Ziebarth brings an ethnic flair into all aspects of her work. Her designs are superimposed on backgrounds colored and shaped like Southwestern landscape images. Ziebarth hand dyes all of her wools, usually working with designers and architects to coordinate her tapestries with decor elements in residences and commercial structures.

PRIMARY PRODUCT: Wool and silk tapestries, rugs and pillows for residential and commercial use. Hand-dyed wool weavings inspired by Southwestern landscapes and figurative forms.

PRICE RANGE: $125 to $10,000.

DIRECT SALES: Yes, by appointment through Boulder studio.

CUSTOM ORDERS: All tapestries are custom designed to suit client's specific design needs.

ONE OF A KIND: All custom work is one of a kind.

CATALOG AVAILABILITY: Slides and photographs are available at no charge.

RETAIL DISTRIBUTION: Boulder Arts and Crafts Co-Op, Boulder, Colorado.

WHOLESALE SHOWROOMS AND REPRESENTATIVES: Rhoda Reiss Gallery and Sandy Carson, Denver, Colorado.

HONORS AND SPECIAL COMMISSIONS: Colorado Bank, Denver, Colorado. HBO Communications Center, New York. Member, American Tapestry Alliance and International Tapestry Network.

SOURCES

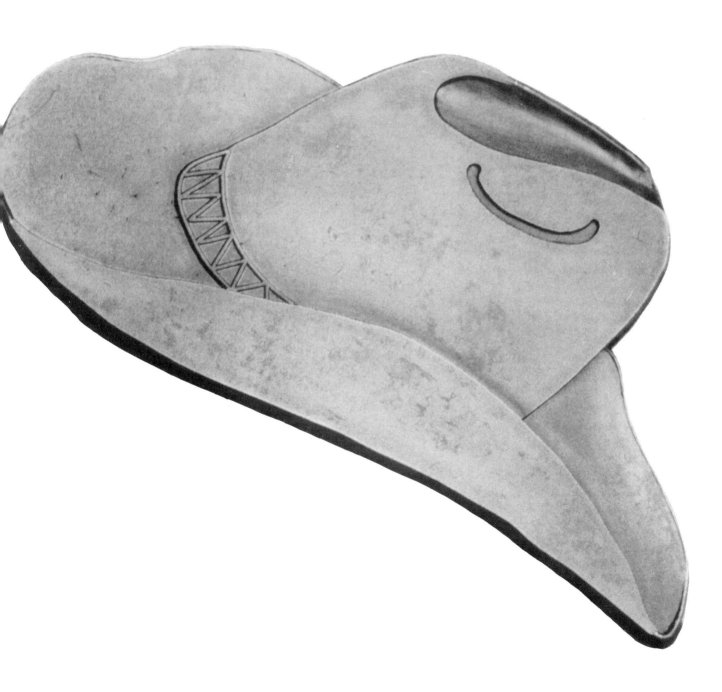

Barrow's
2301 E. Camelback Road
Phoenix, AZ 85016
(602) 955-7550
Contemporary Southwestern furnishings.

Paula Berg Interior Design
7522 E. McDonald Drive, Suite C
Scottsdale, AZ 85250
(602) 951-0165

Beyond Horizons
6137 N. Scottsdale Road, Suite B-104
Scottsdale, AZ 85250
(602) 596-9234
Fine handcrafts.

Contents
4380 E. Grant Road
Tucson, AZ 85712
(602) 881-6900
Contemporary and traditional regional furniture and accessories.

Craftsmen's Cooperative Gallery
614 E. Adams Street
Phoenix, AZ 85064
(602) 253-7770

Rina Forrest
1629 W. Wilshire Drive
Phoenix, AZ 85007
(602) 252-8883
Interior design.

Sangin Trading Company
300 N. 6th Avenue
Tucson, AZ 85705
(602) 882-9334
Traditional and Spanish Colonial furniture styles.

Su Casa
1000 E. Camelback Road
Phoenix, AZ 85014
(602) 277-0101
Contemporary Southwestern furniture and accessories.

Architects' Dozen
3943 Blake Street
Denver, CO 80205
(303) 294-0703
Crafts cooperative.

Boulder Arts and Crafts Cooperative
1421 Pearl Street
Boulder, CO 80302
(303) 443-3683

Country Classics Furniture
975 Garden of the Gods Road
Colorado Springs, CO 80907
(719) 598-7788

Great Things West
P.O. Box 4150
Breckenridge, CO 80424
(303) 453-7239
Just that. High country and Southwestern furniture.

Madeiras
30th and Walnut
Boulder, CO 80301
(303) 443-3078
Traditional and Spanish Colonial furniture.

Nevin Nelson Interior Design
2271 N. Frontage Road West
Vail, CO 81657
(303) 476-5530

Phoenix West Design
7600 E., Arapahoe Road, Suite 107
Englewood, CO 80112
(303) 773-9003
Southwestern furniture and home accessories.

The Slifer Collection
182 Avon Road
Avon, CO 81620
(303) 949-1621
Contemporary and traditional Southwestern furniture and accessories.

Soho West
1730 Wazee Street
Denver, CO 80202
(303) 292-9475
Contemporary Southwestern furniture, accessories, and art objects.

Touch of Santa Fe
6574 S. Broadway
Littleton, CO 80121
(303) 730-2408
Indian and Southwestern collectibles. Custom handcrafted furniture.

NEW MEXICO SOURCES

A
3500 Central SE
Albuquerque, NM 87106
(505) 266-2222
Southwestern contemporary furnishings.

Clay and Fiber
126 Plaza Drive
Taos, NM 87571
(505) 758-8093

Counter Point Tile
1519 Paseo de Peralta
Santa Fe, NM 87501
(505) 982-1247
Fine art tile. Custom designed kitchens, bathrooms, and fireplaces.

Design Center
105 Camino de la Placita
Taos, NM 87571
(505) 758-7800

Dewey Galleries, Ltd.
74 E. San Francisco
Santa Fe, NM 87501
(505) 982-8632
Spanish Colonial furniture and architectural artifacts. Indian textiles and pottery.

Esperanza Fine Furniture
303 Rio Grande NW
Albuquerque, NM 87104
(505) 242-6458
Southwestern furniture and accessories.

Form + Function
328 Guadalupe Street
Santa Fe, NM 87501
(505) 984-8226
The last word in Southwestern lighting.

Garland Gallery
125 Lincoln Avenue
Santa Fe, NM 87501
(505) 984-1555
Functional and fine art glass.

Gondeck
P.O. Box 629
Tesuque, NM 87574
(505) 989-9548
Contemporary Indian pottery and graphics.

Cecily Hughes Design Resources
P.O. Box 8158
Santa Fe, NM 87504
(505) 984-8744

Johnson & Benkert
128 W. Water Street
Santa Fe, NM 87501
(505) 984-2768
The right components.

La Mesa of Santa Fe
225 Canyon Road
Santa Fe, NM 87501
(505) 984-1688
Everything for the tabletop and more.

Lo Fino
201 S. Santa Fe Road
Taos, NM 87571
(505) 758-0298
Ten furniture and lighting craftspeople.
Full interior design service.

Ortega's of Chimayo
Highway 520 at Highway 76
P.O. Box 325
Chimayo, NM 87522
(505) 351-2288 or 351-4215
Spanish textiles and folk art.

SF
418 Cerrillos Road
Santa Fe, NM 87501
(505) 983-9559
Southwestern contemporary furnishings.

Santa Fe Pottery
323 S. Guadalupe
Santa Fe, NM 87501
(505) 988-7687 (988-POTS)

The Shop
208 W. San Francisco
Santa Fe, NM 87501
(505) 983-4823
Southwestern Christmas decorations all year.
Spanish Colonial antiques.

The Taos Company
124-K John Dunn Plaza
Bent Street
Taos, NM 87571
(505) 758-1141
Furnishings and accessories, including own line of
iron furniture.

UTAH SOURCES

Don Brady Interior Design
P.O. Box 434
Park City, UT 84060
(801) 649-4427

Ross Howard Designs
1105 South 800 East
Salt Lake City, UT 84105
(801) 322-5184
Contemporary Southwestern iron furniture and lighting.

The Showroom
1363 South Major Street
Salt Lake City, UT 84115
(801) 467-1213
Southwestern furnishings.

The Southwest Shop
914 East Ninth South
Salt Lake City, UT 84105
(801) 531-8523
Furniture, ceramics, and accessories.

Utah Designer Crafts Gallery
38 West 200 South
Salt Lake City, UT 84101
(801) 359-2770

WYOMING SOURCES

Contract Design
John Thorkildsen
P.O. Box 11
Jackson, WY 83001
(307) 733-5237

Fighting Bear Antiques
P.O. Box 3812
Jackson, WY 83001
(307) 733-2669
Ironwork, furniture, and glass.

Mountain House
P.O. Box 435
Jackson, WY 83001
(307) 733-4227
Regional furniture, ceramics, and textiles.

Other Books from John Muir Publications

Adventure Vacations: From Trekking in New Guinea to Swimming in Siberia, Bangs 256 pp. $17.95

Asia Through the Back Door, 3rd ed., Steves and Gottberg 326 pp. $15.95

Belize: A Natural Destination, Mahler, Wotkyns, Schafer 304 pp. $16.95

Birds of the Eastern National Parks: United States and Canada, Wauer 400 pp. $15.95

Bus Touring: Charter Vacations, U.S.A., Warren with Bloch 168 pp. $9.95

California Public Gardens: A Visitor's Guide, Sigg 304 pp. $16.95

Catholic America: Self-Renewal Centers and Retreats, Christian-Meyer 325 pp. $13.95

Costa Rica: A Natural Destination, 2nd ed., Sheck 288 pp. $16.95

Elderhostels: The Students' Choice, 2nd ed., Hyman 312 pp. $15.95

Environmental Vacations: Volunteer Projects to Save the Planet, 2nd ed., Ocko 248 pp. $16.95

Europe 101: History & Art for the Traveler, 4th ed., Steves and Openshaw 372 pp. $15.95

Europe Through the Back Door, 10th ed., Steves 448 pp. $16.95

A Foreign Visitor's Guide to America, Baldwin and Levine 256 pp. $13.95

Floating Vacations: River, Lake, and Ocean Adventures, White 256 pp. $17.95

Great Cities of Eastern Europe, Rapoport 256 pp. $16.95

Gypsying After 40: A Guide to Adventure and Self-Discovery, Harris 264 pp. $14.95

The Heart of Jerusalem, Nellhaus 336 pp. $12.95

Indian America: A Traveler's Companion, 2nd ed., Eagle/Walking Turtle 448 pp. $17.95

Interior Furnishings Southwest: The Sourcebook of the Best Production Craftspeople, Deats and Villani 256 pp. $19.95 (avail. 9/92)

Mona Winks: Self-Guided Tours of Europe's Top Museums, Steves and Openshaw 456 pp. $14.95

Opera! The Guide to Western Europe's Great Houses, Zietz 296 pp. $18.95

Paintbrushes and Pistols: How the Taos Artists Sold the West, Taggett and Schwarz 280 pp. $17.95

The People's Guide to Mexico, 9th ed., Franz 608 pp. $18.95

The People's Guide to RV Camping in Mexico, Franz with Rogers 320 pp. $13.95

Ranch Vacations: The Complete Guide to Guest and Resort, Fly-Fishing, and Cross-Country Skiing Ranches, 2nd ed., Kilgore 396 pp. $18.95

The Shopper's Guide to Art and Crafts in the Hawaiian Islands, Schuchter 272 pp. $13.95

The Shopper's Guide to Mexico, Rogers and Rosa 224 pp. $9.95

Ski Tech's Guide to Equipment, Skiwear, and Accessories, ed. Tanler 144 pp. $11.95

Ski Tech's Guide to Maintenance and Repair, ed. Tanler 160 pp. $11.95

A Traveler's Guide to Asian Culture, Chambers 224 pp. $13.95

Traveler's Guide to Healing Centers and Retreats in North America, Rudee and Blease 240 pp. $11.95

Understanding Europeans, Miller 272 pp. $14.95

Undiscovered Islands of the Caribbean, 3rd ed., Willes 288 pp. $14.95

Undiscovered Islands of the Mediterranean, 2nd ed., Moyer and Willes 256 pp. $13.95

Undiscovered Islands of the U.S. and Canadian West Coast, Moyer and Willes 208 pp. $12.95

A Viewer's Guide to Art: A Glossary of Gods, People, and Creatures, Shaw and Warren 144 pp. $10.95

2 to 22 Days Series

Each title offers 22 flexible daily itineraries that can be used to get the most out of vacations of any length. Included are not only "must see" attractions but also little-known villages and hidden "jewels" as well as valuable general information.

22 Days Around the World, 1993 ed., Rapoport and Willes 264 pp. $12.95

2 to 22 Days Around the Great Lakes, 1992 ed., Schuchter 192 pp. $9.95 (**1993 ed.** avail. 12/92, $10.95)

22 Days in Alaska, Lanier 128 pp. $7.95

2 to 22 Days in the American Southwest, 1992 ed., Harris 176 pp. $9.95 (**1993 ed.** avail. 12/92, $10.95)

2 to 22 Days in Asia, 1993 ed., Rapoport and Willes 176 pp. $9.95

2 to 22 Days in Australia, 1993 ed., Gottberg 192 pp. $9.95

2 to 22 Days in California, 1993 ed., Rapoport 192 pp. $9.95

22 Days in China, Duke and Victor 144 pp. $7.95

2 to 22 Days in Europe, 1992 ed., Steves 276 pp. $12.95 (**1993 ed.** avail. 1/93, $13.95)

2 to 22 Days in Florida, 1993 ed., Harris 192 pp. $9.95

2 to 22 Days in France, 1992 ed., Steves 192 pp. $9.95 (**1993 ed.** avail. 1/93, $10.95)

2 to 22 Days in Germany, Austria & Switzerland, 1992 ed., Steves 224 pp. $9.95 (**1993 ed.** avail. 12/92, $10.95)

2 to 22 Days in Great Britain, 1992 ed., Steves 192 pp. $9.95 (**1993 ed.** avail. 1/93, $10.95)

2 to 22 Days in Hawaii, 1993 ed., Schuchter 176 pp. $9.95

22 Days in India, Mathur 136 pp. $7.95

2 to 22 Days in Italy, 1993 ed., Steves 176 pp. $10.95 (avail. 1/93)

22 Days in Japan, Old 136 pp. $7.95

22 Days in Mexico, 2nd ed., Rogers and Rosa 128 pp. $7.95

2 to 22 Days in New England, 1992 ed., Wright 192 pp. $9.95 (**1993 ed.** avail. 1/93, $10.95)

2 to 22 Days in New Zealand, 1993 ed., Schuchter 176 pp. $9.95

2 to 22 Days in Norway, Sweden, & Denmark, 1992 ed., Steves 192 pp. $9.95 (**1993 ed.** avail. 1/93, $10.95)

2 to 22 Days in the Pacific Northwest, 1992 ed., Harris 192 pp. $9.95 (**1993 ed.** avail. 1/93, $10.95)

2 to 22 Days in the Rockies, 1992 ed., Rapoport 176 pp. $9.95 (**1993 ed.** avail. 12/92, $10.95)

2 to 22 Days in Spain & Portugal, 1992 ed., Steves 192 pp. $9.95 (**1993 ed.** avail. 12/92, $10.95)

2 to 22 Days in Texas, 1993 ed., Harris 192 pp. $9.95

2 to 22 Days in Thailand, 1993 ed., Richardson 176 pp. $9.95

22 Days in the West Indies, Morreale and Morreale 136 pp. $7.95

Parenting Series
Being a Father: Family, Work, and Self, *Mothering* Magazine 176 pp. $12.95
Preconception: A Woman's Guide to Preparing for Pregnancy and Parenthood, Aikey-Keller 232 pp. $14.95
Schooling at Home: Parents, Kids, and Learning, *Mothering* Magazine 264 pp. $14.95
Teens: A Fresh Look, *Mothering* Magazine 240 pp. $14.95

"Kidding Around" Travel Guides for Young Readers
Written for kids eight years of age and older.
Kidding Around Atlanta, Pedersen 64 pp. $9.95
Kidding Around Boston, Byers 64 pp. $9.95
Kidding Around Chicago, Davis 64 pp. $9.95
Kidding Around the Hawaiian Islands, Lovett 64 pp. $9.95
Kidding Around London, Lovett 64 pp. $9.95
Kidding Around Los Angeles, Cash 64 pp. $9.95
Kidding Around the National Parks of the Southwest, Lovett 108 pp. $12.95
Kidding Around New York City, Lovett 64 pp. $9.95
Kidding Around Paris, Clay 64 pp. $9.95
Kidding Around Philadelphia, Clay 64 pp. $9.95
Kidding Around San Diego, Luhrs 64 pp. $9.95
Kidding Around San Francisco, Zibart 64 pp. $9.95
Kidding Around Santa Fe, York 64 pp. $9.95
Kidding Around Seattle, Steves 64 pp. $9.95
Kidding Around Spain, Biggs 108 pp. $12.95
Kidding Around Washington, D.C., Pedersen 64 pp. $9.95

"Extremely Weird" Series for Young Readers
Written for kids eight years of age and older.
Extremely Weird Bats, Lovett 48 pp. $9.95
Extremely Weird Birds, Lovett 48 pp. $9.95
Extremely Weird Endangered Species, Lovett 48 pp. $9.95
Extremely Weird Fish, Lovett 48 pp. $9.95
Extremely Weird Frogs, Lovett 48 pp. $9.95
Extremely Weird Insects, Lovett 48 pp. $9.95 (avail. 10/92)
Extremely Weird Primates, Lovett 48 pp. $9.95
Extremely Weird Reptiles, Lovett 48 pp. $9.95
Extremely Weird Sea Creatures, Lovett 48 pp. $9.95
Extremely Weird Spiders, Lovett 48 pp. $9.95

Masters of Motion Series
For kids eight years and older.
How to Drive an Indy Race Car, Rubel 48 pages $9.95
How to Fly a 747, Paulson 48 pages $9.95
How to Fly the Space Shuttle, Shorto 48 pages $9.95 (avail. 12/92)

Quill Hedgehog Adventures Series
Written for kids eight years of age and older.
Quill's Adventures in the Great Beyond, Waddington-Feather 96 pp. $5.95
Quill's Adventures in Wasteland, Waddington-Feather 132 pp. $5.95
Quill's Adventures in Grozzieland, Waddington-Feather 132 pp. $5.95

X-ray Vision Series
For kids eight years and older.
Looking Inside the Brain, Schultz 48 pages $9.95
Looking Inside Cartoon Animation, Schultz 48 pages $9.95
Looking Inside Sports Aerodynamics, Schultz 48 pages $9.95
Looking Inside Sunken Treasure, Schultz 48 pp. $9.95 (avail. 12/92)
Looking Inside Telescopes and the Night Sky, Schultz 48 pp. $9.95 (avail. 12/92)

Other Young Readers Titles
Habitats: Where the Wild Things Live, Hacker and Kaufman 48 pp. $9.95 (avail. 10/92)
Kids Explore America's Hispanic Heritage, Westridge Young Writers Workshop 112 pp. $7.95
The Indian Way: Learning to Communicate with Mother Earth, McLain 114 pp. $9.95
The Kids' Environment Book: What's Awry and Why, Pedersen 192 pp. $13.95
Rads, Ergs, and Cheeseburgers: The Kids' Guide to Energy and the Environment, Yanda 108 pp. $12.95

Automotive Titles
How to Keep Your VW Alive, 15th ed., 464 pp. $21.95
How to Keep Your Volkswagen Alive (Spanish Edition) Muir 224 pp. $10.00
How to Keep Your Subaru Alive 480 pp. $21.95
How to Keep Your Toyota Pickup Alive 392 pp. $21.95
How to Keep Your Datsun/Nissan Alive 544 pp. $21.95
The Greaseless Guide to Car Care Confidence: Take the Terror Out of Talking to Your Mechanic, Jackson 224 pp. $14.95
Off-Road Emergency Repair & Survival, Ristow 160 pp. $9.95

Ordering Information
If you send us money for a book not yet available, we will hold your money until we can ship you the book. Your books will be sent to you via UPS (for U.S. destinations). UPS will not deliver to a P.O. Box; please give us a street address. Include $3.75 for the first item ordered and $.50 for each additional item to cover shipping and handling costs. For airmail within the U.S., enclose $4.00. All foreign orders will be shipped surface rate; please enclose $3.00 for the first item and $1.00 for each additional item. Please inquire about foreign airmail rates.

Method of Payment
Your order may be paid by check, money order, or credit card. We cannot be responsible for cash sent through the mail. All payments must be made in U.S. dollars drawn on a U.S. bank. Canadian postal money orders in U.S. dollars are acceptable. For VISA, MasterCard, or American Express orders, include your card number, expiration date, and your signature, or call (800) 888-7504. Books ordered on American Express cards can be shipped only to the billing address of the cardholder. Sorry, no C.O.D.'s. Residents of sunny New Mexico, add 5.875% tax to the total.

Address all orders and inquiries to:
John Muir Publications
P.O. Box 613
Santa Fe, NM 87504
(505) 982-4078
(800) 888-7504

INTERIOR FURNISHINGS SOUTHWEST
c/o John Muir Publications
P.O. Box 613
Santa Fe, NM 87504

Please send me _____ copies of IFS at . . . .$ _____19.95_____ per copy
       plus postage and handling charges . . . . per copy
New Mexico residents _____ . % sales tax . . . . per copy

                                                           Total . . . . per copy
Enclosed is my check or money order for . . . .$ _____
Make checks payable to John Muir Publications.
NAME _____
STREET _____
CITY _____ STATE _____ ZIP _____

COMMENTS

What do you find especially useful in this book? _____
_____
What would you like to see in future editions?
A particular craftsperson? _____
Certain information? _____
A companion volume of art and accessories? _____
Other? _____

1548